Three
Centuries
of
Social
Mobility
in America

Three Centuries of Social Mobility in America

Edited and with an introduction by
EDWARD PESSEN
The City University of New York

D. C. HEATH AND COMPANY
Lexington, Massachusetts Toronto London

To Alex

CONTENTS

III THE COMPLEX MOBILITY PATTERNS OF THE EARLY INDUSTRIAL ERA, 1860-1900

IV THE TWENTIETH CENTURY: NEW DIMENSIONS, NEW APPROACHES, INCONCLUSIVE MOBILITY PATTERNS

FOREWORD

I wish to acknowledge the very great help given to me by the late Edwin C. Rozwenc. I never had the pleasure of meeting Professor Rozwenc, yet even on paper, in our correspondence concerning the progress of this book, his great knowledge, good sense, keen wit, and integrity clearly shone through. His sharp but kindly questions and his good advice led me to reevaluate a number of my original notions, to the undoubted benefit of the final manuscript. His professionalism drove him to undertake critical editing of the first draft even while he was recovering from major surgery. He was a fine and courageous man.

I wish also to acknowledge the contribution of a young colleague of mine, Gail Benick. The skepticism she expressed about a particularly important point led me to view it afresh and attain a surer grasp of the issue in question than I had had before.

The dedication is to my grandson.

INTRODUCTION

Americans have long believed that the society they created in the New World is not simply different from that of the Old but that it is better. Its superiority has been thought to consist above all in the greater opportunity here for persons of whatever background to rise as high as their individual talents permit. In the words of two sociologists of a generation ago, American society, unlike European, supposedly enables its citizens to "attain the position for which they are individually qualified, irrespective of family status." Recent historical studies of popular thought demonstrate that the "rags-to-riches" myth and variations on it have been a central theme of the American Dream from the seventeenth century to the present. In effect, Americans believed that social mobility was the rule in this country long before the sociologist Pitirim Sorokin in 1927 defined and first aroused scholarly interest in the concept.

In the wake of Sorokin's pioneering classic, hundreds of separate studies have been conducted, primarily by his fellow sociologists, to assess the nature and extent of social mobility in American society.

No sociological research is more important. For these studies have not simply tested the relative accuracy of a popular idea. The investigation of social mobility goes to the very root of the society. Whether individuals can move into higher or lower prestige groups or classes, the actual extent to which they do, whether opportunity increases or decreases over the course of time, are prime indicators of the quality of a society or, more specifically, of the degree to which it is a social democracy. And since a widespread belief in the accessibility of success and eminence acts as a kind of social cement, helping to muffle and deflect the critiques of dissidents, another significance of mobility studies is that the results they disclose can either undermine or strengthen social harmony.

Sociological research has been focused almost exclusively on the twentieth century, relying typically on information conveyed by living respondents to questionnaires and/or interviews. A book such as this is possible only because historians too have recently entered the field, examining earlier periods for traces of social mobility. The Colonial and Revolutionary periods, the early nineteenth century, the "era of the common man" before the Civil War, and the early industrial era, or the decades following Appomattox, have all been investigated. Not the least positive consequence of the scholarly examination of earlier periods is that historical comparisons of social mobility rates for the twentieth and for earlier centuries no longer need depend on surmise. Where sociologists once had to rely on the intuitive, unsubstantiated, or slightly documented generalizations of an Alexis de Tocqueville or a Frederick Jackson Turner about preindustrial mobility patterns, they now have access to generalizations that, if far less sweeping than earlier ones, are far more valuable, based as they are on abundant historical data rather than random impressions.

Now that the social mobility patterns of almost the entire American past appear to have been subjected to investigation, it might seem that the time was at hand to answer the great questions: What has been the rate of social mobility over the course of American history? Has social mobility increased or diminished? What precise trends does the evidence disclose? Alas, clear and satisfying answers cannot yet be given. And there is reason to think it will be a very long time indeed before anything resembling definitive answers can be attempted.

The most recent research, particularly that done by sociologists, is increasingly sophisticated, detailed in its coverage, refined in its methodology. It is precisely these exacting studies that disclose most forcefully the complexity of the subject. For social mobility as for other issues of great significance, scholars of similar ability and integrity reach different conclusions even when they draw from what seems to be similar evidence.

No clear historical trends are discernible, while what trends there are are interpreted differently by scholars. This is so for a number of reasons.

Complexity of Social Mobility

The concept of social mobility appears to be relatively simple. Sorokin himself, for example, seemed to be quite optimistic about the possibility of uncovering important truths. Scholars, he said, had been "speculating too much and studying the facts too little." Let them abandon speculation for the "somewhat saner method of collecting the facts and studying them patiently," and before long they would understand the "characteristics of this process [of] vertical circulation." A half century of subsequent research has confounded these hopes, confirming the adage: the more we know, the more we know how little we know.

The concept of social mobility is deceptively simple. Three modern sociologists have advised us that it is a "complex multidimensional concept consisting presently of an indeterminate but substantial number of components." According to another scholar social mobility is "just motion through a property space," while to study mobility is "to study paths of points." The fact that even trickier definitions abound perhaps explains why Seymour Martin Lipset and Reinhard Bendix, two of the leading modern students of the subject, have written that the concept of social mobility is ambiguous.

Fortunately, most specialists appear ready to settle for simpler, more workable definitions, such as Sorokin's, that by social mobility is understood any movement by an individual "from one social position to another"; or Lipset's and Bendix's, that it refers to "the process by which individuals move from one position to another in society—positions which by general consent have been given specific hierarchical values"; or Bernard Barber's, that the term means "movement, either upward or downward, between higher and lower social classes" or "social roles."

Unfortunately, even the clearest definitions of social mobility are not as clear as they seem. In the words of one recent criticism of Barber's definition, "pending the further elaboration of 'movement' and 'social class,' the concept of social mobility so framed cannot serve as an analytical tool."

The twin ingredients of most definitions of social mobility are position and movement. Scholars have gone about the task of measuring these in divergent ways, relying on different criteria in assessing

position, using varied methodological approaches in tracing movement. Some have sought to determine the rate of movement or
change experienced by group or family members across the generations—intergenerational studies. Other scholars have pursued intragenerational research that focuses on changes within the lifetimes
of the same individuals. Where some intergenerational studies have
compared the standing of fathers in their maturity with the standing
of their sons in their youth, others have confined themselves to comparing only the mature positions attained by members of both generations. It is obviously very difficult, if not impossible, to synthesize
studies that, in the words of one scholar, are "not comparable in
study design [or] sample composition."

Position is no less difficult to measure than movement. For how
is position or class to be determined? Shall income, wealth, lifestyle,
informal contacts, uses of leisure, religious denomination, formal
education, residence, or other criteria, together or singly, be investigated? The obvious significance of such subjective criteria or variables as reputation and prestige, whether of residence, religious
affiliation, or other of the *objective* indices of class is yet further assurance that no perfect measure can be devised for rating the position or standing of individuals at any point in time. And further
bedeviling the issue is the fact that the status of a seemingly hard
indicator of position may change over time. A study showing that
children lived on the same street and belonged to the same clubs as
their fathers might be revealing either of continued eminence or
marked decline, depending on circumstances not indicated in the
data.

Occupation as Indicator of Social Position

Most social mobility studies have in fact relied on occupational data
as the chief if not the sole clue to position. A recent popular article
on social mobility advises that "there are two [sic] rather different
ways in which you can study social mobility"; either by comparing
"the occupations of sons with those of their fathers" or by tracing
"the movements of individuals through their various occupations."
Would that it were so!

Occupations offer not necessarily the best clue to social standing
but the most available one. Whether for the living or the dead, occu-

pational information is in longer supply and is more accessible than evidence on their reputations, their fortunes, or the prestige of their friends. This is not to say that occupations are not a valuable expression of "position in society." In the judgment of Otis Dudley Duncan and Peter M. Blau, two modern authorities, "the occupational structure is the foundation of the stratification system of contemporary industrial society," the "connecting link between different institutions and spheres of social life," and the root of prestige, as of economic, and political hierarchies.

The great problem in working with occupations is how to categorize or rank them. Such ranking must be done in order to evaluate the move from one occupation to another. If a person's occupation is an objective fact, the status of that occupation is not. Subjective factors cannot be kept out of any scheme for ranking occupations. Thus the North-Hatt measure, popular with sociologists since it was devised in 1949, ranks occupations according to the popular appraisals of their prestige disclosed in a survey of a cross-section of the population.

To keep occupational studies manageable, scholars have found it necessary to create a hierarchy of occupational categories, with each category containing occupations of assertedly similar standing. There are almost as many ways of categorizing as there have been scholars devising them. Some are relatively simple, dividing occupations into white-collar, blue-collar, and agricultural, or, as in a recent suggestion by a young historian, into the five levels of unskilled, semiskilled, skilled, low and high white-collar. As I glance at the tables used in five major studies of mobility in the twentieth century, it is clear that the difficulty in relating one set of findings to the other is that each employs a different system for classifying occupations. A change that connotes stability in one study would be taken as upward mobility in another.

For all their usefulness, occupations are far from a perfect measure of social position. It has been found that they do not correlate significantly with other components or variables of class position. Individuals of "high-status occupation" can belong to low-status social circles. Occupational strata are "internally differentiated" as well as "socially heterogeneous." That is, there are merchants and merchants, some scratching out a living, others possessed of vast fortunes, some of obscure family, others belonging to the most envied social sets. Even Paul Hatt, whose work stressed the value of occupations to social mobility studies, conceded that a man's occupation was an imperfect index to his position in a "stratified social system." Also detracting from the value of some occupational mobility studies are methodological errors committed by their authors.

Many researchers have overlooked significant features of the occupational careers of their subjects. Men typically change their jobs over the course of time. Yet, as Lipset and Bendix note, "as most current [1963] research is done, the man who has been a skilled worker or an independent businessman for the past twenty-five years is classified in the same category as the man who has been in the occupation for six months." A man is classified as white-collar "at the end as well as at the beginning of his career, though he began as a sales clerk and ended as an executive vice-president." Insufficient attention has been given to measuring the size of the gaps between such occupations as plumbers and carpenters, on the one hand, and between doctors and salesmen, on the other. The need for refinements has been urged, not only to differentiate lawyers from engineers, among professionals, but to distinguish "independent practitioners" from other types and "solo lawyers" from "firm lawyers."

Intrinsic weaknesses and methodological problems notwithstanding, it seems clear that, in the future as in the past, studies of social mobility will continue to focus on occupational changes. Certainly the growing number of historians' studies of past mobility continue to emphasize occupational changes. Yet, the historians' approach is not identical to the sociologists'.

Historians' Studies of Social Mobility: Special Features

In addition to providing useful information that makes possible more meaningful comparisons between social mobility in the twentieth and earlier centuries, the historians' investigations have several other uniquely positive features. At best their work is informed by a rich evocation of, and sure feel for, the social context in which particular patterns of social movement occur. Their language is less prone to be esoteric and jargon-ridden than that of sociologists and is therefore more understandable to general readers. While the passage of time diminishes the availability of evidence, most dramatically by the death of persons who could have responded to questionnaires and interviews, there is another consequence of this harsh fact. The data used by historians are hard: when carefully checked for accuracy, they do indeed disclose the occupations, wealth, residences, club memberships, or whatever it is that they seek to discover. Where volunteered statements, if they do not highly distort the truth, are often "highly colored by [the] status conceptions" that are so important to living respondents, dead men tell no lies: the only acceptable data about them are accurate or verified data. Their obliviousness to refinements of methodology lead some historians boldly to draw conclusions about the mobility patterns revealed by their research. If some of these conclusions are overdrawn or unwarranted, the data underlying them are nevertheless useful.

But if the historian's innocence has certain positive consequences, it also has negative ones. The methodology employed by some historians is implicit, with all of the weaknesses attendant on informality. Their work is often imprecise, relying too heavily on impressionism, marred by poor sampling techniques and questionable analysis. One historical study of intragenerational wealth mobility advises that it measures success by whether or not the individual grew richer over a given time span. There is something seriously wrong with an approach that judges successful the man whose assets increased from $40 to $50 and a failure the poor fellow whose wealth dropped from $750,000 to $725,000! The chief shortcoming of historical mobility studies is their unidimensional character. That is, they focus almost entirely on revealing patterns of social mobility. When it comes to explaining or interpreting the data, historians invariably fall back on conjecture or surmise. While their judgments are often interesting and insightful, they are hardly the product of rigorous multivariate factor analysis. Their methodology is primitive, their notion of subject matter narrow, not approximating the complexity and rich diversity of much of the recent sociological research.

Sociologists' Studies of Social Mobility: Special Features

Not that the mobility studies done by sociologists are free of lapses. In fact the characteristic theme of most recent treatises on methodology is the abundance of errors to be found in earlier sociological studies of mobility. Noncomparable samples have been measured as though they were comparable. Statistically insignificant coefficients of correlation have been misinterpreted. In an otherwise valuable study, a scholar reporting on various features of the later social and economic achievement of a group of high school students fails to compare these with the achievements of other members of the ethnic group under study or of the broader school population, data in both cases that were available. In gathering evidence on the ancestors of twentieth-century subjects, outstanding sociologists have relied on the sparse material offered by notoriously unreliable encyclopedias. Whoever has a mind to do so can find other examples of questionable judgment in the literature. Such mistakes are inevitable, of course. They do not detract from the solid accomplishments of recent sociological scholarship.

Preoccupation with refining their tools of analysis has been accompanied by improved techniques for measuring social mobility rates. Nor have sociologists limited themselves to seeking mathematical expressions for social mobility rates at different points in the twentieth century. What most distinguishes their recent studies from those done by historians is their ever widening scope, as well as their greater methodological sophistication. In contrast to historians, who continue to act like the children of Sorokin, searching exclusively for evidence of social movement and trying to ascertain its extent, sociologists have also sought to discover the factors that underlie or cause mobility to occur and to isolate as precisely as possible the comparative role played by each of these factors. Instead of relying on conjecture or on a random, essentially rationalist, approach to this problem, sociologists have employed factor analysis to establish the correlation and possible causal connection between a given factor and the observed rate of social mobility that accompanies it.

This is not to say that the search for causes has solved all problems or somehow been marked by unprecedented success. As Duncan and Blau have observed, while a number of recently researched factors obviously "play a role in determining the amount and pattern of mobility observed at different times, we are so far from understanding how these factors combine that our conjectures are virtually gratuitous." The scholarly investigation of the causes of social mobility has if anything multiplied the questions that remain unanswered about social mobility. But it has also enriched the discussion, adding both to its interest and significance. For what is knowledge of patterns or results without knowledge of their causes?

Actually, the sociologists' search for the causes of social mobility breaks down into two separate and distinctive searches. In the first, they attempt to discover the causes of the vertical mobility rate, whatever it may be, hoping consequently to be able to explain why the rate is as high, low, or middling as it is. In the second, they put aside their attempt to explain the rate of social mobility, focusing instead on the reasons certain individuals and not others experienced whatever mobility occurred. Fruitful and fascinating studies of the second sort have been done, but the reader should keep in mind that the kind of vertical mobility explored by this form of research could occur in closed as well as open societies and would in fact be ruled out only in a perfectly rigid caste society which allocated all places, ranks, and occupations according to the standing of one's parents.

What Accounts for Changes in the Rate of Social Mobility?

Perhaps the great difficulty in answering this question explains why most recent sociological research has apparently bypassed it. The answer must combine a number of broad social, economic, and technological factors, none of which can be isolated with real precision. Owing largely to Natalie Rogoff's significant study two decades ago, much of the recent discussion has centered on the issue of structural change.

Structural change has been defined as "changes in the size of the various occupations [that] reflect changes in the demand for occupational services, which, in turn, often have their source in technological advances, as exemplified by the declining demand for farm workers consequent to improved farming methods and higher farm productivity." Such structural changes "require a redistribution of manpower." A number of important studies conclude that the alleged increase in twentieth-century rates of upward occupational mobility is due primarily to such changes in the nation's economic and occupational structure. The phasing out of lower-status occupations, in this view, simply propelled workers and their sons into jobs that were more rewarding both in prestige and in real wages. According to Lipset and Bendix, "widespread social mobility has been a concomitant of industrialization and a basic characteristic of industrial society."

Other scholars, however, have questioned the thesis that technological developments invariably result in greater economic mobility, denying that there is a necessary or statistically significant relationship between "economic development and social mobility." No last word has been said on this matter. It does seem clear that certain structural changes unavoidably enhance the likelihood of upward occupational mobility. Attempts to weigh the precise effects of such changes in particular contexts have fallen short of precision. In their famous 1955 study, Warner and Abegglen settled for a most impressionistic series of comments about the impact of structural changes on the mobility patterns revealed by their research, not even attempting to use precise analytic techniques. Where such techniques have been utilized, the results to date have been less than definitive.

What does seem certain is that this issue will continue to receive a great deal of attention. For in assessing the relative opportunity provided by different societies at different times, some scholars appear to discount the significance of upward movement induced by technological or structural factors in contrast, say, to vertical movement that, in Professor Rogoff Ramsoy's recent words, is "independent of such secular trends." Such analyses leave the layman with the impression that upward movement independent of structural change is somehow purer, more praiseworthy, or a truer sign of equal opportunity than mobility induced by impersonal societal change.

Why Are Certain Individuals Rather Than Others Socially Mobile?

Most of the recent sociological scholarship has dealt with this question, no doubt because relatively definitive answers to it can be reached. The backgrounds of the vertically mobile portion of the population have been compared with those of the immobile in an attempt to discover what factors account for upward movement. A variety of factors have been isolated. Studies have been undertaken of the effect on individual mobility of religion or membership in particular denominations, urban residence, family size and age ranking, geographical mobility and the extent of one's footlooseness, personal aspirations and goals, emotional balance, sex, attractiveness, and other qualities. Each of these appears to play a part, but the extent of that part appears to differ depending on who has done the investigation. As was noted at the outset, sociologists no less than other scholars are prone to interpret evidence in their own unique ways, influenced by the almost limitless array of experiences and subjective qualities that differentiate one observer from another.

Certain factors have been studied with particular intensity because of their great importance and interest. Education, whether in terms of level of schooling achieved or quality of schools attended, is one of these. The sensitive matter of innate, or congenital, ability and intelligence and their relationship to social mobility has been substantially if inconclusively researched. For a long time social mobility scholarship focused almost exclusively on intergenerational studies that sought to discover the occupations and prestige of their subjects' fathers, because social origins were conceived to be the most important factor involved in social position. While specialists no longer accord that factor its former preeminence, social origins continue to fascinate scholarly researchers. One suspects that the "laity" still believe that parental or family status is the chief explanation of whatever station an individual achieves.

The Changing "Populations" of Social Mobility Studies

Studies of social mobility patterns, whether done by sociologists or historians, have broadened their focus in recent decades. Unlike earlier investigations, that stressed the social origins of socioeconomic elites, contemporary research has examined the backgrounds or the later status of middle- and lower-class individuals and groups. Modern scholars continue to explore the backgrounds of elites, if in more sophisticated ways than did Taussig and Joslyn two generations ago. Most contemporary research goes beyond elites, however. Today's studies are concerned with lawyers, doctors, the professions in general, entire communities, particular age groups, ethnic groups, and, in the most comprehensive studies, individuals who hold every possible occupation. While such work indubitably adds to the breadth and representativeness of social mobility studies, it offers yet one more testimony that indisputable answers are beyond our reach. (A reader of Stuart Adams's studies of the social mobility experienced by professionals will find a social universe markedly unlike the one drawn by Robert Perrucci from roughly similar material.) Whether due to the noncomparability of their samples or "groups of orientation," their unlike methodologies and grasp, or their unique biases, sociologists continue to arrive at different conclusions.

Mabel Newcomer was doubtless right when she wrote in 1955 that there are certain questions concerning social mobility that cannot be answered, no matter how excellent the technique and how wide the net of the scholar studying them. Yet, if perfection is out of the question, it is nevertheless likely that our perceptions of social mobility will become fuller and more complex, providing better answers than we now have to the most intriguing questions.

The selections that follow indicate some of the varied approaches scholars have taken in studying social mobility. The essays are divided into four sections, each representing not simply a different chronological period but an era that was qualitatively unlike the others, above all in its social and technological characteristics.

Readers who anticipate striking changes in the rates or patterns of vertical mobility from one era to another are in for a surprise. The burden of the sociological studies is that changes in the twentieth century have been less than clear-cut. Historians' studies of earlier centuries reveal similarly ambiguous trends. Perhaps the clearest as well as the most significant finding of the historical studies is that vertical mobility before the twentieth century was not nearly so pervasive as sociologists and general readers thought it was.

I THE MIXED PATTERN OF THE COLONIAL AND REVOLUTIONARY PERIODS

The eminent New Yorker Cadwallader Colden wrote an English friend in the eighteenth century that "the most opulent families in our memory have arisen from the lowest rank of the people." The fact that almost every colony had well-known examples of men who had moved from rags to riches led colonial scholars to conclude that the social ladder was swiftly and regularly climbed in the seventeenth and eighteenth centuries. This cheerful generalization was related to the impressionistic methodology of the scholars who put it forward. Discovering, for example, that Daniel Dulany, Dr. Charles Carroll, and perhaps two other wealthy men of colonial Maryland had started with little or nothing, they concluded that swift upward movement was nearly universal. Substituting data on entire populations or social groups for chance evidence on a handful of men, modern scholars conclude that in Dulany's Maryland, "for the mass, advance was by comparison glacial."

What has replaced the earlier happy picture of pervasive fluidity is not a grim picture but a mixed one. In many new communities in colonial America, opportunities for poor men were far better than in England. But not everywhere. Seventeenth-century Salem's rich had had "considerable wealth" to start with. A recent detailed study of more than 1,000 Massachusetts immigrants in 1637 notes that their subsequent fates in America were largely determined by their status on arrival. Masters flourished; servants remained humble. The prospects for poor young men in New England communities such as Dedham, Massachusetts, were bleak almost from the beginning. As Jackson T. Main's comprehensive study of Revolutionary society reveals, marvelous opportunities for men in modest circumstances continued in rural communities into the eighteenth century, but "mobility diminished as the community grew older." The pattern discerned by Bernard Bailyn in Virginia during the century prior to the Revolution was not from rags to riches, but rather from substantial material and social advantages to membership in the elite upper crust of the colony. Scattered studies indicate that American artisans and small farmers in town and country often improved their situation during the eighteenth century, but many of these changes for the better were not of the substantial sort that indicates upward mobility. That is, they did not alter the social category or class of their beneficiaries.

William A. Reavis

THE MARYLAND GENTRY AND SOCIAL MOBILITY, 1637–1676

William A. Reavis's study of the backgrounds and social origins of seven-teenth-century Maryland gentry was one of the first mobility studies by a historian to employ a quantitative rather than an impressionistic approach. One of the salient points of this essay is the observation that most of Mary-land's gentlemen were Englishmen who had not held that high status before their arrival in America. They accomplished their upward social movement simply by boarding ship for the New World; "shipboard mobility," not "com-ing up through the ranks," was the most popular route to eminence.

The study of social structure is a nebulous thing at best, and it has suffered from the tendency of historians to rely almost exclusively upon diaries and memoirs, leaving the quantitative approach to the sociologists. But man in the mass *is* accessible even to the historian, and court records provide one of our best sources in this regard, particularly in the colonial period, when a man's social status was generally made a part of the public record.

The *Archives of Maryland* contain seven volumes devoted to the records of the Maryland Provincial Court from 1637 until 1676. In those years, 330 men who may be described as gentlemen appeared in the court. When labeled at all, they were called *Esq., Gent., Mr.,* or they were given a military or naval rank. Esquire was used almost exclusively for the Calvert inner circle. Of the entire group, 275 (83 percent) were recognized as gentlemen from their first entry in the records, and have thus been dubbed "immigrant" gentlemen, while 55 (17 percent) rose from the ranks of the Maryland commoners, and have been labeled "indigenous" gentlemen. With the exception of the inner circle, the immigrant gentleman was usually identified as *Gent.* from 1637 to 1650, while the indigenous gentleman was labeled *Mr.* From 1650 to 1665 both groups were usually labeled as *Mr.* and from 1665 to 1676 as *Gent.* Table 1 lists the first appearance of im-

From William A. Reavis, "The Maryland Gentry and Social Mobility, 1637–1676," *William and Mary Quarterly* 14 (July 1957): 418–428. Reprinted by permission. Foot-notes deleted.

TABLE 1
Maryland Gentry

Year	Immigrant Gentry	Indigenous Gentry	Total
1637	25	0	25
1638	3	0	3
1639	6	0	6
1640	0	0	0
1641	0	0	0
1642	11	0	11
1643	4	0	4
1644	2	0	2
Records Destroyed, 1645–1646			
1647	4	3	7
1648	3	2	5
1649	2	3	5
1650	6	6	12
1651	21	2	23
1652	13	1	14
1653	9	1	10
1654	13	0	13
1655	13	3	16
1656	5	1	6
1657	11	1	12
1658	13	7	20
1659	3	3	6
1660	5	0	5
1661	11	2	13
1662	0	2	2
1663	8	5	13
1664	12	2	14
1665	3	0	3
1666	7	0	7
1667	3	0	3
1668	8	1	9
1669	10	0	10
1670	9	1	10
1671	1	1	2
1672	4	0	4
1673	9	3	12
1674	9	2	11
1675	5	1	6
1676	4	2	6
Totals	275	55	330

migrant and indigenous gentry in the Maryland Provincial Court, the latter group in their first appearance as gentlemen.

Considering the immigrant gentlemen first, it is important to ask just what proportion of this group had been, or would have qualified as, gentlemen in England. It has been observed that the English gentleman had the "prestige of birth . . . acquired in three generations of wealth or achievement leading to exemption from gainful labor. . . ." Accepting this definition, it is obvious that few genuine English gentlemen of the early seventeenth century would have migrated to the New World simply to plant tobacco. For what reasons, then, and in what numbers did the gentry come?

Those who emigrated mainly to participate in the rewards of Maryland officialdom were probably all valid English gentlemen. The Calverts had a huge grant of land from the king, but this grant would do the family little good unless colonists could be moved to the New World in large numbers. To staff such a project the Calverts had to recruit a trusted "inner circle" of gentlemen of means and position who could be enticed to America by the promise of a share in the Calvert largess. As Donnell M. Owings has shown very clearly, this largess was distributed through the grant of provincial offices, in the form of salaries and fees of a princely nature.

But this Calvert inner circle was never large: if the 4 Calverts are excepted, only 13 of the 275 immigrant gentry held positions on the Provincial Council during periods of Calvert hegemony for as long as five years. They were Robert Clarke, Thomas Greene, Thomas Gerard, John Lewger, Giles Brent, Henry Coursey, Thomas Trueman, Baker Brooke, Jerome White, Jesse Wharton, William Evans, Edward Lloyd, and Thomas Hatton. Only 5 of these men were included among the 28 gentry who appear in the records in 1637–1638. It can certainly be argued that a higher proportion of the original colonists were Calvert retainers who either returned to England or died or became alienated from the Calvert rule, and who thus had no opportunity to serve on the Provincial Council for as long a period as five years. Even so, the group of genuine English gentlemen, who were primarily attracted to America by a promise of a part of the Calvert largess, was small.

Those English gentlemen who came to Maryland mainly in the pursuit of adventure were even smaller in number. The records suggest that practically all who came for this reason, like Francis Trafford Esq. and WilliamTalbott Esq., stayed but a year or two and then returned to England. The American wilderness held little continuing attraction for gentlemen assured in England of economic, political, and social standing; once the aura of adventure had worn off they were eager to return to remembered comforts.

English gentlemen who migrated primarily because of religious discrimination probably included most of the original group of Catholic gentry and some of the Puritans who came up from Virginia. But the fact that the estates of deceased Maryland gentlemen contained so little of value besides the lands given out by the Calverts indicates that this group could not have been very large; for if they had been gentlemen of means, it is reasonable to assume they would have managed to bring a good portion of their wealth with them.

Examination of the records of the Provincial Court shows that not more than 50, and possibly fewer, of the 275 immigrant gentry can be placed in one of the above groups. That means that at least 225 members (82 percent) of the Maryland immigrant gentry had not been real English gentlemen at all; they were either "gentlemen" of the fringe variety (those whose fortunes were on the wane, or possibly the younger sons of gentlemen, who found themselves with nothing but a famous name), or, more probably, they were English middling sort who filled the void in the Maryland upper stratum caused by the shortage of true English gentlemen. Thus it seems likely that the trip from England to America allowed scores of men to step a notch upward in the social scale without even having to serve an apprenticeship as commoners in the New World. This "shipboard mobility" has been generally ignored by historians, but it is an important phenomenon of the period of settlement on any frontier. In seventeenth-century Maryland it was far more significant numerically than was the "coming up through the ranks" by commoners, although both were based upon the same lack of valid gentry and the same frontier emphasis upon individual initiative and ability. The latter required a certain period of economic and social growth made possible by cheap lands and frontier opportunities for individual initiative; the former required only an air of distinction as one debarked from the ship.

Turning to the indigenous gentry, it is apparent from Table 1 that the accession of Maryland commoners to the status of gentleman was relatively constant after the first eight years. As we have seen,

17 percent of the 330 Maryland gentlemen appearing in the Provincial Court were of this type. These 55 gentlemen averaged twenty-five entries each in the Provincial Court records during an average of twelve years as commoners. They ranged all the way from Nicholas Gwyther, who took four years to move from commoner to gentleman (sixteen entries as a commoner), to William Hatton, who spent twenty-six years as a commoner before he became accepted as a gentleman (thirty-two entries as a commoner).

While there was considerable social mobility in Maryland throughout the seventeenth century, it is easier to gauge it than to determine just how it took place. Certainly one factor to be considered would be the accumulation of riches. A considerable gulf existed between the average net worth of commoners and gentlemen in seventeenth-century Maryland: out of the fifty-five itemized and evaluated estates listed in the records of the Provincial Court, the thirty-nine commoner estates had an average valuation of 3,695 pounds of tobacco, while the eighteen gentry estates averaged slightly over five times as much. This was primarily because of the great differences in landholdings between the two classes: while Lord Calvert was rather liberal in his grants to many of the immigrant gentry, his policies toward the lower classes were much more restrictive, and many were kept in a state of semitenancy for at least a generation. This situation did not remain static: after 1660 there was a considerable inflation in land values, and there were numerous sales of land to commoners, both by the proprietor and by individual gentlemen. The credit structure of provincial finance, based on the annual crop of tobacco, made it easy for commoners with little capital to buy as much land as they could profitably farm, and many others simply drifted off to the frontier and squatted. In either case, land was available which the commoners could not have dreamed of possessing in England, and by tradition the ownership of land has always carried with it the aura of gentility.

But there are many indications that the division between the two classes was not entirely economic. Many gentry estates had lower valuations than some commoners': the estate of Mr. Zachary Mottershead was virtually worthless after debts and death expenses were deducted, while James Jolly, a commoner planter and mariner, left an estate worth 37,367 pounds of tobacco, larger than most of the gentry estates. Both classes owned indentured servants about equally, and it is interesting to note that the commoner John Grammar owned more indentured servants (ten) than did any gentleman whose estate is listed in the records. Moreover, "wealthy" Marylanders were in reality land-poor; besides their indentured servants, livestock, boats, and an occasional slave, their personal property was of such a limited and frontier nature (even in the case of the Calverts) that it was almost negligible.

The main route upward for commoners lay in public service. In 67 percent of the cases, accession to higher social status was preceded by appointment to an office identified with the gentry class: all provincial posts, county commissioners, county sheriffs, county surveyors, commissioned ranks in the militia, ship captains, and professional attorneys. It can be argued that officeholding had some relationship to economic standing since the county offices, at least, paid very little and had to be supplemented by planting. But the relationship of wealth to officeholding was at best only secondary.

In the rural areas of England the gentry had always held the local offices, so it is not surprising that officeholding was the main avenue to gentility in Maryland. What is significant is the fact that only 52 percent of the immigrant gentry ever held *any* provincial or county office. This fact, coupled with the constant formation of new counties, gave many commoners the chance to fill important local offices, an opportunity which would have been practically nonexistent in England. Thus in the newer counties of Baltimore, Dorchester, Somerset, and Cecil, all of which had only a few hundred inhabitants each in 1675, many commoners made the transition to gentry status.

The same thing was happening in the older counties, where just as many openings seem to have existed despite the greater number of immigrant gentry available to fill them. In 1668 George Beckwith became the Calvert County coroner and was recognized as a gentleman; in 1664 the commoner William Marshall was appointed Charles County commissioner after twenty years in Maryland, as Zachary Wade had been the year before. In 1663 Thomas Leitchworth and Tobias Norton became Calvert County commissioners after six years and seven years, respectively, as commoners. Apparently, because of the rough work involved in frontier planting, many of the immigrant gentlemen had little time for officeholding, and their apathy gave many new men their chance.

Very often commoners worked their way up through a succession of minor offices. Robert Vaughan, who had been a sergeant in the militia, was appointed a captain in 1647, and thus became a gentleman automatically. Philip Land served as the undersheriff of St. Mary's County while a commoner, but when he was appointed sheriff in 1650 he became a gentleman. Edward Packer served on juries constantly from 1638 to 1652; in the latter year he was appointed jury foreman, and the clerk inscribed a *Mr.* before his name from then on. Richard Smith served as a lay attorney for some years, and he became a gentleman when he was appointed attorney general in 1657. In 1651 Miles Cooke was mate for Captain Richard Husbands aboard the *Hopeful Adventure;* in 1659 Cooke obtained command of the *Baltimore* and assumed gentry status. James Thompson, while still a commoner, served as clerk of the orphans' court and the Calvert County court. Finally, in 1664, he was made clerk of the Provincial Court and accorded himself the rank of gentleman.

Some members of the indigenous gentry exhibited amazing progress in the social scale; while the majority probably came from among the upper commoners, there are some significant exceptions. James Langworth and James Linsey came to Maryland as indentured servants; Langworth rose in time to be a commissioner of St. Mary's County, a lay attorney, and a captain in the militia, while Linsey was appointed a Charles County commissioner sixteen years after achieving his freedom. John Jarbo, Henry Adams, and William Marshall all began as laborers; in time Jarbo became a lieutenant colonel in the militia and a St. Mary's County commissioner, while Adams and Marshall became Charles County commissioners and sheriffs within twenty years after their first appearance in the records. Other indigenous gentry started higher in the commoner group, but they climbed higher too: Samuel Chew, Edward Packer, John Hatch, Richard Banks, Robert Vaughan, and John Price all served on the Provincial Court for short periods.

As might be expected, many commoners came close to achieving the status of gentleman but were never quite accepted. Daniel Clocker was a significant example of this group. He first appeared in the Provincial Court in 1648 as a newly freed servant who acquired enough "freedom land" to get started as a planter. He was illiterate, but he served as a juror and lay attorney, and in 1655 was appointed a commissioner of St. Mary's County, serving for a year in that capacity. In 1661 he was appointed as executor for the estate of

Colonel John Price, and in 1669 he became overseer of the highways in St. Mary's County. In the 1670s he was regularly a juryman until his death in 1676. The importance of the relationship between social status and political office is suggested by the fact that at no time other than the year he spent as a St. Mary's County commissioner was he marked as a gentleman; the fact that he was not so marked thereafter prevented him from being classed in the indigenous gentry.

The effect of family ties on social status was mixed: sometimes they helped and at other times they had no apparent influence. James Johnson married the daughter of Mr. Thomas Hatton in 1650, and in 1655 he was appointed a commissioner of St. Mary's County, becoming a gentleman after fourteen years as a commoner. Thomas Courtney, on the other hand, married the daughter of Mr. Thomas Taylor in 1664 and received one hundred acres of land as his wife's dowry. Although Courtney was very active in the courts and as constable for St. Mary's Hundred, he was never accepted as a gentleman.

Only about one-third of the sons of gentry were accorded the rank of gentleman as soon as they appeared in the records. It is difficult to distinguish between elder and younger sons, but it appears that most of the latter began as commoners, although some eventually achieved the status of gentleman. The Hatton family had three males who were immediately accepted as gentlemen and one who took twenty-six years to achieve that status. Three members of the Thompson family were marked as gentlemen immediately and three had to work up through the ranks of the commoners. The Adams, Browne, Hall, Mitchell, Morgan, Price, Smith, Taylor, Thomas, and Wade families all had one male who was accorded gentry status on first appearance in the records, one who served a period of time as a commoner before becoming a gentleman, and others who remained commoners all their lives. Thus, while marriage and blood relationship, as well as riches, were factors in determining the gentry status, the big factor, as we have seen, was officeholding.

The upward movement of commoners was facilitated by the failure of the Calverts to enforce class distinctions in legal and property matters that existed in Old England. In a frontier environment and under the pressures of simultaneous struggles for control with democratic elements and with the Puritans, the Calverts simply could not allow special privileges in court for the gentry. It is true that by statute gentlemen were excluded, for at least a few years, from such debasing punishment as whipping, but in all other matters the Provincial Court tended to be firm, yet fair, with both classes. In 1658, for example, both Mr. Henry Hooper and the commoner John Cornelius were found guilty of swearing in court, and they were fined ten pounds of tobacco each. In 1648 Edward Cummings and in 1650 Mr. Luke Gardiner were found guilty of slander, and both fines were remitted upon apology in open court. In 1675 Thomas Taylor, commoner, complained to the court that Thomas Taylor, Gent., "an assault did make and him did beate wound and evill handle and him imprisoned and so imprisoned a long time deteined and other enormities." The jury found for the commoner, and the court awarded damages of 2,000 pounds of tobacco. In 1653 Henry Hyde testified that Mr. Lawrence Starkey had threatened to make him a perpetual servant; the court ordered Hyde released at the end of his term with freedom dues as agreed.

The value of a gentleman's word in court actually declined considerably during the seventeenth century, possibly as a reflection of the changed nature of the gentry. Two cases may be cited to illustrate this trend. In 1642 Mr. Thomas Gerard was able to win a suit concerning a sow by assuring the court that he had never promised the animal as was charged by a commoner. By contrast, in 1661 Mr. Thomas Mathews was sued for £10 wages by Thomas Walker, his former indentured servant, and although Mathews swore that the money had never been promised, the court awarded the £10 to Walker. It was not unusual for a commoner to administer the estate of a gentleman, as Joseph Edlowe did for the estate of Mr. Robert Wiseman in 1651. In 1658 Mr. William Eltonhead's estate was appraised by four commoners, and in 1650 Mr. Thomas Hatton and Captain William Mitchell agreed to arbitration of their suit by two men, a gentleman and a commoner.

From 1637 to 1643 all cases in the Provincial Court were decided by gentlemen sitting as judges; however, after that time almost all of the cases were decided by jury. Out of fifty-five jury cases examined, 16 percent had all-commoner juries, even though most of the cases involved a gentleman either as plaintiff or defendant. When, in 1672, Mr. James Neale and his son were tried for hog stealing, both were found guilty by commoner juries. When Mr. John

Blomfield, in 1675, sued Philip Russell for failing to live up to a contract, the all-commoner jury found for Blomfield.

In the mixed juries a gentleman was generally chosen as foreman, but in 15 percent of those cases a commoner was chosen instead. Almost half of the mixed juries contained only one gentleman, and seldom were more than two or three assigned. The few juries which contained 50 percent gentry or more seem to have been in trials of more than usual interest, such as that in 1652 when Captain William Mitchell was tried for adultery, blasphemy, and murder, and that in 1653 when two Indians were tried for murder. Gentlemen did, at times, demand a place in the jury box, but it was more an effort to get a front row seat than to control the administration of justice.

By 1676 Maryland had grown from about 200 inhabitants to over 20,000, and the colony's transition from frontier to settled, rural status meant that it would be more and more difficult for a new arrival to make the transition from commoner to gentleman. Only by moving westward, or by migrating to the unsettled frontier areas of South Carolina and Georgia, could he hope to match the mobility which had characterized the first settlers who established the Maryland social structure from 1637 to 1676. The heritage of an individualistic frontier tradition would always allow more social mobility in Maryland than had been possible in England, but the days of free-wheeling social ascent were over.

Russell R. Menard

THE SOCIAL MOBILITY OF INDENTURED SERVANTS

In contrast to William A. Reavis, Russell R. Menard has studied social mobility in seventeenth-century Maryland from the bottom up. Where earlier generalizations about the fates of and opportunities available to indentured servants

From Russell R. Menard, "From Servant to Freeholder: Status Mobility and Property Accumulation in Seventeenth-Century Maryland," *William and Mary Quarterly* 30 (January 1973): 37–64. Reprinted by permission of publisher and author. Footnotes deleted.

after they gained their freedom were essentially speculations drawn from a few examples, Mr. Menard's conclusions are firmly grounded in comprehensive evidence concerning an entire servant generation. Striking opportunities for men of humble birth and station marked the period before 1660. Thereafter, opportunities declined sharply, if they did not absolutely dry up.

Miles Gibson, Stephen Sealus, and William Scot all arrived in Maryland as indentured servants in the 1660s. They completed their terms and soon accumulated enough capital to purchase land. Thereafter, their careers diverged sharply. Gibson, aided by two good marriages, gained a place among the local gentry and served his county as justice of the peace, burgess, and sheriff. At his death in 1692, he owned more than 2,000 acres of land and a personal estate appraised at over 600 pounds sterling, including nine slaves. Sealus's career offers a sharp contrast to that of his highly successful contemporary. He lost a costly court case in the mid-1670s and apparently was forced to sell his plantation to cover the expenses. He spent the rest of his days working other men's land. By 1691, Sealus was reduced to petitioning the county court for relief. He was "both weake and lame," he pleaded, "and not able to worke whereby to maintaine himselfe nor his wife." His petition was granted, but the Sealus family remained poor. Stephen died in 1696, leaving an estate appraised at £18 6s. William Scot did not approach Gibson's success, but he did manage to avoid the dismal failure of Sealus. He lived on his small plantation for nearly forty years, served his community in minor offices, and slowly accumulated property. In his will, Scot gave all seven of his sons land of their own and provided his three daughters with small dowries.

Although interesting in themselves, these brief case histories do not reveal very much about the life chances of servants in the seventeenth century. They do suggest a range of accomplishment, but how are we to tell whether Scot, Sealus, or Gibson is most typical, or even if any one of them represents the position that most servants attained? Did servitude offer any hard-working Englishman without capital a good chance of becoming, like Miles Gibson, a man of means and position in a new community? Or did servitude only offer, as it finally offered Stephen Sealus, a chance to live in poverty in another place? Perhaps Scot was more typical. Did servitude promise poor men a chance to obtain moderate prosperity and respectability for themselves and their families? How much property and status mobility did most servants manage to achieve in the seventeenth century? This essay examines the careers of a group of men who immigrated to Maryland in the seventeenth century in order to provide some of the data needed for answers to such questions.

The study of mobility requires an assessment of a man's position in society for at least two points in his career, a task that the general absence of census materials, tax lists, and assessment records makes difficult. Nevertheless, a study of mobility among servants is possible because we know their place in the social structure at the beginning of their careers in the New World. Servants started at the bottom of white society: they entered the colonies with neither freedom nor capital. Since we can define their position on arrival, measuring the degree of success they achieved is a fairly simple task. We can, as the capsule biographies of Gibson, Sealus, and Scot demonstrate, describe their progress in the New World. A study of the fortunes of indentured servants and the way those fortunes changed over time provides a sensitive indicator of the opportunities available within colonial society.

The broadest group under study in this essay consists of 275 men who entered Maryland as servants before the end of 1642, although the main concern is with 158 for whom proof exists that they survived to be freemen. Not all the men who came into Maryland as servants by 1642 are included in the 275. No doubt a few servants escape any recorded mention, while others appear who are not positively identified as servants. One large group falling into this latter category included 66 men, not specifically called servants, who were listed in the proofs of headrights as having been transported into the colony at the expense of someone else to whom they were not related. It is probable that all of these men emigrated under indentures, but since proof was lacking they have been excluded from the study.

The mortality rate among these servants was probably high. One hundred and seventeen of the 275—more than 40 percent—did not appear in the records as freemen. The deaths of 14 of the missing are mentioned, but we can only speculate on the fate of most of the servants who disappeared. Some may have been sold out of the province before their terms were completed, and some may have run away, while others may have left Maryland immediately after becoming freemen. A majority probably died while still servants, victims of the unusual climate, poor food, ill housing, hard work, or an occasional cruel master, before they had a chance to discover for themselves if America was a land of opportunity.

For the 158 who definitely survived the rigors of servitude, opportunity was abundant. Seventy-nine to 81 (identification is uncertain in two cases) of the survivors, about 50 percent, eventually acquired land in Maryland. To be properly interpreted, however, this figure must be understood within the context of the careers of those who failed to acquire land. Fourteen of those who survived servitude but did not acquire land in Maryland died within a decade of completing their terms. Another 25 left before they had lived in the colony for ten years as freemen. These figures are conservative, for they include only those for whom death or migration can be proven. Twenty-five of the 158 survivors appear only briefly in the records and then vanish without a trace, presumably among the early casualties or emigrants. Furthermore, there is no reason to believe that those who left were any less successful than those who remained. At least 11 of the 25 known emigrants became landowners in Virginia. Only 13 to 15 of the 158 servants who appeared in the records as freemen (less than 10 percent) lived for more than a decade in Maryland as freemen without becoming landowners.

Those who acquired land did so rapidly. The interval between achieving freedom and acquiring land, which was discovered in forty-six cases, ranged from two years for Richard Nevill and Phillip West to twelve for John Norman and Walter Walterlin. Francis Pope, for whom the interval was seven years, and John Maunsell, who took eight, came closer to the median of seven and one-half years.

The holdings of the vast majority of those who acquired land were small. Most lived as small planters on tracts ranging in size from 50 acres to 400 acres, although fourteen former servants managed to become large landowners, possessing at least 1,000 acres at one time in their lives. Zachary Wade, who owned over 4,000 acres at his death in 1678 and about 5,000 acres in the early 1670s, ranked with the largest landowners in Maryland.

Inventories of personal estates, taken at death, have survived for 31 of the 158 former servants. Analysis of the inventories reinforces the conclusion that most of these men became small planters. About 60 percent of the inventories show personal property appraised at less than 100 pounds sterling. Men whose estates fell into this range led very simple lives. In most cases, livestock accounted for more than half the total value of their personal possessions. At best their clothing and household furnishings were meager. They either worked their plantations themselves or with the help of their wives and children, for few of these small planters owned servants and even fewer owned slaves. In Aubrey Land's apt phrase, they led lives of "rude sufficiency." But they fared no worse than the bulk of their compatriots and probably better than if they had remained in England.

Not all former servants remained small planters. Twelve of the thirty-one left estates appraised at more than 100 pounds. Men such as John Halfhead, Francis Pope, and James Walker could be described as substantial planters. Their lifestyle was not luxurious, but their economic position was secure and their assets usually included a servant or two and perhaps even a slave. Two men, Zachary Wade and Henry Adams, gained entry into the group of planter-merchants who dominated the local economy in the seventeenth century. Wade, whose estate was appraised at just over 400 pounds, was wealthier than 95 percent of his contemporaries, while Adams left an estate valued at £569 15s. 1d. when he died in 1686.

There are still other measures of mobility which confirm the picture of abundant opportunity for ex-servants that the study of property accumulation has indicated. Abbot E. Smith has estimated that only two of every ten servants brought to America in the seventeenth century became stable and useful members of colonial society, but if we take participation in government as indicative of stability and usefulness, the careers of the 158 men who survived servitude demonstrate that Smith's estimates are much too low, at least for the earlier part of the century.

Former servants participated in the government of Maryland as jurors, minor officeholders, justices of the peace, sheriffs, burgesses, and officers in the militia. Many also attended the Assembly as freemen at those sessions at which they were permitted. The frequency with which responsible positions were given to ex-servants testifies to the impressive status mobility they achieved in the mid-seventeenth century. Seventy-five or seventy-six of the survivors—just under 50 percent—sat on a jury, attended an Assembly session, or filled an office in Maryland. As was the case with landholding, this figure must be understood in the light of the careers of those who failed to participate. Fourteen of the nonparticipants died within a decade of becoming freemen; another twenty-seven left the province within ten years of completing their terms. There is no reason to assume that those who left did not participate in their new homes— two of the twenty-seven, John Tue and Mathew Rhodan, became justices of the peace in Virginia, while two others, Thomas Yewell and Robert Sedgrave, served as militia officer and clerk of a county court respectively. If we eliminate the twenty-five who appeared but fleetingly in the records, only sixteen or seventeen (slightly more than 10 percent) lived for more than a decade in the province as freemen without leaving any record of contribution to the community's government.

For most former servants participation was limited to occasional service as a juror, an appointment as constable, or service as a sergeant in the militia. Some compiled remarkable records in these minor positions. William Edwin, who was brought into the province in 1634 by Richard Gerard and served his time with the Jesuits, sat on nine Provincial Court juries and served a term as constable. Richard Nevill, who also entered Maryland in 1634, served on six Provincial Court juries and was a sergeant in the militia. A former servant of Gov. Leonard Calvert, John Halfhead, served on eleven juries and attended two sessions of the Assembly. John Robinson managed, in five years before his death in 1643, to attend two Assemblies, sit on three Provincial Court juries, and serve as constable and coroner of St. Clement's Hundred.

A high percentage of the 158 survivors went beyond service in these minor posts to positions of authority in the community. Twenty-two of them served the province as justice of the peace, burgess, sheriff, councillor, or officer in the militia. They accounted for 4 of Maryland's militia officers, 12 burgesses, 16 justices, 7 sheriffs, and 2 members of the Council.

For nine of the twenty-two former servants who came to hold major office in Maryland, tenure was brief. They served for a few years as an officer in the militia or as a county justice, or sat as burgess in a single session of the Assembly. During most of John Maunsell's twenty years in Maryland, participation was limited to occasional service as a juror. In 1649, he was returned as burgess from St. Mary's County. Daniel Clocker, who started out in Maryland as a servant to Thomas Cornwallis, compiled an impressive record of minor officeholding. He sat on numerous provincial court juries, served St. Mary's County as overseer of the highways, and was named to the Common Council of St. Mary's City in 1671. In 1655, when many more qualified men (Clocker was illiterate) were barred from office because of their Catholicism or suspect loyalty, he was appointed justice in St. Mary's County, a post he held for three years at most. Clocker was appointed militia officer by the rebellious Governor Josias Fendall in 1660, but again his taste of power was brief. John Cage, also a former servant to Cornwallis, was appointed to the Charles County bench in April 1660, but sat for only six months. Although Cage lived in Maryland for eighteen years after his brief term as justice, his participation was limited to infrequent jury duty. James Walker sat as justice in Charles County for a little more than two years. He lived in Maryland for more than thirty years, but this is the only recorded instance of his holding office.

Thirteen of the twenty-two men who acquired office could count themselves among Maryland's rulers in the first few decades following the founding of the province. Two even reached the Council, although neither became a major figure in the provincial government. John Hatch first participated as a provincial court juror in February 1643. By December 1647, he had been appointed sheriff of St. Mary's County. He was elected to the Assembly from St. George's Hundred in 1650 and from Charles County in 1658 and 1660. Hatch also sat as justice in Charles County from 1658 to 1661. He was appointed to the Council in 1654 and served until 1658. His son-in-law, Governor Fendall, again elevated him to the Council in 1660 during the rebellion against Lord Baltimore. Although after 1661 he was excluded from major office because his loyalty to the proprietor was suspect, he did manage to compile an impressive record of accomplishment for a man who entered Maryland as a servant. Robert Vaughan also entered Maryland as a servant, probably to Lord Baltimore. Vaughan attended the 1638 session of the Assembly as a freeman. He must have been an able man, for he was already both a sergeant in the militia and constable of St. George's Hundred. In 1640, he was returned as burgess from St. Clement's Hundred. He moved to Kent Island in 1642, probably at the urging of Governor Calvert, who sorely needed loyal supporters on the island which was a hotbed of opposition to his interests. Vaughan sat as justice of Kent for twenty-six years before he died in 1668 and served as an officer in the militia for at least that long. He was a member of the Council in 1648.

Although Hatch and Vaughan were the only former servants to reach positions of importance in the provincial government, eleven others became men of real weight in their counties of residence. These eleven averaged more than ten years on the bench, more than three sessions as burgess, and just under two years as sheriff. Zachary Wade, formerly a servant to Margaret Brent, was returned to the Assembly from St. Mary's County in 1658 and from Charles County from 1660 to 1666. He sat as justice of Charles County in 1660 and was reappointed in 1663. Wade served on the bench for a year and then stepped down to take a term as sheriff. He returned to the bench in 1667 and sat until his death in 1678. Henry Adams was brought into Maryland in 1638 and served his time with Thomas Greene, who later became governor. He was first appointed to the Charles County bench in 1658 and served continuously as justice until his death in 1686, with the exception of one year, 1665–1666, during which he was sheriff. Adams also represented Charles County in the Assembly in 1661, 1663–1664, and in every session from 1671 to 1684, when illness prevented him from assuming his seat. Nicholas Gwyther started out in Maryland as a servant to Thomas Cornwallis. Although he was never appointed justice and sat only once in the Assembly, his seven years as sheriff of St. Mary's County and three years as sheriff of Charles County made him one of the mainstays of Maryland's county government.

The significant role played by former servants in Maryland's government in the mid-seventeenth century and the opportunities available to industrious men can also be seen in an examination of the officials of Charles County in the years immediately following its establishment in 1658. Six justices were appointed to the Charles County bench by a commission dated May 10, 1658. Four of them— John Hatch, James Lindsey, Henry Adams, and James Walker—began their careers in Maryland as servants. In the next three years, four more ex-servants—John Cage, James Langworth, Francis Pope, and Zachary Wade—were appointed justices. Hatch, Wade, and Adams also represented the county in the Assembly in this period. Nicholas Gwyther, another former servant, was Charles County's first sheriff; four of the five men who immediately succeeded Gwyther were former servants. In the late 1650s and early 1660s, Charles

County was governed by men who had entered the province under indentures.

The accomplishments of those former servants who were especially successful were recognized by the community through the use of titles of distinction. At least 19 of the 158 survivors acquired the title of mister, gentleman, or esquire and retained it until they died. The 13 men who achieved positions of importance in the colony's government were all honored in this fashion. Office was not, however, the only path to a title. John Courts, for example, rode to distinction on his son's coattails. Although his father acquired a substantial landed estate, John Courts, Jr., started from humble beginnings, nevertheless married well, and, perhaps as a result of his father-in-law's influence, gained appointment to the Charles County bench in 1685. He represented the county in the Associator's Assembly and was appointed to the Council in 1692, a position he held until he died ten years later as one of Maryland's wealthiest men, leaving an estate worth over £1,800, including thirty slaves, and six servants. John Courts, Sr., was regularly addressed as mister after his more illustrious son was appointed to the Council. A few other men were honored with titles for part of their lives, but lost them before they died, as in the case of John Cage, who was only called mister during his brief tenure as justice.

Although the personal history of each of these 158 men is unique, common patterns may be discerned. We can construct a career model for indentured servants in Maryland in the middle of the seventeenth century which should reveal something about the way opportunity was structured and what options were open to men at various stages in their lives. We can also identify some of the components necessary for constructing a successful career in Maryland.

As a group, the indentured servants were young when they emigrated. While they ranged in age from mere boys such as Ralph Hasleton to the "old and decripit" Original Browne, the great majority were in their late teens and early twenties. Age on arrival was determined in thirty-six cases with a median of nineteen. Probably most were from English families of the "middling sort," yeomen, husbandmen, and artisans, men whose expectations might well include the acquisition of a freehold or participation in local government.

The careers of these men suggest that a few had formal education. Robert Vaughan and Robert Sedgrave both served as clerks in county court, a position requiring record-keeping skills. Cuthbert Fenwick was attorney to Thomas Cornwallis, who was probably the wealthiest man in Maryland in the 1630s and 1640s. It seems unlikely that Cornwallis would have allowed a man without education to manage his estate during his frequent absences from the province. These men were, however, not at all typical, for most of the 158 survivors were without education. Total illiterates outnumbered those who could write their names by about three to two, and it is probable that many who could sign their names could do little more.

A servant's life was not easy, even by seventeenth-century standards. Probably they worked the ten to fourteen hours a day, six days a week, specified in the famous Elizabethan Statute of Artificers. Servants could be sold, and there were severe penalties for running away. They were subject to the discipline of their masters, including corporal punishment within reason. On the other hand, servants had rights to adequate food, clothing, shelter, and a Sunday free from hard labor. Servants could not sue at common law, but they could protest ill-treatment and receive a hearing in the courts. Cases in this period are few, but the provincial court seems to have taken seriously its obligation to enforce the terms of indentures and protect servants' rights. No instances of serious mistreatment of servants appear in the records in the late 1630s and early 1640s. Servants were worked long and hard, but they were seldom abused. Moreover, the servant who escaped premature death soon found himself a free man in a society that offered great opportunities for advancement.

None of the indentures signed by these servants has survived, but it is possible to offer some reasonable conjecture concerning the terms of their service. John Lewger and Jerome Hawley, in their *Relation of Maryland,* offered some advice to men thinking of transporting servants into the province and they also printed a model indenture. A servant was to work at whatever his master "shall there imploy him, according to the costume of the Countrey." In return, the master was to pay his passage and provide food, lodging, clothing, and other "necessaries" during the servant's term "and at the end of the said term, to give him one whole yeeres provision of Corne, and fifty acres of Land, according to the order of the countrey." The order or custom of the country was specified in an act passed by the October 1640 session of the Assembly. Upon completion of his term the servant was to receive "one good Cloth Suite of Keirsey or Broadcloth a Shift of white linen one new pair of Stockins and Shoes two hoes one axe 3 barrels of Corne and fifty acres of land five whereof at least to be plantable." The land records make it clear that the requirement that masters give their former servants fifty acres of land cannot be taken literally. In practice, custom demanded only that a master provide a servant with the rights for fifty acres, an obligation assumed by the proprietor in 1648. If a servant wished to take advantage of this right and actually acquire a tract, he had to locate some vacant land and pay surveyor's and clerk's fees himself.

The usual term of service, according to Lewger and Hawley, was five years. However, they suggested, "for any artificer, or one that shall deserve more than ordinary, the Adventurer shall doe well to shorten that time . . . rather than to want such usefull men." A bill considered but not passed by the 1639 Assembly would have required servants arriving in Maryland without indentures to serve for four years if they were eighteen years old or over and until the age of twenty-four if they were under eighteen. The gap between time of arrival and first appearance in the records as freemen for the men under study suggests that the terms specified in this rejected bill were often followed in practice.

Servants were occasionally able to work out arrangements with their masters which allowed them to become freemen before their terms were completed. John Courts and Francis Pope purchased their remaining time from Fulke Brent, probably arranging to pay him out of whatever money they could earn by working as freemen. Thomas Todd, a glover, was released from servitude early by his master, John Lewger. In return, Todd was to dress a specified number of skins and also to make breeches and gloves for Lewger. George Evelin released three of his servants, Philip West, William Williamson, and John Hopson, for one year, during which they were to provide food, clothing, and lodging for themselves and also pay Evelin 1,000 pounds of tobacco each. Such opportunities were not available to all servants, however, and most probably served full terms.

On achieving freedom there were three options open to the former servant: he could either hire out for wages, lease land and raise tobacco on his own, or work on another man's plantation as a sharecropper. Although custom demanded that servants be granted the rights to fifty acres of land on completing their terms, actual acquisition of a tract during the first year of freedom was simply impracticable, and all former servants who eventually became freeholders were free for at least two years before they did so. To acquire land, one had to either pay surveyor's and clerk's fees for a patent or pay a purchase price to a landholder. The land then had to be cleared and housing erected. Provisions had to be obtained in some way until the crop was harvested, for a man could not survive a growing season on a mere three barrels of corn. Tools, seed, and livestock were also necessary. All this required capital, and capital was precisely what servants did not have. Wage labor, sharecropping, and leaseholding all offered men a chance to accumulate enough capital to get started on their own plantations and to sustain themselves in the meantime.

Wages were high in mid-seventeenth-century Maryland, usually fifteen to twenty pounds of tobacco per day for unskilled agricultural labor and even higher for those with much needed skills. These were remarkable rates given the fact that a man working alone could harvest, on the average, no more than 1,500 to 2,000 pounds of tobacco a year. Thirty-two of the 158 survivors were designated artisans in the records: 11 carpenters, 4 blacksmiths, 5 tailors, 4 sawyers, 2 millwrights, a brickmason, mariner, cooper, glover, and barber-surgeon. These men probably had little trouble marketing their skills. At a time when labor was scarce, even men who had nothing but a strong back and willing hands must have found all the work they wanted. However, few of the 158 men devoted themselves to full time wage labor for extended periods. Instead, most worked their own crop and only hired out occasionally to supplement their planting income.

Nevertheless, some men did sign contracts or enter into verbal agreements for long-term wage labor. There were some differences between their status and that of indentured servants. They probably could not be sold, they could sue at common law for breach of covenant, and they may have possessed some poltical privileges. There were severe restrictions on their personal freedom, however, and their daily life must have been similar to a servant's. Wages ranged from

1,100 to 1,500 pounds of tobacco a year plus shelter, food, and clothing. Ex-servants occasionally hired out for long terms, perhaps because of heavy indebtedness or lack of alternative opportunities, or perhaps because of the security such contracts afforded. Recently freed servants may have found long-term wage contracts an attractive means of making the transition from indentured laborer to free colonist. While long-term wage labor was, in a sense, a prolongation of servitude, it could also serve as a means of capital accumulation and an avenue of mobility.

The records reveal little of the extent or conditions of sharecropping in the 1640s, but it is clear that several of the 158 former servants did work on another man's plantation for a share of the crop. By the 1660s—and there seems no reason to assume that this was not also the case in the earlier period—working for a "share" meant that a man joined other workers on a plantation in making a crop, the size of his share to be determined by dividing the total crop by the number of laborers. Contracts often required the plantation owner to pay the cropper's taxes and provide diet, lodging, and washing while obliging the cropper to work at other tasks around the plantation. The status of such sharecroppers seems indistinguishable from that of wage laborers on long-term contracts.

Most of the 158 former servants established themselves as small planters on leased land immediately after they had completed their terms. There were two types of leases available to ex-servants, leaseholds for life or for a long term of years and short-term leaseholds or tenancies at will. Although these forms of leaseholding differed in several important respects, both allowed the tenant to become the head of a household. As householders, former bondsmen achieved a degree of independence and a measure of responsibility denied to servants, wage laborers, and sharecroppers. Heads of households were masters in their own families, responsible for the discipline, education, and maintenance of their subordinates. They formed the backbone of the political community, serving on juries, sitting in Assembly, and filling the minor offices. The favorable man/land ratio in early Maryland made the formation of new households a fairly easy task and servants usually became householders soon after completing their terms.

In many ways there was little difference between land held in fee simple and a lease for life or for a long term of years. Such leases were inheritable and could be sold; they were usually purchased for a lump sum and yearly rents were often nominal. Terms varied considerably, but all long-term leaseholds provided the tenant a secure tenure and a chance to build up equity in his property. Such leases were not common in seventeenth-century Maryland, although a few appear on the private manors in St. Mary's County in the 1640s. Probably men were reluctant to purchase a lease when they could acquire land in fee simple for little additional outlay.

Tenancies at will or short-term leaseholds, usually running for no more than six or seven years, were undoubtedly the most common form of tenure for recently freed servants. In contrast to long-term leases, short-term leaseholds offered little security, could not be sold or inherited, and terminated at the death of either party to the contract. Their great advantage was the absence of an entry fee, a feature particularly attractive to men without capital. Since land was plentiful and labor scarce, rents must have been low, certainly no higher than 500 pounds of tobacco a year for a plantation and perhaps as low as 200 pounds. Rent for the first year, furthermore, was probably not demanded until after the crop was in. No contracts for the 1640s have survived, but later in the century tenants were often required to make extensive improvements on the plantation. Although tenure was insecure, short-term leaseholding afforded ample opportunity for mobility as long as tobacco prices remained high. In the 1640s and 1650s, leaseholding benefited both landlord and tenant. Landlords had their land cleared, housing erected, and orchards planted and fenced while receiving a small rental income. Tenants were able to accumulate the capital necessary to acquire a tract of their own.

Prior to 1660, small planters, whether leaseholders or landowners, frequently worked in partnership with another man when attempting to carve new plantations out of the wilderness. Much hard work was involved in clearing land, building shelter, and getting in a crop; men who could not afford to buy servants or pay wages often joined with a mate. Partners Joseph Edlow and Christopher Martin, John Courts and Francis Pope, John Shirtcliffe and Henry Spinke, and William Brown and John Thimbelly were all former servants who arrived in Maryland before the end of 1642. They must have found their "mateships" mutually beneficial, since, except for Martin who died in 1641, all eventually became landowners.

Some men—about 10 percent of those former servants who lived in Maryland for more than a decade as freemen—did not manage to escape tenancy. Rowland Mace, for example, was still a leaseholder on St. Clement's Manor in 1659, after which he disappeared from the records. The inventory of the estate of Charles Steward, who lived on Kent Island as a freeman for more than forty years and was frequently called planter, indicates that he was operating a plantation when he died in 1685, but Steward failed to acquire freehold title to a tract of his own. A few others acquired land, held it briefly, and then returned to leaseholding arrangements. John Maunsell had some prosperous years in Maryland. He arrived in the province in 1638 as a servant to William Bretton and served about four years. He patented 100 acres in 1649 and added 500 more in 1651, but he could not hold the land and in 1653 sold it all to William Whittle. He then moved to St. Clement's Manor, where he took up a leasehold, and was still a tenant on the manor when he died in 1660. John Shanks, although he too suffered fluctuations in prosperity, ended his career on a more positive note. Entering Maryland in 1640 as a servant to Thomas Gerard, he must have been quite young when he arrived, for he did not gain his freedom until 1648. In 1652 he patented 200 acres and also purchased the freedom of one Abigail, a servant to Robert Brooke, whom he soon married. He sold his land in 1654, and, following Maunsell's path, took up a leasehold on St. Clement's Manor. Shanks, however, managed to attain the status of a freeholder again, owning 300 acres in St. Mary's County when he died in 1684. His inventory—the estate was appraised at just under 100 pounds—indicates that Shanks ended life in Maryland as a fairly prosperous small planter.

Most of the 158 former servants, if they lived in Maryland for more than ten years as freemen, acquired land and held it for as long as they remained in the province. Almost any healthy man in Maryland in the 1640s and 1650s, if he worked hard, practiced thrift, avoided expensive lawsuits, and did not suffer from plain bad luck, could become a landowner in a short time. Tobacco prices were relatively high, and, while living costs may also have been high, land was not expensive. Even at the highest rates a 100-acre tract could be patented for less than 500 pounds of tobacco, and even the lowest estimates indicate that a man could harvest 1,200 pounds in a year. Again barring ill-health and misfortune, retaining land once acquired must not have been too difficult a task, at least before tobacco prices fell after the Restoration.

Hard work and thrift were, of course, not the only paths to land-ownership. For some the fruits of office cleared the way. William Empson, for example, was still a tenant to Thomas Baker in 1658, after ten years of freedom. In 1659, Nicholas Gwyther employed him as deputy sheriff, and in the next year Empson was able to purchase a plantation from his former landlord. Others charmed their way to the status of freeholder. Henry Adams married Mary Cock-shott, daughter of John Cockshott and stepdaughter of Nicholas Causine, both of whom were substantial Maryland planters. To the historian, though perhaps not to Adams, Miss Cockshott's most obvious asset was 1,200 acres of land which her mother had taken up for her and her sister Jane in 1649.

For most former servants progress stopped with the acquisition of a small plantation. Others managed to go beyond small planter status to become men of wealth and power. What was it that distinguished the 13 former servants who became men of importance in Maryland politics from the other 145 who survived servitude?

Education was one factor. We have already seen that a few of the 158 probably possessed some formal training. Early colonial Maryland did not have enough educated men to serve as justices or sheriffs, perform clerical and surveying functions, or work as attorneys in the courts. Under such conditions, a man proficient with the pen could do quite well for himself. Men such as Cuthbert Fenwick, Robert Vaughan, and Robert Sedgrave found their education valuable in making the transition from servant to man of consequence. While approximately 60 percent of the 158 who survived servitude were totally illiterate, only 2 of the 13 who came to exercise real power in Maryland and only 7 of the 22 who held major office were unable to write their names.

Marriage played a role in some of the most impressive success stories. Henry Adams's marriage has already been mentioned. Zachary Wade married a niece of Thomas Hatton, principal secretary of Maryland in the 1650s. James Langsworth married a Gardiner, thereby allying himself with a very prominent southern Maryland family. Cuthbert Fenwick married at least twice. We know nothing of his first wife, but Fenwick found fame and fortune by marrying in 1649 Jane Moryson, widow of a prominent Virginian, a niece of Edward Eltonhead, one of the masters of chancery, and a sister of William Eltonhead, who sat on the Maryland Council in the 1650s.

It would be a mistake, however, to overestimate the significance of education and marriage in the building of a successful career. Certainly they helped, but they were not essential ingredients. Nicholas Gwyther became a man of consequence in Maryland, but married a former servant. John Warren served as justice of St. Mary's County for nine years, but could not write his name. Daniel Clocker and John Maunsell both held major office in Maryland. Both were illiterate and both married former servants. Clearly, Maryland in the middle of the seventeenth century was open enough to allow a man who started at the bottom without special advantages to acquire a substantial estate and a responsible position.

It seems probable that Maryland continued to offer ambitious immigrants without capital a good prospect of advancement throughout the 1640s and 1650s. But there is evidence to suggest that opportunities declined sharply after 1660. True, the society did not become completely closed and some men who started life among the servants were still able to end life among the masters. Miles Gibson is a case in point, and there were others. Philip Lynes emigrated as a servant in the late 1660s and later became a member of the Council and a man of considerable wealth. Christopher Goodhand, who also entered Maryland as a servant in the later 1660s, later served as justice of Kent County and left an estate appraised at nearly 600 pounds. However, in the latter part of the century men such as Gibson, Goodhand, and Lynes were unusual; at mid-century they were not. As Table 1 illustrates, the chances that a former servant would attain an office of power in Maryland diminished sharply as the century progressed.

This reduction in the proportion of former servants among Maryland's rulers is directly related to basic demographic processes that worked fundamental changes in the colony's political structure. The rapid growth in the population of the province during the seventeenth century affected the life chances of former servants in at least two ways. First, there was a reduction in the number of offices available in proportion to the number of freemen, resulting in increased competition for positions of power and profit. Secondly, there was an increase in the number of men of wealth and status available to fill

TABLE 1
Servant Officeholders, 1634–1689
(Former servants serving as burgess, justice of the peace, and sheriff in Charles, Kent, and St. Mary's counties, Maryland, 1634–1689, by date of first appointment.)

		Servants	
	New Officials	*Number*	*Percent*
1634–1649	57	11–12	19.3–22.8
1650–1659	39	12	30.8
1660–1669	64	9	14.1
1670–1679	44	4–5	9.1–11.4
1680–1689	46	4	8.7

positions of authority. In the decades immediately following the founding of the province there were simply not enough men who conformed to the standards people expected their rulers to meet. As a consequence, many uneducated small planters of humble origins were called upon to rule. Among the immigrants to Maryland after the Restoration were a number of younger sons of English gentry families and an even larger number of merchants, many of whom were attracted to the Chesapeake as a result of their engagement in the tobacco trade. By the late seventeenth century, these new arrivals, together with a steadily growing number of native gentlemen, had created a ruling group with more wealth, higher status, and better education than the men who had ruled earlier in the century. As this group grew in size, poor illiterate planters were gradually excluded from office. Table 2, which focuses on the educational levels of all major officeholders by measuring literacy, demonstrates the degree and rate of change.

Former servants also found that their chances of acquiring land and of serving as jurors and minor officeholders were decreasing. Probably the movement of prices for tobacco and land was the most important factor responsible for this decline of opportunity. During the 1640s and 1650s, the available evidence—which, it must be admitted, is not entirely satisfactory—indicates that farm prices for Chesapeake tobacco fluctuated between one and one-half and three pence per pound. After 1660, prices declined due to overproduction, mercantilist restrictions, and a poorly developed marketing system

TABLE 2
Illiterate Officeholders, 1634–1689

(Illiterates serving as burgess, justice of the peace, and sheriff in Charles, Kent, and St. Mary's counties, Maryland, 1634–1689, by date of first appointment.)

		Illiterates	
	New Officials	*Number*	*Percent*
1634–1649	57	16	28.1
1650–1659	39	9	23.1
1660–1669	64	17	26.6
1670–1679	44	1	2.3
1680–1689	46	4	8.7

that allowed farm prices to sink far below those justified by European price levels. By using crop appraisals and other data from estate inventories, it is possible to construct a fairly dependable series for farm prices of Maryland tobacco from 1659 to 1710. In the 1660s, prices averaged 1.3d per pound. For the 1670s, the average was just over a penny. During each of the next three decades the average price was less than a penny per pound. Falling tobacco prices were not, however, the only obstacle to land acquisition, for while tobacco prices were going down, land prices were going up. V. J. Wyckoff has argued that the purchase price of land increased by 135 percent from 1663 to 1700.

One consequence of these price changes was a change in the nature and dimensions of short-term leaseholding. In the 1640s and 1650s, tenancy was a typical step taken by a man without capital on the road to land acquisition. However, falling tobacco prices and rising land prices made it increasingly difficult to accumulate the capital necessary to purchase a freehold. In the 1660s fragmentary results suggest that only 10 percent of the householders in Maryland were established on land they did not own. By the end of the century the proportion of tenants had nearly tripled. Tenancy was no longer a transitory status; for many it had become a permanent fate.

A gradual constriction of the political community paralleled the rise in tenancy. In years immediately following settlement, all freemen, whether or not they owned land, regularly participated in government as voters, jurors, and minor officeholders. At the beginning of the eighteenth century a very different situation prevailed. In a proclamation of 1670, Lord Baltimore disfranchised all freemen who possessed neither fifty acres of land nor a visible estate worth forty pounds sterling. This meant, in effect, that short-term leaseholders could no longer vote, since few could meet the forty pounds requirement. Furthermore, by the early eighteenth century landowners virtually monopolized jury duty and the minor offices. In the middle of the seventeenth century, most freemen in Maryland had an ample opportunity to acquire land and participate in community government; by the end of the century a substantial portion of the free male heads of households were excluded from the political process and unable to become landowners.

Evidence for this general constriction of opportunity can be seen in the careers of the children of the 158 survivors. No attempt was made at a systematic survey of the fortunes of the second generation, but enough information was gathered in the course of research to support some generalizations. In only one family did the children clearly outdistance the accomplishments of their father. John Courts's son, John Jr., became a member of the Council, while his daughter, Elizabeth, married James Keech, later a Provincial Court justice. Of the 22 former servants who came to hold major office in Maryland, only 6 either left sons who also held major office or daughters who married men who did so. The great leap upward in the histories of these families took place in the first generation. If the immigrants managed to become small, landowning planters, their children maintained that position but seldom moved beyond it. If the immigrants were somewhat more successful and obtained offices of power, their children sometimes were able to maintain the family station but often experienced downward mobility into small planter status.

In order to provide more direct evidence that opportunities for men who entered Maryland without capital were declining, an effort was made to study the careers of a group of servants who arrived in the 1660s and 1670s. The problems encountered were formidable. The increase in population and the fact that by this time servants could end up in any one of ten counties in Maryland made simple name correlation from headright entries unreliable. To surmount this difficulty an alternative approach was developed. In 1661, in order to regulate the length of service for those servants brought into the colony without indentures, the Assembly passed an act requiring that masters bring their servants into the county courts to have their ages judged and registered. Using a list of names from this source simplified the problem of identification by placing the servants geographically and providing precise information about their age and length of service. Even with these additional aids, career-line study of obscure men proved difficult and the sample disappointingly small. However, the results did confirm inferences drawn from data about price changes and tenancy and offered support for the argument that as the century progressed, servants found it increasingly difficult to acquire land and participate in government.

From 1662 to 1672, 179 servants were brought into the Charles County Court to have their ages judged. Only 58 of the 179 definitely appeared in the records as freeman, a fact which in itself suggests declining opportunities, since there does seem to be a relationship between a man's importance in the community and the frequency of his appearance in the public records. Of the 58 of whom something could be learned, only 13 to 17—22 to 29 percent—eventually became landowners. Furthermore, none acquired great wealth. Mark Lampton, who owned 649 acres in the early 1690s, was the largest landowner in the group and the only one who owned more than 500 acres. Robert Benson, whose estate was appraised at just over 200 pounds, left the largest inventory. Lampton was the only other one of the 58 whose estate was valued at more than 100 pounds.

A study of the participation of these men in local government indicates that opportunities in this field were also declining. Only twenty-three to twenty-five of the fifty-eight sat on a jury or filled an office, and the level at which they participated was low. Only one, Henry Hardy, who was appointed to the Charles County bench in 1696, held major office. A few others compiled impressive records as minor officeholders. Mathew Dike, for example, sat on eight juries and served as overseer of the highways and constable, while Robert Benson was twice a constable and fourteen times a juryman. For most of these men, however, occasional service as a juror was the limit of their participation. Five of the twenty-three known participants served only once as a juror, while another six only sat twice.

The contrast between the careers of these 58 men and the 158 who entered Maryland before 1642 is stark. At least 46 of the 58 lived in the province as freemen for over a decade. In other words, 50 to 57 percent lived in Maryland as freemen for more than ten years and did not acquire land, while 36 to 40 percent did not participate in government. Only about 10 percent of the 158 who arrived in the earlier period and lived in the colony for a decade as freemen failed to become landowners and participants.

How successful, then, in the light of these data, was the institution of servitude in seventeenth-century Maryland? The answer depends on perspective and chronology. Servitude had two primary functions. From the master's viewpoint its function was to supply labor. From the point of view of the prospective immigrant without capital, servitude was a means of mobility, both geographic and social; that is, it was a way of getting to the New World and, once there, of building a life with more prosperity and standing than one could reasonably expect to attain at home. Its success in performing these two quite different functions varied inversely as the century progressed. Prior to 1660, servitude served both purposes well. It provided large planters with an inexpensive and capable work force and allowed poor men entry into a society offering great opportunities for advancement. This situation in which the two purposes complemented each other did not last, and the institution gradually became more successful at supplying labor as it became less so at providing new opportunities. Some men were always able to use servitude as an avenue of mobility, but, over the course of the century, more and more found that providing labor for larger planters, first as servants and later as tenants, was their permanent fate.

Jackson T. Main

SOCIAL MOBILITY IN REVOLUTIONARY AMERICA

Jackson T. Main's examination of social mobility is part of his remarkably comprehensive study of American society and social structure in the period of the American Revolution. Mr. Main has studied mobility in diverse milieus in every geographical section, ranging from newer communities along the frontier to the great eastern seaboard cities. The strength of his work in addition to its comprehensiveness is its reliance on substantial evidence gathered from inventories of estates, wills, tax assessment records, and other primary data. In view of the disparities of the evidence for different communities, some of his conclusions are more solidly grounded than are others. The reader should bear in mind that some of the allusions to the improved lot of various groups are not thereby examples of upward mobility.

Mobility in the Revolutionary era was of two types: movement from place to place ("horizontal" mobility) and movement upward or downward in society ("vertical" mobility). The two were essentially connected, for it was above all a man's ability to move to a new location that gave him a chance to rise.

Horizontal mobility needs little discussion. Americans were of "an unsettled disposition" by inheritance, for everyone was either an immigrant or descended from one. The lure of cheap fresh land, the attraction of the city, the excess of population in long-settled communities, and perhaps certain cultural factors such as the reduced importance of the family kept people moving about. One observer believed that "it is scarcely possible in any part of the continent to find a man, amongst the middling and lower classes of Americans, who has not changed his farm and his residence many different times." The intent, he continued, was not "merely to gratify a wandering disposition; in every change he hopes to make money." Immigrants started as city workers and ended as farmers or country artisans; indentured servants in a farming community obtained their freedom, took up land, followed a trade, or hired themselves out in

From "Mobility in Early America," in Jackson Turner Main, *The Social Structure of Revolutionary America* (copyright © 1965 by Princeton University Press; Princeton Paperback, 1968), pp. 164–196. Reprinted by permission of Princeton University Press. Footnotes deleted.

some other village; the sons of yeomen went west, north, south; entire families departed and others arrived to replace them. Indeed this constant movement makes the process almost impossible to study in detail.

One reason for horizontal mobility was the decreasing chance to rise in older rural areas. Even before 1700 good land in some coastal regions was unobtainable except by purchase from individuals. The price of land near the cities and along major waterways rose very rapidly. Mittelberger observed that near Philadelphia, cultivated farms cost £16 per acre and even uncleared land was priced at £5 to £8, so that it was hard for German immigrants to establish themselves. Even in the Piedmont of northern Virginia, according to Schoepf, it was expensive to buy land, "and hence the incessant migrations to the farther regions." The young man, indentured servant, or free immigrant thus found his opportunity restricted in many parts of the country, and moved elsewhere in search of a fortune.

Vertical mobility therefore varied with the place, and must be studied along the Eastern seaboard as well as on the frontier. It varied with the individual too. The principal authority on indentured servants believes that they "were much more idle, irresponsible, unhealthy, and immoral than the generality of good English laborers." Land was seldom given to them when their term was up, and one student has found that only about one in ten servants had the qualities necessary to obtain it. Another 10 percent became artisans, but the rest failed—died, became landless workers, or returned to England. These opinions are based upon servants of the pre-Revolutionary years. By 1763 the quality of these immigrants had improved; yet it remains true that the native Americans had an advantage over the foreign born. Probably more important was the degree of skill which the individual possessed. Mobility also varied with the objective, for the young man could easily become a small property holder but few replaced rags with riches. The study of mobility during the years 1763–1788 therefore requires examination of several different problems: the upward progress of the landless servant or worker into the ranks of the small farmer, measured both in settled areas and on the frontier; and mobility into the colonial upper class, rural and urban.

European travelers and Americans all agreed that the young man could easily achieve economic independence. Contemporaries insisted that immigrants, even indentured servants, could "acquire an

easy and honest competency." Indeed there are many instances of
the sort. Western lands were cheap and so easily obtained that
artisans who saved their money could migrate. Even laborers, it was
reported, refused to work long for high wages before they took
up land. "The laboring man will never be so much lost to a sense of
his interest and independence, as to toil for others for small wages,
when, by removing a little further off, he may possess, in his own
right, perhaps a better farm than any of us do at present," predicted
"Genesea."

Observers recorded that one could start as a small farmer and
acquire real wealth. Planters in South Carolina, wrote "Mechanic" in
1783, had emigrated fifty years before, many "from the lowest classes
of mankind," borrowed money, become rich, and now their descen-
dants had hundreds of slaves and lived lavishly. Travelers recorded
astonishing examples. A North Carolina planter owned 1,500 acres
worth at least £3,000, which his father had bought for £30. A South
Carolinian started with five slaves and ended with an annual income
of £5,000 to £6,000. Jonathan Boucher, the Maryland clergyman, arrived with nothing in 1759 and by 1772 was worth £3,500 plus his
income as minister. Governor Cadwallader Colden wrote that in
New York, "the most opulent families in our own Memory, have
arisen from the lowest Rank of the People." The opportunities were
well summarized by James Iredell, the Scottish immigrant who became an eminent lawyer. In England, he wrote, he would have remained for some years in a dependent and insecure position,
whereas in America he was sure of at least an independent income,
and he had "a moral certainty of acquiring such an income every
year as will maintain me genteely. A young country is the fittest for
a young man without a fortune, and however unpromising or dis-
agreeable it may be at first, a steady attentive perseverance will in
all likelihood be at last successful."

These individual instances or opinions prove only that a few men
made their fortunes in the New World. But how general was such
success? Did the landless really acquire property, or were there only
a few who by their good fortune created an appearance, while in
reality most of the landless remained poor? And at the other end of
the economic scale, were the wealthy merchants and landowners
self-made men, or did they start with advantages, the sons of merchants and planters and professional men? The answers can be

found by examining mobility on the frontier, in settled farm communities, and in the towns.

The records of Lunenburg County, Virginia, afford an exceptionally good opportunity to study mobility on the frontier. Tax lists for 1764 show the number of tithes (white men and Negroes over twenty-one) and the amount of land held by each landholder. White tithes were named. Some held land, some did not. Of the latter, most were listed separately, probably signifying that they were heads of families, but others were listed as subordinate to a landholder, their names being indented below that of the farmer. Among these, many bore the same name as that of the landowner, and were doubtless sons who were as yet dependent upon their fathers; while others had quite different names, and were probably hired workers or indentured servants (the few overseers are identified as such). Eighteen years later the first post-Revolutionary tax lists begin. The records of 1782 furnish us with a presumably complete list of landowners and nonlandowners in almost all of the counties, with the amount of land, slaves, horses and cattle held. These records make possible an examination of the degree to which residents of a Virginia county moved from one place to another or changed their economic status as measured by the ownership of land—which in agricultural Virginia was crucial.

Lunenburg was settled principally by small farmers. A few well-to-do planters were present, but there had been little large-scale land speculation. Therefore the county was reasonably typical of that great area south of the James known as the "Southside," typical also of part of the northern Piedmont and of equivalent areas elsewhere in the South. Indeed a majority of Virginians and probably most Southerners lived at one time or another in similar areas. By 1764 it was rapidly ceasing to be a frontier: two new counties, Charlotte and Halifax, were to be created out of it the following year. More than half of the men had land, as was characteristic of the areas which were recently settled. Among those who were not landholders, half were members of landowning families, while the rest were equally divided between heads of families and dependent workers. The great majority of landholders belonged to the small farmer class—nearly three-quarters held between 100 and 500 acres (the median being 340). Some large planters were already present, and there were six estates of more than 2,000 acres, but the wealthiest 10 percent of the men had less than 40 percent of the land, a percentage typical of frontier communities, and there were no large slaveholders. In short, Lunenburg was in an early stage of its development.

Most of the residents of the county were, of course, recent arrivals, and many of them were still on the move. This is especially the case with those who had not acquired land and who did not have relatives in the county. These were men who obviously had started without property, for if their families had possessed some means, they surely would have purchased land at once. They formed a considerable part of the population—there were, in fact, over 100 of them. Of these more than one-third left the county. They were joined in their emigration by a handful of the landless who did have local family connections; and in addition about 1 out of 12 landowners also went west. Altogether perhaps 1 out of 5 Lunenburgers moved on. The major movement however was into, not out of the county: by 1782 at least 150 men had entered Lunenburg and acquired land, thus increasing the landholding population by 50 percent. Meanwhile the original population much more than reproduced itself, so that the total number of landowners doubled between 1764 and 1782.

What became of the men who in 1764 occupied the bottom of the economic ladder? If one lived in a Lunenburg—that is, in an area recently settled and still being developed, in a society still highly mobile—the chance to rise was excellent. Among the approximately 150 men who had not acquired land in 1764 and whose careers can be traced with some probability, at least three-fourths had done so by 1782.

This estimate is based partly on inference. There is a gap in the records during the Revolutionary War years, and when tax lists are again available it is evident that many of the men had gone. No vital records have been preserved, so that it is impossible to determine whether the man not listed had died or moved away. He may have acquired land and then died, or sold it, leaving no trace of the transaction. The only safe procedure is to eliminate such a person from our calculations. In many cases the man himself vanishes, but someone with the same surname appears in his stead as a landowner. If the name is a common one in the area, then the relationship is doubtful, but if the name is unusual, probably the landless worker of 1764 acquired a farm, died, and left it to a son (or a wife or daughter) who became the taxpayer of 1782. For example, John Mason had no land in 1764, but Nathaniel and William held 100 acres in 1782. The chances are good that John acquired this property and left it to his children. So also James Vaughn probably inherited his 640 acres from Michael.

The chance for error is greatly increased when we attempt to trace the careers of the men who left the country, or who at all events are not known to its records after 1764. Where a man's name was uncommon, we are probably justified in assuming that one who turns up in the records elsewhere is the same man. The John Broughton who patented 160 acres in Bedford County, or the Philip Poindexter, Sr., who paid taxes on 353 acres in Mecklenburg County in 1782, are in all probability the same men who are missing in the Lunenburg records. In the case of Poindexter, indeed, his son Philip Jr., who was listed with him in 1764, is also recorded. But we can hardly be certain about a man with so ordinary a name as Thomas Hill. The decisive factor in many of these cases is the location of the county: the general course of migration was into adjacent areas and especially into the counties lying directly west. Therefore Thomas Hill of Stafford, far to the north, must be disregarded, but the Thomas Hills of Halifax (100 acres) or of Pittsylvania (400 acres) are strong possibilities, especially when it is discovered that many Lunenburg names are found in those counties. Moreover if some men are in this way considered to have acquired land who did not actually do so, the error is compensated for because other Lunenburgers probably became landholders without our knowing it. Land patents do show what the colony or state sold, and a few individuals can be traced in this way, but private sales cannot always be traced; moreover Lunenburg is not far from the North Carolina border, and undoubtedly some of the drifters ended life as respectable Tar Heel farmers. Thus the error, if such it is, of counting Thomas Hill among those who acquired land, is counteracted by the equal error of including John Nunn among those who did not, when in fact he may have bought a farm elsewhere.

Altogether, eliminating the men who simply disappear, probably 60 percent of the nonlandholders of 1764 became farmers in Lunenburg, and another 14 percent secured land elsewhere. If full information could be obtained, especially about North Carolina holdings and about the number of deaths, we might find the actual total to be nearly 80 percent.

The most interesting men are those who did not have the advantage, as far as names reveal the situation, of any family relationship. These men obviously were on their own, being unable to secure land upon their entrance into Lunenburg, and without a relative to help them locally. Indeed about half of them were dependent workers. Yet of this large group—over 100 persons—very nearly two-thirds had obtained land by 1782. In all but a dozen cases the records clearly show the man himself, or one of identical name, securing land; in the others the relationship is probable rather than certain. Overseers, usually thought to be drifters, were successful in acquiring property: 9 of them did so in Lunenburg and 2 obtained land elsewhere—a total of 11 out of 14. In addition, one who already owned 480 acres in 1764 held 1,172 acres and 2 slaves in 1782.

Mobility occurred among the landowners too. There was a slight movement downward as well as upward, for among the nearly 300 Lunenburg landholders in 1764 about one-fourth vanished from the tax lists and were not replaced by a relative. Most of these had not really lost ground. Some had always been residents of other counties where they continued to own land; some are known to have died; and two dozen or so moved from Lunenburg and acquired land elsewhere, thus holding their own, economically, or even advancing. There remain only 4 landholders in 1764 who appear on the tax rolls of 1782 without land, plus 13 more who are not on the later lists and who could not be traced. Some of them doubtless had died or moved to North Carolina. Therefore the number who became poorer was extremely small. The owners of large estates (over 500 acres) were quite apt to lose part of their property—indeed rather more of them did so than retained their land intact. On the other hand a compensating number of smaller farmers increased their acreage. Thus among the landowners, about as many rose as fell, and the great majority held their own.

Accordingly, of the entire population in 1764, landless as well as landed, over half remained in the same status, whether high or low, in 1782; about one out of twelve moved downward; and one-third moved up. Since our records tend to exaggerate the proportion which lost ground, it seems probable that the net upward mobility rate (those who rose minus those who fell) was about 25 percent. But this is not the whole of the story, for into Lunenburg poured a great immigration, creating new large estates to replace the old, and adding over 100 families to the small farmer class. Thus Lunenburg, as it developed out of the frontier stage, created opportunities for many of her native sons to rise, and yet could provide scores of immigrants with farms. Just as some of the landless Lunenburgers moved into Pittsylvania or Charlotte or Halifax and took up land, so the poor sons of Tidewater families found homes and property in Lunenburg.

That the high rate of mobility on the Virginia frontier was the rule is shown by Charles Grant's work on Kent, Connecticut, a typical New England frontier town. Kent was founded before 1740. According to Grant, its society during the first half-century or so contained a very large "middle class" of small property owners, and a small "poor class" of men assessed, for tax purposes, at £29 or less. The latter usually comprised between one-fourth and one-third of the population. Most of the "poor" undoubtedly were landless, for the poll assessment alone was £18. A few of those paying a higher tax probably lacked land also, but these must be omitted from consideration. Grant then divides this poor and presumably landless class into three categories: "poor transients" who left without acquiring land; "poor climbers" who remained and improved their economic status, presumably acquiring land; and "permanent pro-letarians" who remained but did not succeed.

Four tax lists from 1740 to 1777 show that there were all told 150 persons classified as poor (about one-fourth of the men), of whom 43 percent left, 44 percent rose, and 13 percent remained but did not rise. In Lunenburg, the gap in records between 1765 and 1782 makes precision impossible, but there seem to have been even fewer "permanent proletarians." The proportion who left was about the same, and the proportion who remained and succeeded was somewhat larger in the Virginia county. Grant did not try to follow the immigrants, but he was able to demonstrate that among those who stayed in Kent, 77 percent acquired land. "The most obvious conclusions about the 'hired hand poor,'" Grant observed, "would seem to be these: from 1740 to 1777 they were temporary poor, temporary hired hands. The greater part of them stayed in Kent and soon saved or borrowed enough to buy a farm of their own."

Goshen, Connecticut, is not far from Kent and was settled about the same time. In 1751 the town contained a slightly larger proportion of "poor," using Grant's definition, and perhaps also more land-less. At any rate one-third of the men had no land according to the tax list of that year. Goshen was primarily an agricultural community, though one out of six paid some sort of a faculty tax. Of those who had no land, the majority left before 1771, when another tax list permits comparison. Of those who remained, 71 percent probably obtained land. Among Goshen's landless in 1771 who stayed in the town until 1782 (again most of the landless men departed), as high as 86 percent may have obtained land.

These Goshen lists also make possible conclusions based upon assessed property generally. In 1751, 31 percent of the men paid a tax on less than £30 worth of property (heads, oxen, horses, cattle, swine, acres, and faculty). Twenty years later, over half of them had left, but among those who remained, five-sixths had increased their wealth, one in fact being among the town's well-to-do men. Meanwhile the poor men of 1751 had been replaced in 1771 by nearly twice as many new poor men, about two-thirds of whom had immigrated from other towns, the remainder having been born in Goshen (one of whom had previously owned more property). By 1782 an even larger number had left, while of those remaining, four-fifths rose. Most acquired only small property, but once again a newcomer attained high rank. The native-born residents were naturally much more successful than the immigrants: half improved their positions within the town; while the great majority of the newcomers who had drifted to Goshen drifted right out again. Once more in 1782 those who had left were replaced—but now only just replaced—by another group of poor immigrants. It is impossible to trace those who departed, but records of other frontiers demonstrate that many of them eventually settled down.

When the frontier stage had ended, and society became stable, the chance to rise diminished. All the land worth owning was now occupied, and land prices rose, so that the sons of pioneers and the newcomers could not so easily improve their positions. Mobility therefore diminished as the community grew older. Grant found that by 1796, when Kent had become a well-established, primarily subsistence farm community, the mobility rate sharply declined. Half of the poor left, and of those who remained, half did not improve their position. The final stage of this process is represented by Lancaster County, in the eastern part of Virginia's Northern Neck. Tax lists of 1773, nearly complete, record the names of all men and their land, if any. These names can be compared with the tax lists of 1782 and of subsequent years. Lancaster was not quite typical of the eastern counties in that only 46 percent of the men were land-less—a higher proportion than in Lunenburg, but lower than the average. The median farm was 260 acres, smaller than that farther west. Large estates were less numerous than in Virginia generally, and the concentration of property, though greater than in Lunenburg, was less than normal for a Tidewater county, the wealthiest 10 percent owning 45 percent of the land.

The opportunities for acquiring land within the county were limited, especially by contrast with the situation nearer the frontier. In Lunenburg, over half of the landless stayed at home and obtained land there, but in Lancaster, only one-third succeeded in doing so. Moreover Lunenburg was only a step from the real frontier, so that another 14 percent could obtain land in nearby areas; but this was not so easy in Lancaster, where only 3 percent are known to have become farmers farther west. Therefore the mobility rate was half that of the Southside County. There is no significant difference in the histories of those whose tax was paid by someone else and those paying taxes themselves.

It is possible that errors in research techniques have somewhat exaggerated the difference between the rate of mobility in the two counties, because for reasons not clear there were more men in Lancaster who disappeared without trace. But to eliminate them from our calculations does not affect the basic situation except to increase greatly the possible rate of mobility: in Lancaster, among those whose futures can be traced with certainty, 52 percent obtained land, while in Lunenburg no less than 85 percent did so. Whatever method is chosen for determining the exact ratio, the proportion of men who acquired land was exceedingly high in both counties, and far higher in Lunenburg.

The rate of mobility among landholders was also much lower in the eastern county. In Lunenburg, nearly as many farmers added to their holdings as lost them, and half of those who disappeared from the Lunenburg records secured land elsewhere. In Lancaster considerably more men lost than gained. Moreover the spectacular influx which occurred in Lunenburg was not duplicated in the eastern county, where there were only 28 more landholders in 1782, a gain of slightly over 10 percent compared with Lunenburg's 200 percent. From every point of view, mobility was enormously higher in the frontier county.

This conclusion is confirmed by comparing the Richmond County quitrent rolls for 1765 with its tax list for 1782. Since only landowners were given in the former, it is not possible to trace the fate of the landless, except by inference, but mobility among those with land can be analyzed.

Richmond is located just west of Lancaster and was similar in its socioeconomic characteristics. The concentration of property was about the same, and the proportion of landless differed only slightly in 1782. There were 200 landholders in 1765, of whom the great majority—nearly four-fifths—remained in the county seventeen years later. Whereas in Lunenburg there was considerable mobility among the farmers, nearly 30 percent decisively increasing or decreasing their holdings, in Richmond there was almost no movement at all. The same amount of land remained in the same families. A number of new landholders appeared by 1782, but there were only one-fourth more than before; moreover, some of them (such as Charles and Robert Wormeley Carter) were not in fact mobile, being residents of adjacent counties. Almost none of the 1765 landowners increased their holdings to any extent, but more than two dozen had lost a significant part of their property by 1782.

As to Richmond County's landless, some inferences are possible. The 1782 tax lists included all men, and the proportion of landed to landless at that date is therefore known. Assuming that this ratio did not change much between 1765 and 1782 (and there was no major change in Lancaster), about 150 men did not own land at the earlier period. Some 90 new names appear on the land lists of 1782, but not all of these were landless previously, for we know that some of them had resided outside the county, where they may have been farmers. In Lunenburg, about 30 percent of those who took up land between 1764 and 1782 had lived in the county at the earlier date; all the rest were newcomers. The proportion of those who were residents was presumably higher in Richmond, where there was much less movement in and out. Perhaps it is a reasonable assumption that half of the new landowners in 1782 had been nonlandholding residents of the county earlier. If so, then about 45 out of 150 landless men acquired land within the county, or just 30 percent, almost the same proportion as the known 32 percent in Lancaster, and again contrasting sharply with the 55 percent or so in Lunenburg. Richmond and Lancaster alike demonstrate that when an area ceased to be a frontier region and became a settled commercial farm community, both horizontal and vertical mobility declined.

In Lunenburg, at least three-fourths of the landless men became farmers; in Lancaster and Richmond slightly over one-third did so. Chester County, in Pennsylvania, represents a Northern equivalent of the Lancaster-Richmond type. The 1765 tax list, like the Virginia records, names all of the adult men, and itemizes their acreage and certain farm animals. There are available tax lists for this and other Pennsylvania counties during the next two decades, a time span equal to that of the Virginia records. As in Virginia these records are incomplete, but again inferences are possible.

Chester County lies in the southeastern corner of the state. The townships selected for examination are in the eastern part (now Delaware County) just west of Philadelphia, and in the southern section bordering Delaware and Maryland. The region had been settled for many decades and was a commercial farm area in 1765. Not quite half of the men were landless. These men were of three sorts. About 40 percent were heads of families, paying their own poll tax, and usually (though not always) owning a few farm animals. Another 40 percent were called "Single Men," or sometimes "Freemen." They seem to have paid their own tax but owned no farm animals. Presumably they were free laborers or artisans. Finally, one-fifth of the men were called "inmates." These were evidently servants, perhaps indentured, and the category also included some adult sons of the farmers. The tax lists did not always separate the inmates from the single men (two out of eight studied did not), but the latter were clearly more numerous.

The Pennsylvania records, like those of Virginia, have their serious shortcomings. For most of the counties there are no tax records before the 1780s, so that a man might have acquired land and died, and we be none the wiser. Some men doubtless moved to Maryland, where it has not been feasible to follow them; others may have gone to Virginia and even conceivably to the Carolinas (though from Chester this is most unlikely). There is also the same difficulty with names. Thus William Walter, single man of Haverford, is different from the William Walter of Concord and William Walter of Pikeland, so that it is impossible to know which of them is referred to in subsequent records. We know only that the Haverford Walter did not obtain land in his home town.

The eight townships studied contained 277 men without land in 1765. Of these, 72 disappear or cannot be certainly identified. Twenty percent obtained land within the township of origin by 1784. There was a good deal of local movement out of the township to adjacent towns, which were almost always slightly to the west, and occasionally someone moved farther away. Altogether nearly 40 percent of the landless finally became landowners.

Among the landless men, those who were heads of families had the best chance of rising. About 46 percent of them are known to have obtained land, and if the men who disappear or whose names preclude certainty are eliminated, 61 percent eventually became farmers. Those who did not succeed were sometimes artisans, one of whom, a blacksmith, became an "inmate" much later (if this is the same person); while a storekeeper also apparently failed and sank into the same lower status. Two were schoolmasters and seven were called laborers. These men sometimes moved two or three times, never improving their rank.

The "Single Men" did not do as well, perhaps because they lacked the incentive of a family. Only 36 percent, or 47 percent of those definitely identified, obtained land. The "inmates" are the most interesting of all, for we are here presumably dealing with indentured servants. Their mobility was least of the three groups, being 29 percent of the whole number, or 45 percent of those about whom it is possible to be certain. This is an unexpectedly high figure, since these servants have been assumed to be of inferior potential. The inmates often were or became skilled workers, and frequently moved around. Out of the 17 who obtained land, 5 were artisans and 1 was or became a schoolmaster. These inmates, when they did obtain land, usually secured only a few acres, though Reuben Roberts owned 170, James Denning 200, and John Russel the same quantity. They were apt to succeed in some town other than that in which they began.

There are other points of interest. The men with some skill other than farming met with a high degree of success. Out of 70 landless artisans in the whole county, between 55 and 60 percent acquired land. Of course others may have prospered without investing in real estate. On the other hand those without a trade, identified as laborers, succeeded less than half of the time and were especially apt to vanish without trace. Pennsylvania offered great opportunities to the men who had or acquired a skill, but the unskilled were likely to fail, as usual.

The geographical mobility which occurred, insofar as it can be traced, ordinarily consisted of a removal from one town to an adjacent town, or perhaps a few towns away. It was usually, though not always, in a westerly direction. There seems to have been remarkably little migration to Philadelphia even among the artisans. The movement, though limited geographically, was considerable: among over 200 landless men who can be traced, nearly half moved at least once.

The general mobility of Chester County residents was almost identical to that in Lancaster County. Of all the landless, 38.5 percent are known to have obtained land, compared with 35 percent in Lancaster; and of those whose success or failure is certainly known, 52 percent succeeded, exactly the same proportion as in the Virginia county. This evidence indicates that the mobility rates which were found in the southern state have a general application.

These scattered case studies show that the American who started without land had an excellent chance of becoming a yeoman farmer. Mobility into the upper class of rural society, however, was much more limited. In order to analyze the social origins of the great landowners, we once again turn our attention to Virginia.

In a previously published article entitled "The One Hundred," I have listed the wealthiest Virginians in 1787 according to tax lists of that year. Actually one of these turns out to have been a Londoner; several ought not to have been included (such as Patrick Henry and James Madison), and there may have been other Virginians richer than those on the list; but it is reasonably representative of the great planter class. All of these men were large landowners, though several were primarily merchants and others were lawyers. Most of them lived in the Tidewater counties, especially in the Potomac and James River valleys. They all owned more than 4,000 acres, and almost half had 10,000 acres, in addition to nearly 100 slaves. Certainly each held more than £10,000 worth of property.

Of the 100, 79 or 80 inherited all of their wealth. These were members of the First Families—the old, established aristocracy of the colony which survived the Revolution intact: the Randolphs, Harrisons, Fitzhughs, Nelsons. Nine more started near the top, as sons of well-to-do though not wealthy men. Examples are David Patterson, whose father was a substantial planter, and who bought 40,000 acres in the West out of commercial profits; Muscoe Garnett, third generation, whose father was a burgess; and Joseph Jones of Dinwiddie, great-grandson of the immigrant, and member of a respectable, perhaps even prominent, family of planters. Two others inherited part of their wealth and cannot really be considered mobile. There remain at the most 10 men who were self-made. Four of these were immigrants. Roger Atkinson, English-born, married a Virginia girl of good family and amassed wealth in what was then the newly developed southern Piedmont. Nicholas Davis, a Welsh immigrant, became a Richmond merchant and married the widow of a Randolph, herself an heiress. William Ronald, also a merchant, bought large tracts in the Southside; and David Ross, a merchant from Scotland, accumulated a fortune during the Revolution and was for the time being the richest man in the state. The other half-dozen apparently were native born, of humble parentage (unless James Henry of King and Queen is the same person as Judge James of the eastern shore). Practically all of the mobile planters had risen through commercial or legal activities, and centered their agricultural pursuits in the Southside—the Lunenburg County area, where mobility was the rule.

The economic opportunity of the city dweller was somewhat greater than that of the American in an older farm community. The skilled laborer, who began as a journeyman wage worker and aspired to become a master, lived in a rapidly expanding community where there was always more room near the top. The Philadelphia tax list of 1769 contains the names of over 100 men, identified as artisans, who were not assessed for any property although only a small amount made one a taxpayer. Of these about one-fourth had disappeared by 1774 and cannot be found in any other tax records of the colony. Another group of men are untraceable because their names are too common. Of the rest, about 45 percent succeeded in acquiring property, almost always within the city. This rate of success is about equal to that in Chester County, though much less than that on the frontier.

The opportunity of rising into the ranks of large property holders was of course much more limited. Manufacturing during the colonial period was seldom profitable enough to permit an artisan to become truly wealthy, and few men could start from scratch and hope to reach the top. Nevertheless the prosperous artisans consisted to an unusual degree of men who had improved upon their father's economic position. The Philadelphia tax list of 1769 includes nearly sixty artisans who were assessed for £50 worth of property. Probably these men owned £2,000 or more. The economic status of a good many parents is unknown, probably because in many cases it is unknowable; but there remain thirty-one whose social origins can be identified. These men comprise a fair cross-section of the city's well-to-do artisans. They were engaged in a score of trades, and included the owners of fairly large business enterprises such as distilleries, who perhaps ought to be termed manufacturers rather than artisans. Slightly more than half of this prosperous group had decisively improved upon their fathers' economic position. Few of them were truly self-made: probably not more than half a dozen, about one out of five, started from scratch as Franklin, for example, had done. Characteristically their fathers were artisans, or rarely farmers, who could provide the son with the advantage of a respectable, middle-class, usually urban background.

The opportunities in Boston were about the same. The 1771 assessment list does not distinguish artisans, but that of 1780, though incomplete, can be used. Identified are forty-eight artisans (including the manufacturers) who were rated at £150 or more. These men belonged to the top 15 percent of all taxpayers. The fathers of forty can be identified. As in Pennsylvania, the man who started from the bottom was unusual, accounting for only one out of four. However about 60 percent of the artisans had acquired more property than their parents. The superior success rate of the Bostonians may be due to some local factor, but is more probably an effect of the Revolution. In any case the aspiring artisan had reason for optimism.

Merchants, as we have seen, had considerably more wealth than did artisans, and they were less often self-made men. The members of the New York Chamber of Commerce, in particular, were a select group. There were fifty-nine of them during the chamber's first year of existence (1768–1769). The great majority, perhaps all of the members, were large property owners. Probably most of New York's commercial upper class was included.

About two-thirds had been born in the colonies, principally in New York. Among these the majority, and about 45 percent of the whole number, belonged to the colony's elite families. There were, for example, two Crugers, a Beekman, a Gouverneur, a Low, a Reade, a Van Dam, four Waltons, and a Watts. They were related by marriage to each other, to the large landholders, and to various merchants of lesser origin (Duyckinck, Keteltas, Lynsen).

Some of the natives, though not of the established upper class, began part way up the socioeconomic ladder. Examples are Nicholas Hoffman, son of a well-to-do farmer, and Laurence Kortright, whose father was perhaps wealthy but who was not of the elite. The rest, about one-fourth of the natives, rose from humble or obscure parentage. We know of Edward Laight only that his father Edward was an immigrant. The same is true of Elias Debrosses. Isaac Sears's father had only moderate means; John Thurman's was a baker; and there are several so little known that even their birthplace is doubtful.

Among the foreign-born a few had advantages. Theophylact Bache, of English birth, son of an excise collector, had an uncle who was a successful merchant and who left him £300. Thomas Buchanan's father was a wealthy Glasgow merchant, while Peter Hasenclever's was a rich merchant and manufacturer. William Seton's uncle was a banker. However the great majority of the immigrants arrived without a head start; though they may have belonged to families of status, as far as their colonial experience was concerned they were *nouveaux riches*.

The background of these merchants, as far as is known, was almost entirely urban. Probably not far from half had wealthy fathers, almost all of whom were merchants. Another group, perhaps one out of five, came from well-to-do families, and were therefore not really mobile. There remain 40 percent who had risen from well down the social scale. The figure may be too high, for among the men about whose background nothing is known there may be some who started with advantages. However there could have been few such because prominent families are, obviously, conspicuous. Taking everything into account, then, it is certain that between one-third and two-fifths of the merchants in pre-Revolutionary New York City were self-made men.

Unfortunately no such select list of New York merchants is available for the postwar period. There does exist, however, a directory for 1786 which identified many of the residents by their occupation. The first 100 men designated as "merchants" were selected for study. The term "merchant" was doubtless loosely applied, and there were probably men so designated who had little property. However a distinction was made in the directory between merchants and shopkeepers, thus presumably differentiating between wholesalers and retailers; so that most of the men included certainly were well-to-do.

The significant characteristic of this merchant class was the much higher proportion of self-made men. Only one-fourth were sons of wealthy landowners or merchants. At most another tenth came from well-to-do families. This contrasts strikingly with the situation prior to the war, when about 60 percent had had a head start in life. Two-thirds of the postwar merchants had made their way up. Among these, roughly two out of three were natives of the state. Some of them came from artisan families, but a majority were farmers' sons. The rest—about one-fourth of the whole number—were apparently immigrants, for there is no trace of their surnames in the extensive collection of published wills or in genealogies. Some may have come from prosperous backgrounds, perhaps set up in business by a merchant father or uncle; but it is plain that the majority of New York's merchant class—probably 60 percent at the least—were self-made men. Not all of these merchants were successful, for inventories and tax lists testify that there were poor as well as rich ones. However, the degree of mobility is clearly very high, surpassing that of the pre-Revolutionary period and incomparably greater than that in Virginia.

The 1791 tax list for the city's east ward has survived, and this combined with other sources makes it possible to identify positively a number of those merchants who were well-to-do or wealthy. Some changes doubtless had occurred since 1786, and the data are incomplete, but a list can be compiled that is comparable with the Chamber of Commerce membership. Fewer members of this postwar elite were self-made men than among merchants generally, yet half of them had risen from humble origins. Therefore mobility was higher than the prewar rate of 40 percent.

A similar list of Boston merchants in 1789, again drawn from a city directory, proves that the rate of mobility was about the same in both these cities, though fewer Bostonians were immigrants. As in New York, only one-fourth of the merchants were members of the established upper class. One out of four Boston merchants started as sons of artisans. These artisan fathers were of all trades: coopers (John Breck, father of Samuel), sleighmakers, brewers, masons, hatters, leather dressers, felt-makers (Benjamin Clark, who sent his son to Harvard), tailors, snuff makers, braziers, ropemakers, cordwainers, housewrights, and potters. Many of the craftsmen's sons had been brought up in the family business and later entered trade.

Other merchants, sons of mariners, began their careers before the mast. A few were sons of innkeepers, and thus engaged in commerce from the start. Five had fathers who were ministers and one was descended from a school-teacher. One or two out of ten began life on a farm. All together one-fourth started near the top, one-third were the sons of artisans, shopkeepers, or mariners, 6 percent came from families of professional men, and the remaining three-eighths were farmers' sons, or immigrants, of humble or obscure origin. Probably 70 percent had risen from lower status.

Among the Boston merchants were thirty-two equivalent in income and social rank to the wealthy New Yorkers. As might be expected, far more of them came from wealthy backgrounds than was true of Boston merchants in general: just half were born into wealthy or well-to-do families, usually the sons of merchants. Four were ministers' sons; four were sons of farmers. Artisans rarely reached the top. The backgrounds of four wealthy merchants are unknown, and they were probably immigrants. The rate of mobility—50 percent—is higher than that of the pre-Revolutionary New York Chamber of Commerce, and exactly the same as that of the equivalent postwar New York merchants.

Obviously a larger proportion of prosperous artisans and merchants were of humble origin than was the case with the Virginia elite. However in order accurately to compare mobility in the city and country, the Virginia group should be matched with their economic equals. What were the social origins of the wealthiest townsmen, regardless of occupation?

The Philadelphia tax list of 1765 includes 100 men who were rated at £160 or more—probably the equivalent of £4,000. More than half of these were merchants. Nearly one out of five were professional men, mostly lawyers and doctors. Some owned large amounts of real estate, the rent from which was their primary support. Less than one-tenth were artisans or manufacturers. The economic status of 91 of the fathers has been discovered. Whereas in Virginia only one-tenth of the men had achieved wealth primarily by their own efforts, in Philadelphia one-third had accomplished this. About one-seventh were entirely self-made. Characteristically these *nouveaux riches* were born into an urban middle-class family, the fathers evidently following some trade. A considerable number of Philadelphia's elite—at least one-fourth—were immigrants, as were more than one-third of the mobile men. Many of the Philadelphia 100 had far less property than did the Virginia planters, but even among those who were truly wealthy, one-third had made their own fortunes.

A comparable list of wealthy Bostonians can be obtained from the 1771 assessment roll. The 60 men who, according to this record, were the largest property owners, consisted principally of merchants. About one-fifth were artisans, manufacturers, and the like, and there was a scattering of lawyers, men of leisure, or royal officials. About 30 percent were Harvard graduates. A majority were Congregationalist, but one out of five was an Anglican (who usually became a Loyalist). All but a handful were born in Boston or Charlestown; in contrast to Philadelphia, where one-fourth or more of the upper class were immigrants, only three of these Bostonians came from across the seas. Between 40 and 45 percent were *nouveaux riches;* indeed one-third were self-made men. Most successful Bostonians were city-bred: only three are known to have come from farm families, though a few others may have done so. Most of these upper-class Bostonians were not truly wealthy. Of those whose property was comparable to that of the Virginia 100, only about 20 percent had made their own way up. Still, this represents a mobility rate twice that of the planter elite.

Revolutionary America was a society in flux. The amount of movement from place to place is striking. In the average rural community perhaps 15 percent of the population left in the course of a decade, and even more newcomers arrived. Probably 40 percent of the population, or thereabouts, moved during a few years' time. In general this movement was economically successful. There were some habitual drifters: perhaps 5 percent of the men wandered from one place to another without ever acquiring land, and on the frontier the proportion might be two or three times as great. How-

ever, out of the 30 or 40 percent of the white population who at any
one time were landless, over half, and on the frontier three-fourths
or more, became farmers or townsmen of equivalent status. Many
men who already owned land also moved, and these seem ordinarily
to have held their own. This horizontal mobility helped to maintain
the very high rate of vertical mobility. The opportunity to rise was
good even in older farm areas such as Lancaster and Richmond,
where nearly one-third of the landless acquired real estate within
the county, or in Chester, where even more succeeded. Moreover
if one failed there, opportunities were excellent in the west. In Kent,
Goshen, and Lunenburg, all but a handful of those whose history
is known improved their economic rank. There is even evidence
that the much maligned indentured servants did well. Thus in
America the lower class (excluding the slaves) was a temporary
status for the overwhelming majority of men. Probably not more
than one in twenty whites was a permanent proletarian.

In the cities, the relative ease with which the skilled worker could
obtain credit and open a shop, the generally high wage level which
permitted such workers to save, and the actual accumulation of
property shown by tax lists and inventories—all suggest that the
poor laborer could normally expect to become a small property
owner if he had the ability to learn a trade. In Philadephia the chance
to rise was indeed a good one. At least one-third and probably
over 40 percent of the men who paid no tax in 1769 improved their
economic position during the next few years.

Mobility into the upper class was much more limited. In particular
the landed aristocracy (in Virginia at least) was virtually a closed
group by the time of the Revolution, undoubtedly because most of
the available good land was occupied. Probably the same sort of
elite was developing wherever commercial farming had been conducted for some time. Even the great estates in the west were being
purchased principally by men of established wealth. Commerce, on
the other hand, was a comparatively open field. Before the war, 30
or 40 percent of New York's mercantile upper class were self-made
men, and the proportion both there and in Boston reached 50 percent after the Revolution. These men frequently became large landowners, and indeed most of the *nouveaux riches* in Virginia were
merchants who bought their way into the "one hundred." Here the

existence of cheap western land furthered mobility into the elite as it aided mobility at the lower economic levels.

The chance to rise in the Revolutionary era varied with the circumstances. The frontier offered almost unlimited opportunity. After the frontier stage passed, the mobility rate was reduced. Subsistence farm areas still afforded a fair chance to buy land, but that land was not very valuable and most of the landless men moved on. In commercial farm areas economic opportunities were also diminished because the good land was claimed, land prices rose, and the landholding elite became increasingly exclusive. Farmers seem seldom to have risen into the highest ranks: the way to wealth was primarily through trade or perhaps the law. The social structure of the cities was much more open, especially during a period of rapid expansion such as the war years, though when stagnation set in merchants and artisans had trouble maintaining themselves. But even at such times the city people could join the men from subsistence and commercial farm areas as they moved on to Lunenburg County, to the west of cheap land, ample credit, and high mobility.

II THE SURPRISING IMMOBILITY OF THE "ERA OF THE COMMON MAN," 1820-1850

The Jacksonian era's reputation for high social mobility stems largely from the observations of Alexis de Tocqueville and other influential Europeans who visited the United States in the years before the Civil War. Struck by the vast differences between the Old World and the New—particularly surface differences—they leaped to the conclusion that America was an egalitarian society. They mistook appearances for reality.

While the United States lacked the vestigial feudalism, the formal hierarchical class structure, and the almost palpable deference that characterized western Europe, it was itself an increasingly stratified society. Great fortunes were there to be made as booms in transportation, cotton production and manufacture, shipbuilding, finance and insurance, and international commerce moved the country toward the mature industrialism of the post-Civil War years. These fortunes were made not by mythical upstarts, but by men whose parents and grandparents had already carved out sizable estates. Quantitative studies reveal that small classes of rich men, active in real estate and commerce, held substantial fractions of their communities' wealth by the Revolutionary era. It was the children and grandchildren of the colonial elite who alone were able to brush off the financial panics of 1819, 1837, and 1839, and who had the necessary capital to participate in the great financial, commercial, and entrepreneurial ventures that beckoned. Political historians, relying more on intuition than on evidence, once characterized the era's typical man as an entrepreneur "on the make." The evidence indicates that the typical man was a farmer or artisan of little or no property and with modest to bleak prospects. The man on the make was a man who to a large extent was already made.

Stuart Blumin

RESIDENTIAL AND OCCUPATIONAL MOBILITY IN ANTEBELLUM PHILADELPHIA

Stuart Blumin's study makes heavy use of an invaluable source for students of nineteenth-century mobility: city directories. Fruitful for other inquiries, too, they are particularly helpful in working with the occupational and residential data on which Mr. Blumin relies. As a historian, he attempts to explain the "substantive rates and patterns of mobility" disclosed by his evidence. Without using the term "structural change," Mr. Blumin offers an explanation very much like it, attributing declining opportunities to the maturing merchant capitalist economy and accompanying expansion of low-status jobs. This explanation, of course, is not made with the analytical rigor that informs Mr. Blumin's research into occupational and residential changes. This kind of differentiation between what might be called the mobility researcher's theory and his practice is commonplace.

The measurement of the magnitude of vertical mobility is a particularly important consideration for the student of the American city. For in America, more than in most other countries, this particular measure coincides with one of the central ingredients of the prevailing ideology. "This is a country of self-made men," boasted Calvin Colton in 1844, "than which nothing better could be said of any state of society." More specifically:

> *Money and property, we know, among us, are constantly changing hands. A man has only to work on, and wait patiently, and with industry and enterprise, he is sure to get both. The wheel of American fortune is perpetually and steadily turning, and those at the bottom today, will be moving up tomorrow, and will ere long be at the top.*

Colton's is certainly not a minority view of American culture, nor is it the exclusive property of pre–Civil War propagandists. Rather, it is one of our most durable and widely shared propositions, concerning not only what America is, but also what it should be. In the 1960s we know that for large numbers of individuals the American

Dream is an illusion. Yet we have never surrendered the idea that the best society is a fluid society, and the characteristic response to the problems of poverty and racism, among those who admit their existence, is to restore equality of opportunity.

This paper is an attempt to study vertical mobility in a major American city, Philadelphia, during the period 1820 to 1860, when Calvin Colton and others were elevating the concept of worldly success to its eminent place in American social thought. But, sensitive both to the tentative nature of my results and to the methodological temper of this volume, I have tried to focus here not simply on substantive rates and patterns of mobility. I have sought as well to extend the relevance of this type of study to the general problems of urban historical research. The study of mobility is a complicated operation involving numerous procedures which, when viewed together, may reveal more about the city than simply the fluidity of its social structure. Further on, I shall explore the relevance of the observed mobility patterns to difficult questions of economic change in the antebellum city.

Technical Considerations

The study of mobility may be examined in a number of different ways. Typically, it is the study of intergenerational occupational mobility— that is, the study of the relationships between the occupations of a group of men and those of their sons. These relationships are used to infer the magnitude and pattern of social mobility in the period and place of the son's youth or adult life, depending on whether the son's original or ultimate occupation is recorded. Since social mobility is inferred, occupations are ranked or grouped according to an assumed or empirically derived prestige scale, an example of which is the well-known NORC scale.

It is important to point out, however, that the validity of inferring social mobility from occupational mobility is virtually never examined. Leaving aside the question of whether the inference of social mobility from occupational mobility is valid even in contemporary research, we must recognize the inappropriateness of applying a mid-twentieth-century prestige ranking of occupations to early nineteenth-century conditions. The economy and the occupational structure have changed too much to support such a procedure.

Furthermore, the creation of an accurate ranking system based on pre–Civil War opinion is made especially difficult in light of the amorphous character of surviving historical documents.

A possible solution may emerge, however, from a simple redefinition of the problem. Although recent studies of the concept of success in America claim for it a certain amount of complexity, the straightforward matter of making money has always been its most basic ingredient. In the effusive words of Calvin Colton, success is conceived of entirely in terms of "money and property." Accordingly we may reinterpret the scale of social mobility as the measurement of economic mobility. We probably lose little information in doing so, for the magnitude of one would no doubt closely resemble the magnitude of the other, and it permits us validly to base our ranking or classification of occupations on the more workable basis of the wealth or incomes of the men who worked within each occupation.

Other problems inherent in the application of this method to the past are not as easily overcome. They often arise from the absence or incompleteness of appropriate data, for we must bear in mind that we are attempting to apply a method oriented toward survey research to a society that is no longer susceptible to personal interview. I have discussed these problems in another place, and will return later to the question of validity.

The first step of any occupational mobility study is to define the vertical dimension of the occupational structure—to rank or classify occupations. As the above discussion implies, this was achieved through the use of whatever data were available for determining the average wealth of the members of each occupation. For the closing year of the period, 1860, manuscript federal census schedules were used to rank fifty-one occupations, from import-export merchant to boatman (see Table 1). To assure that the occupational structure was sufficiently stable throughout the period, a similar ranking was created for 1820, on the basis of local tax records. These rankings were compared statistically, resulting in the following rank-order correlation coefficients; Spearmans $r = .759$, Kendall's Tau $= .625$.

These occupational rankings produced few surprises. At the top of Table 1 are the merchants, often merchant-manufacturers, followed by the professionals, manufacturers, and one group of crafts-

TABLE 1
Rank Order of Occupations According to Mean Wealth, 1860
("Journeymen" excluded)

Rank	Occupation	Mean Wealth
1	Merchant	$50,357 [a]
2	Attorney	34,948
3	M.D.	23,879
4	Watchmaker	20,972 [b]
5	Broker	16,961
6	Manufacturer	16,910 [c]
7	Druggist	12,281 [d]
8	Agent	10,369
9	Saddler	9,980
10	Tanner and currier	8,950
11	Brickmaker	8,433
12	Cabinetmaker	7,272
13	Grocer	5,767
14	Bricklayer	4,308
15	Storekeeper	4,062 [e]
16	Carpenter	3,755
17	Teacher	3,746
18	Machinist	3,627
19	Tobacconist	3,512
20	Printer	3,510
21	Baker	3,507
22	Victualler (Butcher)	3,414
23	Coachmaker	3,371
24	Plasterer	3,243
25	Hatter	3,175
26	Cooper	3,020
27	Shipwright	2,935
28	Confectioner	2,662
29	Stonecutter	2,425
30.5	Innkeeper	2,324 [f]
30.5	Gardener	2,324
32	Tailor	2,317
33	Bookbinder	2,300
34	Shoemaker	2,114
35	Blacksmith	2,089
36	Painter	1,788
37	Carter	1,727
38	Tinsmith	1,625
39	Clerk	1,410
40	Stonemason	1,150
41	Salesman	546

Rank	Occupation	Mean Wealth
42	Watchman	$457
43	Conductor	454
44	Domestic servant	328
45	Carpet weaver	186
46	Laborer	180
47	Coachman	170
48	Mariner	113
49	Weaver	106
50	Ironworker	88
51	Boatman	50

Source: *Eighth Census of the United States,* microfilmed manuscript schedules, County of Philadelphia.

[a] Includes only those listed as "merchant," with no further specifications. As a rule, the term "merchant," when unaccompanied by the name of a product, indicates a large-scale, general importer-exporter.
[b] Includes jewelers and silversmiths.
[c] Includes all manufacturers, whether or not a product is specified. The mean for unspecified manufacturers is $1 lower.
[d] Excludes one extreme case, George W. Carpenter, whose wealth was listed at $2,120,000. The mean for druggists, including Carpenter, is $136,147.
[e] Includes those specified simply as "storekeeper."
[f] Includes innkeepers, tavern keepers, and hotelkeepers. These terms appear to be interchangeable, in spite of the fact that a few large hotels existed in Philadelphia in 1860.

men specializing in highly esteemed and expensive products. Lower, but still above the middle range, are several craftsmen, such as tanners and brickmakers, who are more properly considered small manufacturers, as well as such nonmanual businessmen as druggists, agents, and grocers. Storekeepers, innkeepers, and a host of craftsmen form the middle range of the rank order, with clerks and carters intermingled with the lower end of this group. Finally, the last ten ranks consist of unskilled workers, domestic servants, and weavers. Weavers in this period were not master craftsmen, but wage-earning machine operatives. Their wages were little higher than those of unskilled workers.

Missing from the rank order is an army of journeymen craftsmen. Journeymen, as wage-earning and usually propertyless individuals, would logically fall near the bottom of the rank order. Unfortunately, city directories do not include journeymen. Proprietors are regularly reported, and unskilled workers less reliably so, but journeymen craftsmen are almost invariably excluded from the Phila-

delphia directories because the stated purpose of the early directories was to report the names, occupations, and addresses of heads
of household and those who were "in business." Journeymen craftsmen represent the only adult male group that is systematically excluded by these terms.

Thus, we have arrived at a major qualification of our attempt to
calculate rates of occupational mobility—namely, that we cannot
directly observe the mobility experience of one of the most interesting groups in the occupational structure. We will refer later to the
question of the journeyman's opportunity. Here we must simply
declare that our mobility rates will apply primarily to the city's proprietors, a much larger range of individuals than we might at first
expect, and, with a great deal of hesitation, to its unskilled workers.
With regard to this latter group, we will see that we have generated
rates of mobility that are frankly unrealistic. This phenomenon, which
might appear at first to be a striking affirmation of the American
Dream, is actually a product of incomplete directories. The directories were likely to include only those unskilled workers who were
upwardly mobile.

A second important limitation concerns the type of mobility that
proved accessible for study. We have mentioned thus far only the
method of intergenerational mobility, the study of occupational
change from father to son. Equally important, however, is the study
of intragenerational mobility, the study of the occupational history
of individual men. In this Philadelphia study both kinds of mobility
measures were made; the intragenerational measure provided the
more fruitful results.

Intragenerational mobility of course introduces problems of its
own. The tracing of an individual career requires not two but many
observations in the sequential editions of the Philadelphia city directory. With each attempted observation there arises the possibility
of loss of trace due to death, out-migration, incomplete data, or the
spiritual debilitation of the researcher. To minimize these pitfalls, the
tracing process in this study was restricted to a single decade for
each of four separate samples drawn from the city directories of
1820, 1830, 1840, and 1850. A sample of names drawn from the 1820
directory was traced to the 1830 directory. An entirely new sample
was drawn from the 1830 directory and traced through 1840, and so
on until four decades of observations were available. No attempt

was made to exclude individuals from more than one sample, since the samples are sequential, and such an exclusion would have interfered with the comparability of their "age mix."

What follows, then, is a series of matrices measuring the intragenerational occupational mobility of a particular (but rather extensive) subset of the adult male working population of antebellum Philadelphia. It should be noted that these matrices apply not to individual careers in their entirety, but to the magnitude of mobility observed within a given decade. It is the decades that are being measured and compared.

Thus far I have emphasized the factors shaping the study of socioeconomic mobility. The city directories include material on the residential addresses as well as the occupations of the men listed. This means that a second variable, residence, can be used to illuminate further the nature of mobility in the antebellum city. We will consider this point in due course.

Occupational Patterns

Table 2 presents the occupational mobility matrix for the first decade, the 1820s. The fact that it is a five by five matrix requires some explanation, for we have thus far spoken only of a ranking of a large number of individual occupations. To make a mobility matrix serviceable, it was necessary to collapse the rank order to a limited number of categories. In order to retain as much descriptive power as possible, however, and to avoid the influence of an artificial classification scheme, occupations were coded both to retain their individual identities and to produce a number of alternative classification schema. Thus, matrices were produced to reflect five occupational categories, two different sets of four categories, three categories, and the "functional" categories of "nonmanual proprietors," "manual proprietors," "nonmanual employees" and "manual employees." Each of these schema produced results consistent with the others. Accordingly, it was decided to present the results in the form of the most descriptive interpretation of the occupational rank order, the five by five matrix. The first category, the highest, consists mainly of merchants, professionals, and manufacturers, were merchants comprising over half of the category in each sample. In terms of Table 1, it represents those occupations with a mean of wealth

TABLE 2
Occupational Mobility, 1820–1830

1830 Occupational Category	1820 Occupational Category					Total	% of Sample
	1	2	3	4	5		
1	160 (88.9%)	15 (7.5%)	9 (2.0%)	2 (4.3%)	—	186	19.6
2	8 (4.4%)	160 (80.0%)	26 (5.8%)	5 (10.9%)	3 (4.1%)	202	21.3
3	9 (5.0%)	19 (9.5%)	408 (90.5%)	3 (6.5%)	13 (17.8%)	452	47.6
4	3 (1.7%)	2 (1.0%)	2 (.4%)	35 (76.1%)	1 (1.4%)	43	4.5
5	—	4 (2.0%)	6 (1.3%)	1 (2.2%)	56 (76.7%)	67	7.0
Total	180 (100.0%)	200 (100.0%)	451 (100.0%)	46 (100.0%)	73 (100.0%)	950	100.0
% of Sample	19.0	21.0	47.5	4.8	7.7		

of $16,000 or higher. The second category, representing the range in means of approximately $5,000 to $12,000, consists mainly of druggists, grocers, agents, and high-ranking craftsmen. The third category is best described as "craftsmen," although it also includes tavern keepers, minor public officials, dealers, tobacconists, and most teachers. In terms of the rank order it is the "middle class," with means ranging from approximately $1,500 to $4,000. The fourth category represents something of a departure from Table 1, as its few occupations—carter, clerk, accountant, and salesman—are pieced together out of the lower range of the middle category. The final category, representing occupational means under $500, are mostly semiskilled and unskilled laborers and domestic servants.

The most striking feature of Table 2 is the magnitude of upward mobility from the fourth and fifth categories, 21.7 percent and 23.3 percent respectively. Of course, we have already seen that abnormally high rates from these categories were to be expected, and that these rates reflect, to a large degree, the incompleteness of the directories rather than the actual mobility of manual and nonmanual workers. Upward mobility from the other categories is quite a bit lower, with 7.5 percent of the second category and 7.8 percent of the third category moving into higher categories by 1830.

More interesting, perhaps, than these purely quantitative expressions are the specific patterns of occupational change that Table 2 does not reveal. With regard to upward mobility, the most prominent pattern is the tendency for change to occur within situs, that is, between closely related occupations. For example, of the fifteen members of the second category who were upwardly mobile, all but one had become merchants by 1830. Seven of these fifteen had been storekeepers, three were grocers, and the others were sea captains, auctioneers, and agents. Not one had been a craftsman in 1820. Six craftsmen from the third category did move into the first by 1830, but the pattern is not destroyed. Two of the six became manufacturers of products closely related to their skills, and, interestingly, three became high-ranking government officials, a term that applies here to such positions as judge, alderman, and mayor. (As only two members of the 1820 sample were high-ranking public officials in 1820, these three cases hint that politics may have been an important avenue of mobility.)

The pattern of movement between related occupations is preserved in the largest cell of upward mobility, that which represents movement from the third to the second category. Of the twenty-six changes, twenty-two involved closely related occupations. Thus of five men who became retail clothiers, four had been tailors. Both of those who became shoe retailers had been shoemakers. Of the six who became grocers, three had been innkeepers, one was a baker, and one was a butcher. Four cabinetmakers had all come from lower-ranked woodworking crafts. The editor had been a teacher. The pattern is retained even in the badly distorted bottom categories, with "white-collar" employees becoming merchants, storekeepers, and bank cashiers, and manual workers moving into higher manual positions.

Downward mobility presents a somewhat different pattern. Although the rather large movement from the first category (11.1 percent) presents almost a mirror image of movement into that category, the 12.5 percent downward mobility from the second category does not tend to occur between related occupations. Rather, there are two occupations, tavern keeper and minor public officer, neither of which required much investment or skill, that seem to have served as recourse for those who either failed at, or perhaps simply retired from higher-ranked occupations. Just under half of all those who were downwardly mobile into the third category became tavern keepers or officials, and yet these two occupations together accounted for only 5 percent of the third category in 1820.

In both its magnitude and its underlying pattern, then, occupational mobility in Philadelphia in the 1820s suggests a rather stable economic and social order. In subsequent decades this stability appears to break down. Space does not permit a detailed discussion of each of the matrices, but we can at least note that Table 3 and Table 4, representing the 1830s and 1840s respectively, depart from the patterns of Table 2. Specifically, the pattern of movement within situs is considerably weakened. In the most important cell in Table 2, representing mobility from the third to the second category, 85 percent of the cases moved into closely related occupations. In the 1830s this figure is reduced to 56 percent, and in the matrix representing the 1840s it is 37 percent. In the 1820s, as we have seen, none of the high-ranking craftsmen of the second category had moved into the "white-collar" occupations of the first. In the 1830s,

TABLE 3
Occupational Mobility, 1830–1840

1840 Occupational Category	1830 Occupational Category					Total	% of Sample
	1	2	3	4	5		
1	192 (94.0%)	28 (12.3%)	29 (5.6%)	10 (20.8%)	7 (7.5%)	266	24.4
2	5 (2.5%)	162 (71.4%)	25 (4.8%)	2 (4.2%)	6 (6.5%)	200	18.3
3	4 (2.0%)	31 (13.7%)	452 (87.1%)	7 (14.6%)	14 (15.1%)	508	46.6
4	1 (.5%)	4 (1.8%)	6 (1.2%)	22 (45.8%)	5 (5.4%)	38	3.5
5	2 (1.0%)	2 (.9%)	7 (1.3%)	7 (14.6%)	61 (65.5%)	79	7.2
Total	204 (100.0%)	227 (100.1%)	519 (100.0%)	48 (100.0%)	93 (100.0%)	1091	100.0
% of Sample	18.7	20.8	47.6	4.4	8.5		

TABLE 4
Occupational Mobility, 1840–1850

1850 Occupational Category	1840 Occupational Category					Total	% of Sample
	1	2	3	4	5		
1	337 (92.1%)	10 (3.7%)	29 (3.3%)	10 (12.3%)	7 (3.1%)	393	21.4
2	10 (2.7%)	228 (84.4%)	33 (3.7%)	4 (4.9%)	18 (8.0%)	293	16.0
3	8 (2.2%)	21 (7.8%)	785 (88.8%)	8 (9.9%)	38 (16.8%)	860	46.9
4	2 (.5%)	5 (1.9%)	5 (.6%)	47 (58.0%)	4 (1.8%)	63	3.4
5	9 (2.5%)	6 (2.2%)	40 (4.5%)	12 (14.8%)	159 (70.4%)	226	12.3
Total	366 (100.0%)	270 (100.0%)	892 (100.1%)	81 (100.0%)	226 (100.1%)	1835	100.0
% of Sample	20.0	14.7	48.6	4.4	12.3		

these craftsmen comprised one-third of the upward mobility from the second category, and in the 1840s they constituted 60 percent.

Downward mobility reveals a similar change. The tendency for the downwardly mobile to become tavern keepers and public officials is overshadowed in the 1830s by an increase in the number who are downwardly mobile into low-ranking crafts and other manual positions. By the 1840s, even the downward mobility of merchants is affected. In the 1820 sample, fourteen merchants were downwardly mobile, all to other "white-collar" occupations. But in the 1840 sample, fifteen of twenty-three downwardly mobile merchants had assumed manual positions, seven as craftsmen and eight as laborers!

These and numerous other examples seem to indicate a fundamental change in the pattern of occupational mobility in the two decades following 1830. Occupational mobility seems to have lost the orderliness that prevailed in the 1820s. In that decade, mobility was largely a "white-collar" phenomenon, a reshuffling of merchants, grocers, and clerks. Those craftsmen who did advance tended to remain within the general area in which they were trained, usually to become retail merchants of goods they formerly made themselves, or perhaps larger-scale manufacturers of these goods. In the 1830s and 1840s, however, craftsmen comprised a larger and larger proportion of those who were both upwardly and downwardly mobile, and began moving into trades quite different from their own. Merchants and storekeepers, for their part, also began moving into unexpected fields. All of this seems to imply that some kind of basic change in the urban economy may have occurred in the period following 1830. We are not lacking in theories that tend to support this proposition, most notably the "merchant capitalism" theory of John R. Commons. But this is a question to which we must return later. Perhaps it will be interesting to note, however, that in the 1830s downward mobility from the fourth category increased from 2.2 percent to 14.6 percent. The latter figure consists of seven cases, all of whom had been carters. It was in this decade that the streetcar and the railroad first appeared on the streets of Philadelphia.

Strangely, mobility in the 1850s, represented by Table 5, seems to have reverted somewhat to the pattern of the 1820s. Fewer craftsmen participated in occupational change, and larger numbers of them restricted their movements to related trades. Mobility from low-ranking to high-ranking crafts still shows a strong tendency toward un-

TABLE 5
Occupational Mobility, 1850—1860

1860 Occupational Category	1850 Occupational Category					Total	% of Sample
	1	2	3	4	5		
1	181 (90.0%)	13 (8.9%)	17 (3.2%)	9 (20.5%)	4 (2.3%)	224	20.6
2	7 (3.5%)	109 (74.7%)	28 (5.3%)	4 (9.1%)	9 (5.2%)	157	14.4
3	6 (3.0%)	12 (8.2%)	439 (83.8%)	2 (4.5%)	31 (17.9%)	490	45.1
4	7 (3.5%)	4 (2.7%)	13 (2.5%)	25 (56.8%)	8 (4.6%)	57	5.2
5	—	8 (5.5%)	27 (5.2%)	4 (9.1%)	121 (69.9%)	160	14.7
Total	201 (100.0%)	146 (100.0%)	524 (100.0%)	44 (100.0%)	173 (99.9%)	1088	100.0
% of Sample	18.5	13.4	48.2	4.0	15.9		

related areas, but of eleven changes from craftsmen to shopkeepers, ten were within situs. Approximately 46 percent of the changes from the third to the second category involved closely related occupations, which is a moderate reversal from the rapid downward trend of this percentage in the previous decades.

Thus far, I have discussed only the underlying patterns of mobility that do not appear in the matrices themselves. But what of the overall trend in the magnitude of mobility, as measured in the preceding tables? For the sake of simplicity, Table 6 summarizes all four mobility matrices, and is itself summarized on the bottom row, which presents an average upward and downward mobility rate for each decade. Average upward mobility, according to Table 6, follows no stable progression, but rather rises and falls with each decade. Its range lies between 10 percent and 15 percent for each decade, although we have already seen that this average is inflated by the artificially high percentages of the bottom two categories. Downward mobility, on the other hand, increases in magnitude each decade. Actually, the progression is not consistent within each category, but seems to derive from the steady and rather large increase from the third category. This is by far the largest group in each sample, and includes most of the master craftsmen. It may be of some importance to note that downward mobility from this category increased from an unimportant 1.7 percent in the 1820s to 7.7 percent in the 1850s. At the same time, upward mobility from the middle category remained essentially constant. By the final decade the upward and downward mobility experiences of this critical group were about equal in magnitude.

In purely quantitative terms, then, upward occupational mobility appears to have been fairly stable in the four decades immediately preceding the Civil War, whereas downward mobility seems to have gradually increased. This overall pattern holds true whether occupational classifications are derived from our empirical rank order, or whether they are defined functionally, as in Table 7. Must we conclude, then, that the American city failed to generate increasing opportunities for economic advancement in the age of the "self-made man"? Not necessarily. Such a conclusion assumes the validity of inferring economic mobility from occupational mobility, and, as we have seen, this inference may well be invalid. The only statistical procedure that could be brought to bear on this problem in the pres-

TABLE 6
Summary of Occupational Mobility, 1820–1860, in Five Occupational Categories, Expressed as Percentages

Occupational Category	Upward Mobility				Downward Mobility			
	1820–30	1830–40	1840–50	1850–60	1820–30	1830–40	1840–50	1850–60
1	—	—	—	—	11.1	6.0	7.9	10.0
2	7.5	12.3	3.7	8.9	12.5	16.4	11.9	16.4
3	7.8	10.4	7.0	8.5	1.7	2.5	5.1	7.7
4	21.7	39.6	27.1	34.1	2.2	14.6	14.8	9.1
5	23.3	34.5	29.6	30.1	—	—	—	—
Average Mobility	10.0	15.0	11.0	14.1	6.2	6.9	7.3	9.6

TABLE 7
Summary of Occupational Mobility, 1820–1860, in Functional Categories, Expressed as Percentages

Occupational Category	Upward Mobility				Downward Mobility			
	1820–30	1830–40	1840–50	1850–60	1820–30	1830–40	1840–50	1850–60
Nonmanual Proprietors	—	—	—	—	8.4	10.5	11.5	11.0
Craftsmen	5.4	10.4	7.2	9.2	2.6	3.5	4.5	7.2
Clerks, etc.	25.0	37.8	30.0	26.4	—	—	3.7	5.7
Unskilled Workers	21.7	32.1	28.1	28.3	—	—	—	—
Average Mobility	9.1	15.3	12.8	14.9	4.6	6.2	7.1	8.6

ent study was an indirect one, the analysis of variance relating the static variables of occupation and wealth. Its results are inconclusive. Specifically, occupation (regardless of how that term is defined) accounts for approximately one-sixth of the variation in the wealth of the members of the sample drawn from the 1860 census schedules.

Such a relationship does not appear to justify the inference of economic mobility from occupational mobility. Neither does it necessarily invalidate it. What it does suggest is that economic mobility, like social mobility, is a complex phenomenon that is best approached through complex, rather than unidimensional procedures. It is precisely this consideration that leads us to consider a second variable for observing mobility. Perhaps it will prove to be a more valid index of economic mobility. Perhaps it can be combined with occupational mobility to provide a better inference than either variable acting alone.

Residential Mobility

That residence should be that second variable was dictated by the format of the city directories. It is a variable that we would probably have turned to in any event, for residence is a workhorse in the literature of stratification. W. Lloyd Warner's famous (and, admittedly, controversial) Index of Status Characteristics, for example, consists of four variables: occupation, source of income, and two variations of the concept of residence, house type and dwelling area. This, of course, does not mean that we should not be just as skeptical of residence as we were of occupation, and we will subject it to the same examination. It does indicate, however, that we have expanded our methodology in a very important direction.

Since our information extends only to the address of each sample member, "residence" will refer not to the type, size, or value of each house but to its location. Before this concept acquires meaning, therefore, we must discover some means of differentiating one location from another. That is, we must define the neighborhoods of the city, just as we prepared our ranking of occupations. In the present study this was achieved through two methods. First, local tax records were used to define "neighborhoods" in strictly quantitative terms. A preliminary scanning of the tax register indicated that neighborhoods did in fact exist (that houses in a given area of the city had very similar assessments), and that these neighborhoods were much larger than the city's political wards. This means that a Philadelphia ward map, containing average residential assessments within each ward, can be used as a fairly reliable guide to the boundaries of the city's neighborhoods.

Figure 1 presents just such a map, based on the wards and tax records of 1820. The area presented is not merely the City of Philadelphia (the rectangle of fourteen wards stretching between the Delaware and Schuylkill rivers), but also includes those semiautonomous districts ("liberties") that had grown up along the Delaware long before the city itself filled up from river to river. In 1820, population was of urban density throughout each of the eastern city wards and throughout the adjoining districts, but tapered sharply in the western portions of the long wards to the west of Fourth Street. Thus, Philadelphia in 1820 was a city of approximately 120,000 inhabitants, extending some three miles along the Delaware River, with a maximum width of about a mile. In its northern and southern extensions, the distance from the edge of the city to the river was perhaps no more than a half-mile.

The average assessments in Figure 1 reveal a very interesting pattern. Specifically, there is a direct and very pronounced relationship between high average assessment and centrality. The highest averages are in the heart of the city, in four wards comprising a small square of perhaps one-quarter of a square mile. Immediately to the west of this square are wards with somewhat lower averages, and immediately north and south of it are wards with averages that are appreciably lower. These averages, in turn, are significantly higher than those on the perimeter of the city. The fact that the average assessment in each eastern ward is higher than in the ward immediately to its west represents an enlargement of this basic pattern, once the "center" of the city is located—not at its geographic center, but a few blocks west of the Delaware, midway between the northern and southern extremes of dense population.

If we were to rely solely on Figure 1, we would describe the city as a series of radiating zones of affluence, much like the classic theory of Park and Burgess. According to this theory, the central zone is an affluent one, but the first concentric ring is the poorest. Thereafter, the quality of the neighborhood increases, all the way out to the suburbs. The pre–Civil War city, however, seems to present a

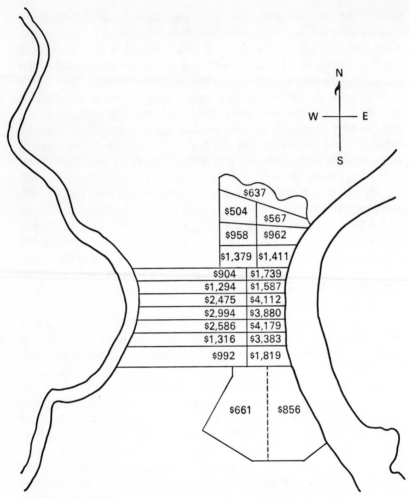

FIGURE 1. Average assessment by wards, 1820 (per taxable inhabitant).

partial reversal of this pattern. The interior zone is the most affluent, the surrounding ring is middle class, and the urban poor are located on the periphery.

In light of the absence of urban transportation systems in the early nineteenth-century city, this reversal of the classic pattern should be no surprise. The major institutions of the city—the port, the banks, the Merchants' Coffee House, the State House, the fashionable and important shops—were all located in its center. Before the omnibus and the streetcar, proximity to these institutions was the first requisite of urban life and, accordingly, the major criterion for judging the desirability of a neighborhood. Yet, to define the city's neighborhoods solely in terms of average ward assessments is clearly to oversimplify a complex matter. Accordingly, Figure 1 (and subsequent maps that were prepared for each decade) was examined in the light of qualitative data, usually in the form of descriptions of the city. Interestingly, the results of these two basic methods coincide quite closely. The following, for example, is from a description of Philadelphia in 1820 by its greatest historian:

> the smart quarter of the city was that in the vicinity of Third and Spruce streets. In the circle of a few blocks, around the spot where Thomas Willing had fixed his home, there were now a number of fine houses. Many substantial Quaker families were settled in Arch street, and some had gone out to Spring Garden and the Northern Liberties where they had built themselves large and comfortable residences. This neighborhood, however, was identified in most minds with butchers, drovers, and market people. The negro and poor white quarters were already in and south of Cedar or South street. Chestnut street was early spoken of as the city's fashionable promenade ground.

Third and Spruce streets ("the smart quarter"), Chestnut ("the city's fashionable promenade ground"), and Arch Street (the home of "many substantial Quaker families") all lay within the small, inner zone as defined by Figure 1. Spring Garden does not appear on our map because it was not yet taxed by the city, but Northern Liberties, just to the north of the city's political boundary and just east of Spring Garden, does. It is largely a "middle class" region, except for its northern extremes, and in the above description it is "identified in most minds with butchers, drovers, and market people." As the public markets of Northern Liberties were located in its southern wards, Oberholtzer's description obviously applies to these wards; in other words, to those with middle-class averages. Finally, the "negro and poor white quarters," south of Cedar Street, are the low-average wards at the bottom of Figure 1. Indeed, only one item in Oberholtzer's description fails to coincide with Figure 1. The "comfortable residences" of Northern Liberties and Spring Garden seem to intrude on our middle-class neighborhood. Actually, subsequent maps indicate that this was merely the advance guard of a northward expansion of the wealthy community.

Thus, it is with some confidence that we have identified three areas, or zones, of Philadelphia, each associated with a particular level of residential life. These zones were defined for 1820 by Figure 1, and then adjusted slightly on the basis of descriptive data. This procedure was repeated for each decade, retaining the three-zone system but changing its boundaries to reflect the growth and history of the city. Within this system, each member of the four directory samples was traced from residence to residence, just as he was traced from occupation to occupation.

Relations between Occupational and Residential Mobility

Table 8 summarizes the residential mobility of each sample. Interestingly, its results are strikingly similar to the overall pattern of occupational mobility in both magnitude and trend. Average upward mobility remained stable for each group through the first three decades, and decreased somewhat during the fourth. Actually, this decline probably reflects an error of judgment in defining the zonal boundaries of 1860. Relative to the previous decades, the proportion of the final sample in the outer zone was quite large, indicating that the inner zones should perhaps have been expanded more than they were. If this had been done, the decline in upward residential mobility would probably have been erased, and mobility would have been stable throughout the forty-year period.

Downward residential mobility also resembles occupational mobility, in that it increased through each decade for all groups. Its magnitude relative to upward mobility, however, was much greater than was the case with the first variable. In the 1820s, upward and downward residential mobility were about equal in magnitude. Thereafter, the latter became increasingly more common. Although the 3:1 ratio indicated in Table 8 is probably inflated, downward residential mobility (as defined here) was perhaps twice as high as upward mobility in the 1850s.

Thus, with both of our measurements we have obtained similar results: stable upward and increasing downward mobility. What, then, do we make of these results? Aside from their intrinsic interest, what

TABLE 8
Summary of Residential Mobility, 1820–1860, Expressed as Percentages

	Upward (Converging) Mobility				Downward (Radiating) Mobility			
	1820–30	1830–40	1840–50	1850–60	1820–30	1830–40	1840–50	1850–60
Zone 1								
To Zone 2					14.3	19.0	19.4	24.1
To Zone 3					4.2	9.2	9.7	11.8
Total					18.5	28.2	29.1	35.9
Zone 2								
To Zone 3					10.3	14.4	21.7	28.3
Average Downward Mobility					14.2	21.4	24.7	31.8
Zone 2								
To Zone 1	11.0	11.3	11.1	9.6				
Zone 3								
To Zone 2	12.4	11.0	12.3	7.8				
To Zone 1	3.7	5.5	3.2	3.8				
Total	16.1	16.5	15.5	11.6				
Average Upward Mobility	13.7	13.9	13.4	10.9				

do they tell us about the fluidity of the urban economic class system? The appropriate statistical analysis of this question (correlating economic mobility with occupational and residential mobility) is not possible with the data that are available, and the "indirect" analysis (of the static variables of wealth, occupation, and residence) is again inconclusive. Specifically, when both nominal variables are combined into a two-way analysis of the variation in wealth, the amount of variation accounted for is not appreciably different from the amount explained by each nominal variable acting alone. This peculiar fact is explained by the correlation between occupation and residence, that is, by the tendency of members of high-ranking occupations to reside in the inner zone, and for members of low-ranking occupations to reside in the outer zone (see Table 9). Thus, for purposes of analyzing variation in wealth, we may use either variable, or we may use both. The same variation is explained in each case.

TABLE 9
Residential Distribution of Occupational Categories, 1820–1860, Expressed as Percentages

	Occupational Category					
	1	*2*	*3*	*4*	*5*	Average
1820 Sample						
Zone 1	60.2	33.0	21.5	23.9	5.5	30.2
Zone 2	26.0	35.5	34.8	45.5	30.1	33.4
Zone 3	13.8	31.5	43.7	30.4	64.4	36.4
1830 Sample						
Zone 1	57.3	37.5	27.3	27.1	22.6	34.7
Zone 2	29.0	32.5	35.4	47.9	32.4	34.0
Zone 3	13.7	29.9	37.3	25.1	45.2	31.3
1840 Sample						
Zone 1	51.4	26.3	17.2	13.6	13.7	24.7
Zone 2	34.7	35.6	37.5	43.1	25.7	35.5
Zone 3	13.9	38.2	45.2	43.2	60.6	39.8
1850 Sample						
Zone 1	51.8	24.7	16.8	9.1	7.5	22.5
Zone 2	26.5	26.7	26.3	34.0	28.4	26.9
Zone 3	22.0	48.7	57.0	56.7	64.2	50.6

Have we added nothing, then, with our second variable? Again, we must remember that it is the dynamic variables of economic, occupational, and residential mobility that we are interested in. We have neither proved nor disproved our basic inference, and we cannot do so until we can find a direct measurement of economic mobility. In this connection, it is interesting to note that we are able to correlate occupational and residential mobility, and that the relationship between them is actually quite weak. As Table 10 indicates, none of our samples reveal a strong direct or inverse relationship between occupational and residential mobility. Perhaps they are essentially unrelated phenomena, each, in turn, unrelated to economic mobility. Or, perhaps they are significant and *additive* components of economic mobility, providing between them a reliable estimate of its magnitude and trend.

If occupational and residential mobility are additive components of economic mobility, we may come closer to a valid inference by combining both nominal variables into a new set of matrices that would represent mobility within both dimensions simultaneously. In the preceding matrices, the inference of each particular sample member's economic mobility depended almost entirely on which variable was being observed. As we have seen in Table 10, those who represented upward and downward mobility in our occupational matrices were not those who were mobile in our residential matrices. The coincidence of overall results has perhaps served to distract our attention from this problem, but it is a significant one nonetheless. What would we be thinking now if mobility rates on each dimension had contradicted the other?

By combining the two variables, we establish what would seem to be more realistic criteria for inferring economic (and probably social) mobility. For example, in the combined matrices, upward occupational mobility that is accompanied by movement to a wealthier neighborhood would be regarded as a clear indication of upward economic mobility. But if the same upward occupational change had been accompanied by movement to a poorer neighborhood, the individual's status could well be regarded as unchanged. In all probability, he achieved the upward occupational mobility only while moving to a neighborhood where the rents were lower and the incomes smaller.

Table 11 summarizes the results of four new five-by-five matrices

TABLE 10
Cross-Classification of Occupational and Residential Mobility, 1820–1860

Residential Mobility	Occupational Mobility			
	Downward	Static	Upward	Total
1820 Sample				
Downward	8	69	9	86
Static	39	674	63	776
Upward	9	74	8	91
Total	56	817	80	953
G = −.041				
1830 Sample				
Downward	10	123	27	160
Static	59	685	88	832
Upward	6	69	24	99
Total	75	877	139	1,091
G = .042				
1840 Sample				
Downward	36	209	28	273
Static	73	1,200	104	1,377
Upward	13	140	32	185
Total	122	1,549	164	1,835
G = .194				
1850 Sample				
Downward	22	131	18	171
Static	61	672	92	825
Upward	8	68	16	92
Total	91	871	126	1,088
G = .157				

representing the combination of the two nominal variables. In the first category of these matrices are those members of the first occupational category who lived in Zone 1 and Zone 2. The second category consists of the remainder of the first occupational category (those who lived in Zone 3) as well as the members of the second

TABLE 11
Summary of Two-Dimensional Mobility, 1820–1860, Expressed as Percentages

Category	Upward Mobility					Downward Mobility				
	1820	1830	1840	1850		1820	1830	1840	1850	
1	—	—	—	—		10.3	9.7	11.7	19.1	
2	9.3	13.6	6.9	12.6		14.2	18.5	18.8	16.0	
3	10.1	12.9	7.3	9.8		11.9	15.3	19.6	26.0	
4	20.9	22.7	18.6	15.4		2.6	4.8	7.8	8.8	
5	23.0	32.4	30.3	31.3		—	—	—	—	
Average	14.4	17.7	14.5	16.6		9.6	12.5	14.5	17.2	

category who lived in Zones 1 and 2. Each occupational category and residential zone is divided in this manner except the lowest occupational category, which is placed entirely in the fifth combined category. The results generated by these matrices are, unsurprisingly, quite similar to those we have observed within each separate dimension. Average upward mobility remained rather stable throughout the period, and average downward mobility gradually increased until it approximated the magnitude of the former. It is doubtful that any other method of classifying and combining occupations and residence, or even the elimination of the built-in errors that we have noted, would have produced results that would contradict this basic generalization.

The question of whether or not these patterns validly indicate the magnitude of economic or social mobility remains largely a matter of conjecture. On the other hand, they do seem to point to a significant alteration of the urban social structure that is itself relevant to the question of fluidity. Specifically, the steady expansion of the magnitude of downward occupational and residential mobility strongly suggests that the lower-ranked occupations and neighborhoods were themselves expanding—that is, the city's lower classes were growing significantly faster than the rest of its population. In addition, the specific patterns of occupational change, in the 1830s and 1840s especially, indicate that this shift in the class pyramid may have been related to a critical change in the city's economic life.

Table 12 sheds a small amount of light on this matter by comparing the relative sizes of occupational groups in 1820 and again in 1860. In this comparison, one significant shift is evident. Although the ratio between nonmanual and manual positions remained about the same, the latter group reveals a significant expansion of unskilled positions and contraction of skilled positions. Thus, the proportion of craftsmen to the adult male working force declined from 56.2 percent to 47 percent, whereas the proportion of unskilled workers increased from 16.7 percent to 23.6 percent. The growth of the unskilled category, furthermore, is more than accounted for by increases in day laborers from 5.8 percent to 13.9 percent.

But the most significant shift in the occupational structure is the one that Table 12 cannot measure, the increase in the number and proportion of journeymen craftsmen. We have already seen that the 1860 census schedules do not generally make the distinction be-

TABLE 12
Proportion of Occupational Groups to the Adult Male Working Force, 1820 and 1860, Expressed as Percentages

	1820 [a]	1860 [b]
Merchants and professionals	21.5	24.2
Manufacturers	1.0	2.3
Total nonmanual proprietors	22.5	26.5
Clerical workers	4.6	2.9
Total nonmanual	27.1	29.4
Master craftsmen	34.3	[c]
Journeymen craftsmen	21.9	[c]
Total craftsmen	56.2	47.0
Day laborers	5.8	13.9
Other unskilled and service workers	10.9	9.7
Total unskilled workers	16.7	23.6
Total, manual	72.9	70.6
Total	100.0	100.0

[a] Edward Whitely, *The Philadelphia Directory and Register for 1820* (Philadelphia, McCarty & Davis, 1820); manuscript tax assessors' lists, County of Philadelphia, 1820.
[b] Manuscript schedules of inhabitants of the County of Philadelphia, Eighth United States Census, 1860.
[c] Not specified.

tween masters and journeymen. Other data, on the other hand, indicate that the number of journeymen in Philadelphia in 1860 was at least 40,000, and was possibly as high as 50,000. From our sample from the census schedules we may project a total craftsman population of approximately 60,000. From these figures, therefore, we may derive a conservative ratio of journeymen to masters of 2:1. This compares to the 1820 ratio of approximately 2:3, indicating a tripling of the proportion of journeymen, relative to masters, in the forty years before the Civil War. When this assumed 2:1 ratio is applied to Table 12, the previously noted changes are enormously heightened. The proportion of master craftsmen to the total work force is reduced by more than one-half, from over 34 percent to approximately 16 percent. The total manual wage-earning class increases from a minority of 38.6 percent to a majority of some 55 percent. In 1820, in other words, there was a skilled, proprietary position for almost every skilled and unskilled wage-earning position. By 1860 the manual, wage-earning jobs outnumbered the manual proprietorship by more than three to one.

It would be difficult to exaggerate the importance of this shift. In 1820, Philadelphia was dominated, numerically and physically, by small shops and shopkeepers. The demand for master craftsmen was great enough to provide any ambitious and competent journeyman with the opportunity to set up his own shop. During the next forty years, the number of shops remained substantially the same. But at the same time the population had quadrupled, and in this new city of a half-million people, a few thousand could no longer dominate the landscape. Nor could a few thousand proprietorships give much hope to forty or fifty thousand journeymen. Never again would this American city be described, as John Fanning Watson once described it, as a place where,

> almost every apprentice, when of age, ran his equal chance for his share of business in his neighborhood, by setting up for himself, and, with an apprentice or two, getting into a cheap location, and by dint of application and good work, recommending himself to his neighborhood.

A Theory and the Data

What had happened to Philadelphia since the days when, as Watson continues, "every shoemaker or tailor was a man for himself"? One important event, no doubt, was the massive immigration of Irish in the 1840s—poor, rural Irish, absolutely unequipped for urban life. The significant increase in day laborers, noted in Table 12, consisted largely of Irish (and to a lesser extent German) immigrants. But a more fundamental answer is suggested by John R. Commons's theory of "merchant capitalism" as the intervening stage between craft and factory production in American history. This theory, first explored by Commons a half century ago in a study of American (and usually Philadelphia) shoemakers, has gradually become the most widely respected interpretation of economic change in the immediate pre–Civil War period. In essence, it states that the rapid expansion of markets, created by the revolutionary developments in transportation, eroded the craft system by giving large merchants increasing control over the production of goods. In the days before the canal and the railroad, indeed before the Jeffersonian embargo and the War of 1812, the large, urban merchants interested themselves but little in American manufacturing. In the 1820s, however, and especially in the 1830s, it was becoming evident to the organizers of trade that the greatest opportunities lay not to the east but to the west and south. This was a trade of an entirely different type—indeed, the reverse of that trade which had occupied urban merchants for generations. Now, instead of importing manufactured goods from Europe and exporting American raw materials, merchants would turn increasingly to the westward and southward shipment of Eastern manufactures, in exchange for grain, meat and cotton. In the exploitation of these new markets, the merchant had numerous advantages over the master craftsman. Only the merchant could afford to invest in a stock of merchandise large enough to make shipments on a profitable basis to Illinois or Alabama. Only the merchant could afford to wait six months for payment, or pay the rent on a large warehouse. Only the merchant had the skill, the credit, and the personal contacts to organize such a trade. As a consequence, the merchant increasingly dominated the craftsman. At first, he merely bought his product. But the advantages of large-scale production, of control over the supply of goods, indeed, of the elimination of the profits of the independent craftsmen, were too obvious. Increasingly the merchant organized production himself, bringing large numbers of journeymen under one roof, training new journeymen in brief periods for specialized tasks, and hiring former masters to serve as foremen. By the mid-1830s, according to Commons, the merchant-manufacturer had emerged into full view in the Philadelphia shoe industry. By the 1840s he dominated it.

The value of Commons's theory in the present context is that it helps to explain the emergence of a large, "blue-collar" working force in a period that precedes, in all but a few industries, the emergence of the mechanized factory. Historians have long recognized the significance of industrialization in shaping the career expectations of the workingman, but in doing so they have tended to miss the significance of the antebellum period. The reason, no doubt, rests in the customary association of industrialization with the mechanization of production, and in the further association of mechanization with the latter decades of the nineteenth century. In the shoemaking industry, for example, mechanization was not fully accomplished

until the 1880s. Yet, from the standpoint of the master and journeyman shoemaker, the industry experienced its most critical changes a
full fifty years earlier.

An extensive report on manufacturing in Philadelphia, published
in 1858, indicates that the same sequence held true for most other
industries as well. The clothing industry seems to confirm Commons's theory in detail. In other industries, such as furniture, carriages, bricks, rope, cigars, brushes, barrels, candy, and hats, it is not
clear just who the manufacturer was—whether he had previously
been an import-export merchant, or whether he had risen from the
ranks of the craftsmen. But in each of these industries it is evident
that the growth of a small number of large producers was accomplished with little mechanization of the manufacturing process. In
each of these industries the mechanized factory may have come
much later. But the working force that is usually associated with this
factory preceded the Civil War.

A number of industries, of course, were mechanized before the
Civil War. In most of these—metals, machinery, paper, beer and ale,
liquor—production had been organized into a few large shops even
before the beginning of our period. The mechanization of the textile
industry before the Civil War is classic, and needs no elaboration for
the nation's third largest area of textile production. Yet, perhaps
ironically, the textile industry is not primarily responsible for the
restructuring of the working population that this paper has explored.
Most of the operatives in the cotton and woolen mills of Philadelphia
were women and children. In this study, we have concerned our-
selves only with their husbands and fathers.

Thus, even though the adult male factory operative was primarily
a phenomenon of the latter nineteenth century, the emergence of a
large wage-earning class was evident around mid-century. The
numerical domination of this class in Philadelphia was probably
achieved in the 1850s, the product of forces that had become visible
in the 1830s and 1840s. It is here that our mobility matrices become
especially revealing. For our proposition of critical change and our
observed patterns of mobility are mutually reinforcing. The expansion of the lower classes tends to explain the observed growth of
downward mobility. In turn, the disruption in the 1830s and 1840s of
stable patterns of occupational mobility seems to reflect the impact
of "merchant capitalism" on the economic life of the city.

In one very important sense, then, economic change in antebellum Philadelphia seems to have lessened opportunity for worldly advancement. But a decline in the extensiveness of opportunity does not necessarily make the success ideology less potent. The American Dream is fed, not by such mundane matters as mobility matrices, but by isolated cases of spectacular success. And in Philadelphia, the very forces that seem to have threatened the extensiveness of upward mobility also seem to have made the stakes a great deal more interesting. The schedules of the 1860 census may give us an interesting perspective on this matter by permitting a tabulation of the distribution of wealth at the end of our period. Figure 2, a Lorenz Curve, reveals that distribution to be one of remarkable inequality. One-third of the sample of male family is described as propertyless. When the curve begins it rises very slowly until it reaches the upper 20 percent of the sample, the bottom 80 percent owning a mere 3 percent of the sample's reported wealth. Even the next to highest 10 percent owned less than their "equal share" of the wealth. Thus, it is only in describing the wealth of the richest 10 percent of the sample that the curve begins to soar. The wealthiest 10 percent owned 89 percent of the sample's wealth. The wealthiest 1 percent owned one-half!

The slope of this curve may be interpreted statistically by calculating the Schutz Coefficient of Inequality, a measure defining absolute equality as 0 and values approaching 1.0 as reflecting increasing degrees of inequality. The Schutz Coefficient for Figure 2 is an understandably high .79. Unfortunately, we cannot compare this measure to earlier points in time, as our earlier data are not comparable to the schedules of the Eighth Census. One item, however, may be of some use. Tabular tax assessment data for the city of Boston seems to provide at least a rough basis for assessing change in the distribution of wealth. If we accept these data on faith, they yield coefficients of .537 for 1820, .637 for 1830, and .694 for 1845. Comparing these figures to .79 for Philadelphia in 1860 reveals a picture of increasing inequality.

In any case, the inequality of the distribution of wealth in 1860 speaks for itself. Philadelphia, on the eve of the Civil War, was a society of extreme economic stratification. Many of its inhabitants were poor, and most were entirely dependent on the continued wages of one or two persons. Opportunities for establishing some

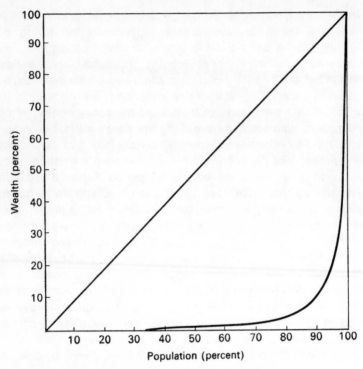

FIGURE 2. The distribution of wealth: Philadelphia, 1860.

other basis of economic support were seemingly on the decline. On the other hand, for those who did dream of economic success, the drama of that dream must have been considerably heightened by the appearance of individual fortunes of unprecedented proportions. Indeed, in these two statements we come to the very heart of both opportunity and change in the antebellum American city. For never before were the rich so rich. And never before were the poor so plentiful.

Gary B. Nash

THE SOCIAL ORIGINS OF
ANTEBELLUM LAWYERS

*Gary B. Nash, author of numerous important studies of society and politics
in eighteenth-century Pennsylvania, provides a nice example of the historian's
treatment of one aspect of social mobility in this essay. Before discussing
the backgrounds of the men who became lawyers in antebellum Philadelphia,
he examines the changing attitudes toward the legal profession—in themselves a significant explanation of some of the changes that occurred in the
kind of men who entered the profession.*

Americans have traditionally recognized social mobility as a valuable
and characteristic feature of their society. Constant movement up
and down the ladder of wealth and status, it is generally assumed,
stems naturally from our healthy insistence on equality of opportunity, on careers "open to talent." A corollary belief, embodied in
a faith in such a system, is that an egalitarian society will necessarily
produce the strongest and most stable institutions.

Recently this American ideal has come under simultaneous attack
from two separate quarters. On the one hand, sociologists and certain historians have amassed an impressive array of statistics to suggest, contrary to traditional belief, that the rags-to-riches career
pattern has been greatly overemphasized, at least for the years since
1870 and probably before. At the same time, other historians, employing hunch, insight, and impressionistic evidence, have accepted the
old "fluidity" school only to tell us that the rapid social and economic ascent of large numbers of nineteenth-century Americans may
have had unsuspectingly injurious consequences, and may have
been, in fact, a part of a far broader pattern of institutional decay
and social confusion.

Neither view of nineteenth-century social mobility—the one quantitative, the other qualitative—has been supported by empirical evidence for the pre–Civil War period. The present essay is a test case
both of the nature and extent of antebellum social mobility and of

From Gary B. Nash, "The Philadelphia Bench and Bar, 1800–1861," *Comparative
Studies in Society and History* 7 (January 2, 1965): 203–220. Reprinted with the
permission of Cambridge University Press. Footnotes deleted.

the effect of the forces of egalitarianism, particularly virulent during this period, on social institutions. To this end attention will be focused on a small segment of society, the legal profession in Philadelphia, as a particular study of institutional change between 1800 and 1860.

I

The legal profession is doubly appropriate for such a study. On the one hand, lawyers have long been regarded as a bulwark of stability and order. Characteristically their work concerns the defense not the alteration of the law, conservation not change. Tocqueville saw American lawyers as "the most powerful, if not the only counterpoise to the democratic element," standing alone to check the people when they became "intoxicated by passion or carried away by the impetuosity of their ideas." The legal profession, he added, was the "most powerful existing security against the excesses of democracy." Lord Bryce, more than a half century later, described similar "conservative instincts" and attachments to "old forms" so characteristic of the legal profession. It was this habitual concern for stability, this resistance to precipitous change, that made lawyers a logical target for those who wished to complete the process of democratization, which they judged to be the natural conclusion of the Revolutionary era.

On the other hand, the legal profession is peculiarly well adapted to a study of upward social mobility. Law throughout the nineteenth century was a favorite occupational goal of ambitious individuals of middle- and lower-class birth. Since colonial days the social prestige of lawyers had been high, the monetary rewards excellent, and the gateways which it opened to politics and finance well known. Moreover, it was relatively free of organizational impediments—the hierarchical structuring characteristic of business or civil service—which would have constricted the flow of aspirants from the lower levels of society. It was, in short, among the most accessible of the sought-after elite professions.

The choice of Philadelphia is not altogether arbitrary. The great prominence of Philadelphia lawyers, dating to the adroitness and profundity of Andrew Hamilton in defending Peter Zenger in 1735, continued throughout the eighteenth and nineteenth centuries, making Philadelphia the cynosure of the legal profession in the early national period. The city's position as the nation's center of commerce and banking until about 1835 encouraged a large and mature legal body. In Philadelphia law was in the air. In City Hall sat the United States Supreme Court at the end of the eighteenth century, as well as the United States Circuit and District Courts. In the nearby State House the Pennsylvania Supreme Court convened. Nowhere in the country could be found such an outstanding body of men expert in commercial, criminal, and maritime law. A British traveler of wealth and education epitomized the prevalent view: "I have never met a body of men," he remarked in 1833, "more distinguished by acuteness and extensive professional information than the members of the Philadelphia bar."

At the same time it is recognized that resistance to the egalitarian ideology was probably abnormally high in Philadelphia. Almost every European observer saw tight-knit upper-class cliques entrenched in Philadelphia to a degree unparalleled in other American cities. Nonetheless, the present study need not suffer from this fact, since it is intended to be illustrative rather than conclusive of the processes which transformed the structure of antebellum American society.

II

Accessibility to the elite professions stood as a fundamental demand of those who spoke for unlimited opportunity in nineteenth-century America. In the legal profession two somewhat opposed movements promised to bring about such equalitarianism. One sought to replace the old office-apprenticeship system of legal education with systematic university training; the other agitated for less stringent educational requirements for admission to the bar. Both tended to lessen the exclusiveness of the bench and bar. In Philadelphia, as in Pennsylvania, the latter movement was less important than in other states because educational requirements for lawyers had long been minimal.

In 1800 the education of lawyers was almost entirely in the hands of practicing members of the profession. Recruits read law in the offices of an established practitioner—a diet of Blackstone, Coke, Grotius, Pufendorf, and reported state trials. The training was painfully arid, often emphasizing memory at the expense of comprehension. William Lewis, a celebrated Philadelphia criminal lawyer, was a typical taskmaster. To one of his students who inquired whether he should read the ponderous Pennsylvania State Trials, Lewis replied, "Not only read, but get them by heart." A second and more important aspect of this system of legal apprenticeship was the close personal relationship between tutor and student. Established lawyers, practicing alone or with one or two partners, often supervised the training of a half-dozen students, directing their reading, instructing them in the preparation of forms and documents, and hovering over them in the daily routine of office work. The novitiates endured weekly question-and-answer periods, accompanied their superiors to court, ate at their tables, and not infrequently married their daughters. All of this led inevitably to a high degree of cohesiveness throughout the legal circle. "Graduates" of law offices had every opportunity to take on the colorations of their preceptors.

As early as 1817 attempts were made in Philadelphia to parallel the apprenticeship system with a program of systematic instruction. In that year the University of Pennsylvania established a series of law lectures with an eye toward building a law curriculum. Apparently for lack of interest the program did not survive the following year. Four years later Peter DuPonceau, a leading light of the Philadelphia bar, organized the Law Academy to supplement the work of the law offices. Although the academy had a continuing existence for more than a century, it evolved more as a professional social and debating society than as an instrumentality of legal education. There is no evidence that these premature starts at systematic legal education received the support of practicing lawyers, who doubtless guarded jealously their prerogatives of legal education.

Further attempts to replace the apprenticeship pattern were made in 1832. In that year the Law Academy petitioned the Board of Trustees of the University of Pennsylvania for the establishment of a Law Department. The motive force appears to have been the law students themselves, who, restive in the confinements of law offices, were eager to follow the example of other areas in establishing a regularized and less inbred program of legal studies under the auspices of a university. That the established lawyers looked apprehensively upon this challenge to their prerogatives is evident in the solid opposition of virtually all of the leading lights of the Philadelphia bar—

Chew, Gibson, Burd, Binney, Chauncey, Hopkinson, Waln, Cad-walader, Sergeant, Ingersoll, Rawle, and Biddle. It is also worthy of note that all of these men, with the possible exception of Gibson, came from the highest strata of Philadelphia society.

In the face of active opposition from the legal profession itself, the university took no action on the proposals of the Law Academy. For nearly two decades the issue lay dormant. Again in 1849, however, law students vociferously appealed for a University Department of Law and the movement was revived. Whether by the decline of the old aristocratic leaders of the bar or by a growing consensus that Philadelphia had fallen behind other parts of the country in legal education, the profession this time offered no resistance. In 1850 George Sharswood, a well-known city lawyer, undertook the leadership of the new Law Department. A man of middle-class background and a Democrat in politics, Sharswood was an ideal person to lead the movement away from a restrictive and circumscribed system of legal education.

In 1850 the new Law Department enrolled its first students, and two years later awarded the degree of Bachelor of Laws for the first time. By 1861, 71 students were enrolled. Prerequisites for admission, in contrast to the standards of most present-day law schools, did not include a collegiate education. Candidates were accepted without regard for college indoctrination as evidenced by the fact that in the first ten classes only 21 of 116 students had more than a high school education. As will be seen later this was a considerably smaller percentage of college graduates than was reaching the bar as a whole, a fact suggesting the opportunity which the Law School afforded to recruits of noncollegiate background. The Law School fees of $10 per term for each course were sufficiently low to open the door to all but the poorest of recruits. It is doubtful that these fees exceeded, or in some cases even matched, the charge made by practitioners for their students.

The second impetus which worked in favor of a broader recruitment of lawyers threatened to make superfluous efforts to entrust legal education to the universities. Concerned with access to positions of influence and wealth, reformers demanded the diminution of requirements for admission to the bar. Especially did they decry long periods of study which militated against ambitious young men of limited means. Nothing less than the abolishment of these "un-

democratic" qualifications was called for. Response to such demands was widespread. Whereas in 1800 fourteen of nineteen states
required between three and seven years of preparation for bar candidates, by 1840 definite periods of legal instruction were required in
only eleven of thirty jurisdictions. The climax was reached in 1860
when only nine of thirty-nine states made such a requirement and
four states required only proof of good moral character and attainment of twenty-one years of age for admission to the bar. Although
Pennsylvania escaped any further reductions of her already minimal
requirements in the 1830s and 1840s, she was not immune to the impact of this movement to deprofessionalize the practice of law as
will be amplified in a following section. Indirectly, however, the
establishment of the University of Pennsylvania Law School abetted
the movement for shorter training. In 1856 the Supreme Court of
Pennsylvania adopted the rule that any recipient of the Bachelor of
Laws degree who had been admitted to the Court of Common Pleas
or the District Court was admissible to the State Supreme Court.
Thus a two-year curriculum at the Law School sufficed to meet all
requirements for admission to the bar.

The half century before the Civil War, then, evinced a dual movement to alter the existing pattern of legal education. On the one hand
a popular crusade moved to diminish educational requirements and
other prerequisites to professional attainment. At the same time,
forces were at work to replace the old apprenticeship system with
professional university education, available without regard to social
status, economic position, or college training. There is no evidence
to suggest that university legal education was intended to broaden
the social spectrum of recruits, or that established lawyers opposed
it to prevent entry from the lower ranks of society. It was, however,
an innovation that was long resisted by the aristocratic elite of the
Philadelphia bar and which, when instituted, broke the exclusiveness
of legal education engendered by the apprenticeship system.

III

If the metamorphosis of legal training presaged changes in the solidarity of the profession, it was but a minor disturbance as compared
with the impact of direct attacks on the bench and bar from 1800 to
1860. Sometimes inspired by party politicians, but often the product

of bipartisan sentiment, these assaults weakened respect for both the judicial process and the legal profession by indicting the motives and methods of the legal fraternity. Movements to make lawyers and judges answerable to the electorate or to supersede them altogether were widespread.

In Pennsylvania the attacks on the legal profession traced back to post-Revolutionary days and before. The postwar animus toward lawyers, however, was related to an aversion to the prevailing system of English common law, and stemmed from the natural reaction against a British system of jurisprudence, as well as from the remembrance of the high incidence of Royalist lawyers at the pre-Revolutionary bar. This early antipathy was heightened during the Confederation period by the frequency with which lawyers utilized their education in the work of debt collection and contract enforcement. The lawyers, with pro-British colorations, indeed often trained at the English Inns of Court, seemed most often to be the wolf at the door.

While a residue of sentiment against the supposedly Anglophilic lawyer remained at the beginning of Jefferson's presidency, the attack, by then, had shifted ground markedly. No longer were lawyers trained at the English Inns; nor was their work primarily the thankless task of collecting wartime debts. Their offensiveness, it was discovered, came instead from their attempts to entrench themselves as a professional aristocracy, fattening their purses at the people's expense. In the demagogic idiom they were parasitical and superfluous agents who had arrogated an important democratic function—the administration of justice.

In Pennsylvania from 1799 to 1810 such attacks, frequently led by Republican-Democrats, sought to reduce the power of the judiciary and to undermine the position of lawyers. At first the incursions were aimed principally at impeaching the Federalist judges on the Pennsylvania Supreme Court. These forays can be identified as purely partisan attempts by the Republicans to add the finishing touches to their political victory of 1800, which had netted them the governorship and the state legislature. While successful, in 1803, in removing Federalist judge Alexander Addison, whose primary transgression was political bias, the attacks failed of their primary purpose—the popular election of judges.

Republican attempts to obtain a friendly Supreme Court were

paralleled by a more general movement to curb the so-called "aristo-cratical" practices of the legal profession. Under the leadership of the acidulous William Duane, stanch Jeffersonian and editor of the popular Philadelphia *Aurora,* a reform movement designed to render justice more accessible to ordinary litigants by the circumvention of expensive lawyers gathered speed. As early as January, 1800, "A Real Democrat" had proposed in a letter to the *General Advertiser* that contestants be allowed to plead their own cases without pro-fessional assistance. This single voice adumbrated a more prevalent feeling which was to arise two years later.

In 1802 a bill was introduced to the state legislature to extend the jurisdiction of justices of the peace, almost always laymen, to civil suits of $100 or less. Since 1794 justices had been empowered to arbitrate cases extending to $60 or less, more on the basis of equity than on technicalities of law. Also available were small claims courts before which litigants could plead without benefit or expense of counsel. Although the bill of 1802 passed both houses of the legis-lature, Thomas McKean, the Republican governor and himself a lawyer, crushed it with a veto. Twice in 1803 similar bills were passed but vetoed by McKean. On the second instance, however, the veto was overridden, in itself indicative of the persistent agitation in favor of the bill.

The fermentation of popular feeling against lawyers continued in 1805. Radical Republicans such as Duane tried to stir public pas-sions by asking ". . . whether the doors of courts shall be shut to 'every man' except lawyers, by requiring dexterity in fiction and non-sensical pleadings and rules, arbitrarily imposed by the monkish priesthood. . . ." In a series of essays entitled *Samson against the Philistines,* Duane asserted, true to the Jeffersonian faith in the abili-ties of the common man, that any good reader could master the ele-ments of law in a single month of solid application or in four months leisure time. All civil actions, he insisted, should be settled by arbi-tration; criminal trial processes should be simplified; and lawyers, if they could not be destroyed root and branch, should be limited in their fees to $5 per case.

There is little evidence to suggest that these individual attacks on the bench and bar ever became a great issue, supported by wide majorities. They were, in part, the pyrotechnics of internecine warfare in the Pennsylvania Republican party, split violently between the Duane–Michael Lieb faction and the McKean–Alexander Dallas wing. That such sorties against the profession were not simply the outpourings of a single hot-tempered Irish demagogue, however, is evident from the rash of petitions and remonstrances which descended on the state legislature. These appeals called for constitutional amendment and invariably listed as major reforms the control of the judiciary through term appointment or election, and the extension of the jurisdiction of lay justices of the peace. Such demands for constitutional revision were numerous in 1805–1806 and reached a new crescendo in 1810. While it is impossible to abstract the purely antilawyer sentiment from these broader appeals for democratic reform, the thread of hostility to the legal profession, fed by zealots such as Duane, is evident throughout the petitions.

Other indications of the growing antilawyer sentiment are not lacking. At the legislative caucus, convened on April 3, 1805 to select a candidate for the gubernatorial election, the conferees agreed "... that the candidate should not be a lawyer, and that a clodhopper should be preferred." This may have been a veiled reference to Governor McKean, but if so it proceeded in large part from his defense of the legal circle, and especially from his triple veto of the $100 civil suit bill, an action which only brought further obloquy to his profession. Lawyers grew uneasy under these attacks. In a letter to Rufus King, minister to England, a prominent Philadelphia lawyer confided in December 1803 that sentiment was abroad to do away with the bar altogether. "All the eminent lawyers," wrote Charles J. Ingersoll, "have their eyes on one city or another to remove to in case of extremes." Peter DuPonceau recalled some years later that in 1805 the bar was subjected to bitter attacks and "constant invective." Of lawyers, he recollected, some advocated "nothing less ... than their entire destruction."

Although direct attacks on lawyers and the judiciary subsided after 1810, lawyers were sensitive throughout the following decades to the suspicion in which they were held by some elements of society. A Philadelphia essayist of the 1820s described the popular view: lawyers were slippery, rascally characters who accumulated a mass of knowledge, purposely complicated to render it unintelligible to the layman, and thus plied their mysterious trade at great personal profit. "If you seal one up in a quart bottle," said the common man of a lawyer, "he will get out through the pores of the cork and the wax."

Such deprecatory feeling continued throughout the 1820s and 1830s when pressure for constitutional reforms was applied intermittently. The primary attention of reformers was focused on political issues, particularly the extension of the electorate's power at the expense of the executive. But purely antilawyer sentiment was not lacking in the continual petitions for a convention to amend the constitution. When at last the convention met in 1838, proposals to circumscribe the powers and influence of the legal profession were foremost among the reform measures. Amendments to render elective various legal offices—prothonotaries, justices of the peace, court clerks, recorders of deeds, and registers of wills—were drafted, debated, and passed. Another article abolished lifetime judicial appointments, prescribing instead tenures of fifteen, ten, and five years. Complementing these revisions were the purely political issues, mostly involving the executive patronage.

Lawyer delegates to the convention were by no means unalterably opposed to the demands of reformers. This lack of unanimity, in itself, speaks for the growing unsolidarity in the legal ranks. While ably defending their profession against the thrusts of antagonists, lawyer delegates frequently conceded the need for judicial reform. Charles Brown, a delegate from Philadelphia and a lawyer of that city, was a leader in the fight to abolish lifetime judicial appointments. He was supported by his compeers Thomas Earle and Joseph Doran, also lawyers of Philadelphia. Other city attorneys such as Jared Ingersoll, John Sergeant, Charles Chauncey and William Meredith were strongly opposed to these measures. It is interesting to note that those in opposition were all men of wealth and distinguished pedigree. This lack of unanimity among lawyer delegates also extended to the question of making lesser legal offices elective. Lawyer delegates from Philadelphia were evenly split on this issue.

The work of the convention was not completed until 1838 when the amendments were submitted to the electorate. Although sanctioned by a majority vote, the narrow margin of victory illustrates again that the urge for reform was not overwhelming. Nonetheless, a bill which tended to bring within the public purview a part of the legal fraternity, was warmly welcomed by a broad section of the electorate. Further changes in 1851 made the judiciary totally responsible to the people for office. In that year an amendment was carried to make state judgeships at all court levels elective.

The first half century of the 1800s, then, gives evidence of a steady and resolute movement to whittle away at the power and autonomy of the legal profession. Although many of the more radical proposals found little appeal with the voters, inroads were made on the breadth and profundity of legal influence through extending the jurisdiction of courts of arbitration, by making the judiciary and certain legal functionaries answerable to the people, and most importantly, by stigmatizing lawyers with a steady barrage of invective which impugned their motives, their democratic instincts, and even their social usefulness.

IV

As salient as were the periodic forays against the bench and bar, and the attempts to recast the mode of legal education, the most important factor in altering the complexion of the legal circle was a changing pattern of social recruitment. Between 1800 and 1860 a new breed of lawyers, or at least an unprecedented admixture of social types, populated the profession with a less homogeneous, less like-thinking group.

A comparative study of the social and economic backgrounds of lawyers during the period 1800 to 1860 may help to illustrate this central point. For the sake of numerical equality, and to obtain the widest possible spread in time, I have selected for study those lawyers admitted to the Philadelphia bar from 1800–1805 and from 1860–1861. The former group totals 101, the latter 98. Such persons are registered in the office of the Prothonotary of Philadelphia and conveniently listed in John Hill Martin's *Bench and Bar of Philadelphia*. Biographical data has not, of course, been found for all of the men. But as the study is comparative, the information derived should yield an accurate picture of changing social characteristics within the profession.

A striking feature of both groups is the uniformity of both ethnic background and nativity. Of the earlier group less than 6 percent of the lawyers whose place of birth could be ascertained were foreign-born, all of these coming from the British Isles. In the later group 6.7 percent of the cases observed were alien by birth, once again the rare examples of foreign birth being those of British-born subjects. This homogeneity is all the more striking when the composition of Philadelphia's population is considered. In 1870, the nearest year for which statistics are available, the foreign-born—almost entirely English, Scotch-Irish, or German—composed 27 percent of the city's inhabitants. No doubt linguistic difficulties, in a profession where forensic abilities counted heavily, blocked the road to the legal profession for most non-English-speaking immigrants. But the relative absence of British-born lawyers, while slightly less in 1860 than in 1800, speaks for the general difficulty of the foreign-born in gaining entrance to the legal circle.

The ethnic uniformity extends also to the fathers of both sets. Sires of the early nineteenth-century lawyers were native-born in 79 percent of the cases in which data was found, the foreign-born tracing their birth to Ireland or England in every case. Of the 1860–1861 attorneys, 87.5 percent had American-born fathers. If lineage is traced farther back the parallel continues. Both groups derived predominantly from English or Scotch-Irish lines, in the earlier group in 95.9 percent of the cases observed; in the latter group in 88.4 percent of cases noted. Thus the bar in both epochs was composed preponderantly and disproportionately of native Americans, for the most part third generation or older, and overwhelmingly of English and Scotch-Irish extraction.

The statistics derived for religious affiliation are more fragmentary, but they indicate no clear difference between the two groups. Among both, Protestants, and especially Presbyterians and Episcopalians, bulk exceedingly large. While these denominations were overrepresented, other less affluent and socially important religious groups such as Catholics, Jews, and Methodists had disproportionately few representatives. In the earlier sample were ten Presbyterians, five Episcopalians, four Quakers, two Congregationalists, one Baptist, and one Freethinker. Among the later group Presbyterians were again most numerous with twelve representatives, being followed by Episcopalians (9), Quakers (2), Baptists (1), and Jews (1). Not a single Catholic and but one Jew, then, was found in the two groups combined. The relative absence of Quakers, especially in the early nineteenth-century era when they were numerically important in Philadelphia, is to be explained in part by their reluctance to take or administer oaths, an action not easily avoidable in the legal profession. The figures on the predominance of Protestants, like the data on nativity and ethnic characteristics, suggest that the legal profession was not easily attainable by members of minority groups, be they the foreign-born or the non-Protestant.

The educational training of the two sets of lawyers marks a significant departure from the similarity noted between lawyers of 1800 and their counterparts of 1860. Even though college training in the early national period was relatively rare, 68 percent of the 1800–1805 lawyers observed were college graduates. Fifteen of these were alumni of the University of Pennsylvania, seven of Dickinson College, and four of Princeton. Others attended scattered Eastern institutions. In contrast, despite the rapid growth of collegiate education after 1800, the 1860–1861 lawyers matriculated at colleges in only 48 percent of the cases noted. Eleven were alumni of the University of Pennsylvania and five graduated from Yale. Other institutions contributed single representatives. The data indicate that in a society notable for increasing numbers of college-trained men, the legal profession was recruiting relatively fewer college graduates. This trend is more than likely to be explained by the broadening range of economic and social backgrounds from which lawyers were being drawn.

The problem of class origins, which is of central importance to this study, is a difficult one. Even contemporary sociologists have not completely solved the identification of social class, and for the nineteenth century the task is still more subjective. A currently used method of class determination, for instance, weights occupation, source of income, type of house, and dwelling area according to an elaborate scale of values. Such a formula is of little help for studies of nineteenth-century mobility, as most of the requisite facts are unrecoverable. For the purposes of the present study only a broad differentiation of classes can be attempted. Without claiming absolute methodological precision, an attempt has been made to determine the class origin of each lawyer for whom data was available, taking into account all relevant factors such as education, dwelling area, father's occupation, descent, education and social position. Broadly defined the upper class includes wealthy landowners, merchants, and manufacturers, and prominent lawyers, doctors, clergymen, and officeholders. The middle class is construed to be prosperous, if not wealthy, farmers, the less successful professional types, shopkeepers, minor officeholders, and bureaucratic functionaries. The lower class includes artisans, laborers, and farmers with small or poor land holdings.

If the two groups of lawyers are thus differentiated by occupational and social background, the evidence corroborates the suggestiveness of the statistics on educational training that in 1860 easier access to the legal fraternity from middle- or lower-class ranks was corroding the homogeneity of an essentially upper-class elite. In the early nineteenth-century group, lawyers came predominantly from families of wealth, status, and importance. Of the forty-three lawyers in the 1800–1805 group for whom family background has been determined, 72 percent were of upper-class derivation. Occupationally, seven were sons of landowners whose considerable wealth allowed them to live at their leisure on large tracts of land, often acquired by colonial ancestors. Such a man was Bayse Newcomb who owned his father's plantation near Mill Pond in Cumberland County, New Jersey—property in the family for two generations or more. John Browne was another. He inherited land in the Northern Liberties section of Philadelphia which later in the nineteenth century sold for more than a million dollars. Others were men of prominence in outlying counties, individuals who had parlayed modest holdings into large estates. Such was Joseph Hemphill, proprietor of one of Chester County's largest and most valuable farms. General William Irvine, a graduate of Trinity College, Dublin, and a Revolutionary War hero, was another. Each a man of wealth and status, they guided their sons into the profession of law.

Eleven of the 1800–1805 lawyers came from families of mercantile interests. In an era when great fortunes were amassed most frequently by landowners and merchants, their fathers were numbered among the most illustrious personages of their communities. Included in this group were Richard Bache, husband of Benjamin Franklin's only daughter and later postmaster general of the United States; Charles Biddle, great-uncle of Nicholas Biddle and vice-president of Pennsylvania; William Coxe, father of Tench Coxe and an affluent city merchant; and John Shee, born in Ardnagraph Castle, Ireland, and collector of the Port of Philadelphia.

Fifteen other lawyers of the early group were sons of professional men—lawyers, doctors, and clergymen. Of these fathers, most were scions of prominent, well-to-do families. Old and heralded Philadelphia names are common in this group: Barnabas Binney, valedictorian of the class of 1774 at Brown and a peer of Benjamin Rush; Ebenezer Bradford, descendant of the governor of Plymouth Colony, recipient of degrees from Princeton, Dartmouth, and Brown and a minister of the Congregational church; William Bradford, Jr., attorney general of Pennsylvania and the United States; Charles Chauncey, eminent lawyer of the illustrious Connecticut Chauncey lineage; John Ewing, provost and professor at the University of Pennsylvania and a leading Presbyterian cleric; Richard Peters, Jr., commissioner of war during the Revolution and a renowned Philadelphia lawyer; and Benjamin Rush, class of 1760 at Princeton and an internationally known colonial physician.

The rest of the earlier lawyers came from middle- or lower-class environments. Four were raised on small farms. One was the son of a tailor and another of an innkeeper. In statistical terms, little more than a quarter of the lawyers could look back on homes which did not fit upper-class description.

By 1860 the preponderance of upper-class representatives reaching the Philadelphia bar was yielding to a strong upward surge of the middle class. Between 1800 and 1860 new recruits at the bar of upper-class background dropped from 72 to 44 percent of the fifty-six cases observed. This drop was almost wholly the result of the success of the middle class in raising its sons to the profession. Whereas middle-class families provided the Philadelphia bar with only 16 percent of its recruits in 1800–1805, six decades later they nearly tripled their contribution, supplying 44 percent of all the lawyers observed. The lower-class representatives remained steady at 12 percent. To be sure, distinguished Philadelphia names were by no means absent in 1860. One can identify a Bache, a Chauncey, a Dallas, a Dorrance, a Pepper, a Dwight, and a Reed. But middle-class families had assumed a new importance.

Occupational statistics reaffirm this trend. Fewer lawyers in the 1860–1861 group, as is shown in Table 1, came from professional and big-business families. Fewer came from homes of landed gentlemen and even farms. But a dramatic increase occurred in that fraction of the bar recruited from small business and clerical families. In 1800–1805 only 5 percent of the lawyers had risen from the ranks of shopkeepers, clerks, tailors and the like. Six decades later such cases were typical of 27 percent of the Philadelphia bar admittees. Lawyers came from the homes of accountants, clerks, and conveyancers, from homes of cordwainers, meat suppliers, grocers, surveyors, trolley-car conductors, hostlers, and artisans. The large business and professional groups, which made up a very small percentage of the total population in the parental generation, were still supplying a disproportionately large share of the lawyers among the sons; but great inroads had been made by the middle class.

TABLE 1
Occupational and Class Origin of Lawyers

Division of Lawyers by Father's Occupation	1800–05	1860–61
Large business: merchant, banker, manufacturer	29.5%	21.5%
Professions	34.0	30.5
Farmer-landowner	29.5	15.0
Small business or officeworker, shopkeeper, accountant, clerk, etc.	5.0	27.0
Worker	2.0	6.0
Division of Lawyers by Father's Class Position		
Upper	72%	44%
Middle	16	44
Lower	12	12

V

"If the present course be pursued," bemoaned a leading member of the Philadelphia bar in 1856, "the past glory of Pennsylvania Jurisprudence, shall never return." So changed was the character of the bar, reflected the author, that in the courtroom "we have sometimes almost been at a loss to know, from the bustle and confusion, and hurry of the occasion, whether it was a *riot* or a *trial,* that was going on." Missing was the social and professional harmony, the cohesiveness that stemmed from the common backgrounds of early nineteenth-century lawyers, and the solidarity and dignity that inspired in the community a "profound respect and veneration." No longer was the profession regarded as an organic part of society, set apart from the generality by purpose, training, and background. No longer was the legal fraternity in Philadelphia characterized by the unity that earlier had bound lawyers together as "a band of confiding brothers."

The disintegration of the bonds of common origin and outlook probably began early after the start of the new century. Popular outcries against lawyers and demands for wider access to the profession began to loosen the hold of the upper class on the bench and bar in the first decades of the century. By 1825, for example, a lawyer of lower-class birth, Edward King, had been raised to president-judge of the Philadelphia Court of Common Pleas, much to the chagrin of the older members of the bar who lamented that "precedents had been violated in thus elevating a man whose birth and position were not up to the old-time judicial standards." Nonetheless, the erosion of the upper-class monopoly continued apace. Constitutional reform in the 1830s and the establishment of systematic and accessible legal education in the 1850s further challenged the old legal oligarchy. By the 1860s, if not before, an egalitarian-minded society was raising to the bar drafts of recruits of modest means and undistinguished antecedents. Diversity characterized their backgrounds, unlike those of their predecessors six decades earlier. As many middle-class sons reached the bar as upper-class representatives. And relatively fewer recruits were possessed of college education. The foreign-born and non-Protestant still found the legal profession unattainable to a great extent, but infusions of middle-class sons had shattered the upper-class hegemony. The aristocratic legal profession, which Tocqueville had identified as the indispensable balance-weight in the democratic system, was steadily giving way to a socially heterogeneous bar.

The changing composition of the profession was paralleled by the erosion of respect for the bench and bar. Persistent agitation brought constitutional revision which made the judiciary subservient to the political vagaries of the people. Other legal positions, long held by professional merit, were transformed into political offices. Lawyers as a class were held suspect of antidemocratic propensities. Moreover, society's need for the professional at all was questioned. Some said that the American democracy had no place for aristocratic lawyers and that Pennsylvania should revert to William Penn's old system of arbitration before disinterested citizen referees. Others would be content merely to see law deprofessionalized.

Of course the legal profession was never in danger of extinction, nor is it evident that the calibre of the bench greatly deteriorated after constitutional reform. But attacks against lawyers epitomized the growing reluctance to recognize social position as a natural structuring of society. There was skepticism that people were organized best when differentiated into organic, interdependent units. And there was a powerful desire to tip the scales of government far to the side of popular rule. Visibly altered by the infiltration from below and by the attacks of egalitarian-minded reformers, the profession had lost some of its old discipline, self-awareness, and homogeneity that had distinguished it previously as a bulwark of institutional stability.

Edward Pessen

THE MYTH OF ANTEBELLUM SOCIAL MOBILITY AND EQUALITY OF OPPORTUNITY

Edward Pessen's interest in the Jacksonian era was first centered on its labor leaders, atypical men whose denunciations of contemporary society testified, he believed, more to their radical state of mind than to the actual state of things in America. His subsequent research into the broader civilization clearly showed that belief in the era's alleged equality of condition and opportunity was based on random impressions rather than substantial data. Evidence on the wealth of every resident in the great Northeastern cities and on the lives of the rich and eminent was examined "to subject the egalitarian thesis to the kind of detailed check it had been previously spared." Pessen, like Stuart Blumin and most others who have focused on the empirical aspect of their investigations, offers a historical explanation for the surprising patterns he uncovered that is not itself based on the kind of research that characterized his fact-gathering.

From Edward Pessen, "The Egalitarian Myth and the American Social Reality: Wealth, Mobility, and Equality in the 'Era of the Common Man,' " *American Historical Review* 76 (October 1971): 1004–06, 1012–18, 1027–29. Copyright © by Edward Pessen. Footnotes deleted.

"In America," wrote Tocqueville, "most of the rich men were formerly poor." The idea that, in the words of Henry Clay, the wealthy and successful were "self-made men," came close to being an article of faith, so widely was it subscribed to by Americans during the era. The common man was constantly reminded that "the most exalted positions" or great wealth were accessible to men of humble origin, since in this country "merit and industry" rather than "exclusive privileges of birth" determined the course of one's career. The merchant prince, William E. Dodge, offered the estimate that 75 percent of the era's wealthy men "had risen from comparatively small beginnings to their present position." If few modern historians would commit themselves to a precise ratio, many have nevertheless agreed that a remarkable movement up the social and economic ladder characterized the second quarter of the nineteenth century. We have evidently convinced our colleagues in sociology, including some of the leading students of social mobility and stratification, that for the Jacksonian period the facts are in: intergenerational economic and occupational mobility were the rule. Actually it is not the facts that are in but rather a continuing series of firmly stated generalizations that essentially do nothing more than assume that the facts would bear them out.

That Tocqueville in some instances was ready to spin his marvelous social theorems by reference more to logic than to pedestrian data is well known. What is fascinating is the extent to which scholars, ordinarily skeptical of unverified observation, have relied on it in discussing the origins of the rich in the "age of the common man."

The social origins and parental status of wealthy citizens of Boston, Philadelphia, New York City, and Brooklyn have been investigated in order to test the belief that typically they were born poor. Information has been gathered on the several hundred wealthiest citizens in each of these great cities. The evidence indicates that some of the best known among the wealthy citizens did in fact have the kind of background ascribed to them by the egalitarian thesis.

John Jacob Astor's story is perhaps improperly described as a rise from rags to riches. There is some question as to the precise wealth or status of his father. Whether the latter was a "very worthy" minor officeholder, as some described him, or a poor man devoted more to tippling than to industry, as he was depicted by others—

for the moment I am prepared to regard the two judgments as contradictory—it seems fairly certain that the great merchant was indeed a self-made man of humble origin. The same can be said, with even more certainty, of his sometimes partner, Cornelius Heeney, who migrated from Ireland apparently with less than a dollar in his pockets, to become one of the wealthiest residents in Brooklyn. Lewis A. Godey, publisher of the popular *Ladies' Book,* John Grigg, and Joseph Sill were wealthy Philadelphians of humble beginnings, while Daniel P. Parker, Ebenezer Chadwick, John R. Adan, and the three Henshaw brothers in Boston also appear to have been of poor or humble birth, as were such New York eminences as Anson G. Phelps, Marshall O. Roberts, Gideon Lee, Saul Alley, and possibly the Lorillard brothers. Stephen Girard's claim that he, too, had been a destitute youth was evidently accepted by most contemporaries, although there is some doubt as to whether it was well founded. Evidence is thus not lacking that some rich men had in fact been born poor. The most interesting feature of such evidence, however, is its uncommonness.

*   *   *

During the age of alleged social fluidity, the overwhelming majority of wealthy persons appears to have been descended of parents and families who combined affluence with high social status. The small number of these families that had been less than rich had typically been well-to-do. Only about 2 percent of the Jacksonian era's urban economic elite appear to have actually been born poor, with no more than about 6 percent of middling social and economic status. Included in the middle are the families of Peter Cooper, William E. Dodge, Gerard Hallock, Joseph Sampson, Cornelius Vanderbilt, Moses Yale Beach, Peter Chardon Brooks, Amos and Abbot Lawrence, Thomas H. Perkins, George C. Shattuck, George Hall, Thomas Everitt, Jr., Samuel R. Johnson, Cyrus P. Smith, and Samuel Smith, all of whom appeared to have been both better off and of higher status occupations than the mechanics, cartmen, milkmen, and laborers who predominated in the cities. The middle category was composed of ministers, petty officials, professionals other than successful lawyers and doctors, shopkeepers, skilled artisans who doubled as small tradesmen, and independent or moderately prosperous farmers. The evidence for these generalizations, inevitably imperfect, requires explanation.

It was of course impossible to obtain reliable information on the family status of all persons, but fortunately abundant evidence exists on the backgrounds of most of the wealthiest persons in the great cities. Data were secured on 90 percent of the more than 100 New Yorkers who in 1828 were assessed for $100,000 and upward, and in 1845 at $250,000 or more; on 85 percent of the more than 100 Bostonians worth $100,000 or better in 1833, and $200,000 or more in 1848; and on about 90 percent of the 75 Brooklynites who in 1841 were evaluated at $60,000 or more. For Philadelphia, as was indicated earlier, the nature of the tax records does not permit them to be used to disclose the assessed total wealth of individuals. One can differentiate the "super rich" of that city from other rich or well-to-do persons only by accepting at face value the sums attributed in the anonymous *Memoirs and Auto-Biography of Some of the Wealthy Citizens of Philadelphia.* (Information was obtained on 70 percent of the 365 persons each claimed by the *Memoirs* to be worth $100,000 or more.) The pattern of the social backgrounds of the urban rich was strikingly similar for all the Northeastern cities. About 95 percent of New York City's 100 wealthiest persons were born into families of wealth or high status and occupation; 3 percent came of "middling" background; only 2 percent were born poor. As small a portion of Boston's 100 wealthiest citizens started humble, with perhaps 6 percent originating from middling families. Philadelphia's statistics differ from Boston's only in that 4 percent of the former city's 365 richest citizens were born into families of middling status; 2 percent of her wealthiest citizens started poor. Cornelius Heeney and John Dikeman were the only wealthy Brooklynites of truly humble origins, with 16 percent born into middling status, and the remaining 81 percent of wealthy or high-status families.

Evidence was not as freely available for the "lesser rich" of the great cities. Data were obtained on about 70 percent of the more than 450 New Yorkers assessed at between $25,000 and $100,000 in 1828, and for 63 percent of the 950 New Yorkers who in 1845 were worth between $45,000 and $250,000; on close to 65 percent of the 260 Bostonians evaluated at between $50,000 and $200,000, in 1833, and on the same percentage of the 400 Bostonians similarly assessed in 1848; and 63 percent of the 100 Brooklynites assessed in 1841 at $30,000 to $60,000. It is of course possible that the backgrounds of the "missing persons" were unlike those of the much larger number of persons for whom information was obtained. It could be argued that the omissions concern less eminent persons, whose families probably were not as wealthy or of as high status as the families whose careers and records are better publicized. Yet a significant feature of the evidence is its disclosure that there appeared to be no difference in the patterns of social origin among the "lesser wealthy" as against the "super rich"; or in the patterns of family background of the relatively little known or unknown rich for whom information was obtained as against the eminent rich.

Many of the era's richest men, while born into relative affluence, managed to carve out fortunes that far surpassed their original inheritances. Such persons were self-made only in a special sense, their careers hardly illustrating what publicists of the era meant by that term. That the children of high-status parents, living in an age of dynamic growth, convert their original advantages into fortunes of unprecedented scope is—as Jackson Turner Main has noted in another context—hardly a sign of social mobility. A family whose adult heads for four or five generations were among the economic elite of their city or community cannot be said to have experienced upward social movement because their always inordinate wealth kept increasing.

The rags-to-riches ideology had so penetrated American thought during the era that publishers whose own compilations contradicted the thesis could manage to convince themselves that it was nevertheless true. Freeman Hunt, devoted and enthusiastic admirer of America's merchants, whom he extolled in his charming *Merchants' Magazine,* could somehow describe Walter Restored Jones of the old, eminent, and wealthy family of Cold Spring, Long Island, truly one of fortune's favorites, as a "self-taught and self-made man." Popular ideology notwithstanding, the era of the common man was remarkable above all for how few rich men were in fact descended of common folk.

When it is compared with earlier periods in American history, the age of egalitarianism appears to have been an age of increasing social rigidity. According to a recent study of seventeenth-century Salem, while "some members of the rapidly emerging elite began their careers propertyless and benefited from the opportunities for investment ... more often they emigrated with considerable wealth which was further augmented by fortuitous investment." Jackson Main has concluded that there was "remarkable opportunity for the man of modern property to become rich" in the late eighteenth century. Main's admittedly imperfect and partial data on the three greatest cities of the Northeast are of special interest. He finds that about one-third of the 60 wealthiest Bostonians of 1771 had started with little or nothing; in 1789 only one-half of a small number of the city's wealthiest merchants had been born into "wealthy or well-to-do families," with the rest scattered among middling or lower status occupations. Of a group of 100 wealthy Philadelphians, about "one third had made their own fortunes." He found that "between one third and two fifths of the merchants in pre-Revolutionary New York City [actually, members of the Chamber of Commerce] were self-made men," while in the years immediately after the Revolution the high "mobility rate" actually went up: "probably 60 percent at the least [of a number of merchants in 1786] were self-made men," and in 1791 50 percent of the wealthiest citizens of the east ward had risen from humble origin.

A recent study of post-Revolutionary New York City concludes that for the period ending in 1815, "the evidence of upward social mobility is marked. Almost two-thirds of the attorneys and merchants in public office had risen above the occupational level of their fathers who were mechanics or farmers." The evidence on the earlier period, scattered and partial though it may be, suggests that a substantial upward economic mobility that had characterized Northeastern urban life came to a halt during the so-called age of the common man. The self-made man, recently shown by William Miller and his students to have been more fantasy than fact in the post–Civil War decades, was evidently a creature of the imagination a generation earlier, at the very time that the great Henry Clay was asserting the phantom's corporeality and ubiquitousness.

A related belief holds that the second quarter of the nineteenth century was "a highly speculative age in which fortunes were made and lost overnight, in which men rose and fell ... with dexterous agility." Tocqueville believed that fortunes here were both scanty and "insecure," wealth ostensibly circulating with "inconceivable rapidity." Contemporary American merchants insisted that theirs was the most precarious of callings, incapable of attaining the "security which accompanied the more pedestrian occupations." True, the eminent Philip Hone had noted the resiliency of businessmen: "Throw down our merchants ever so flat [and] they roll over once and spring to their feet again"; but this optimistic judgment was confided to his private diary. The prevailing view was that the pre-industrial decades were characterized by great intragenerational economic mobility. It has recently been shown, however, that ante-bellum Philadelphia witnessed slight movement up and down the occupational ladder or to and from residential districts of clearly differentiated wealth and status. Another recent study examines the changing economic circumstances of thousands of Bostonians and New York City residents of different wealth levels over the course of a generation. Some generalizations, drawn from its detailed findings, follow.

The richest Bostonians of the early Jacksonian era were invariably among the very richest Bostonians late in the period. Very few persons of the upper-middle wealth level—only 7 percent of that group—moved upward into the wealthy category whose members were each assessed for $50,000 or more. The extent of an individual's early wealth was the major factor determining whether he would be among the rich later. Absolute increases in wealth of any sort followed the rule: the greater an individual's initial wealth, the greater the amount by which it was augmented. A companion rule was that the greater one's original riches, the more likely was he to enjoy an increase. Since the population by mid-century had increased substantially in two decades the ranks of the later rich necessarily had to be filled by many persons who earlier were not among the wealthy. More often than not these newly rich taxpayers were younger members of old families, since fewer than 10 percent of the later group of Boston's rich were new men. Not one member of the $100,000 group of mid-century who had paid taxes earlier had paid them on less than the $20,000 owned by the wealthiest 2 percent of the Boston population. Since many contemporaries claimed that the careers of successful merchants followed an erratic course in this kaleidoscopic economy, changes over short-run periods were also investigated to determine whether persons who started and ended the race strong may have lagged in between. They did not.

In Boston "few new great families sprang up while fewer still fell away" during the era.

New York City's statistics for the period were not an exact replica of the Boston evidence. Since New York was richer all categories of wealth from the upper middle on up experienced greater gains in absolute wealth than did their counterparts in Boston. For the rest the general pattern was remarkably similar for the two great cities. Between the period of Andrew Jackson's first election to the presidency and his death not quite two decades later only one of New York City's fifty richest persons fell from the class of the rich, and even he barely failed to qualify. As in Boston the few New Yorkers who rose from the upper-middle wealth level to the rich during the course of the era "were more often than not from families of great wealth." The "newcomers" were younger members of the great Hendricks, Jones, Lenox, Lorillard, Barclay, Cruger, Grinnell, Bronson, Grosvenor, Hone, Lawrence, Post, Murray, Storm, Ward, Remsen, Schieffelin, and Van Rensselaer families or of "others of like distinction." About 75 percent of the New York City families constituting the plutocracy of the so-called industrial era of the mid-1850s were families that comprised the elite of the merchant-capitalist era of a generation earlier.

Brooklyn assessment data exist for 1810 and 1841. If the earlier date falls before what even the most flexible classifications would consider the "Jacksonian era," that fact hardly detracts from its value. If anything the earlier starting point permits those so inclined to draw conclusions about economic fluidity between the "Jeffersonian" and "Jacksonian" periods. Brooklyn's wealthiest families of the early nineteenth century remained among the wealthiest families of the 1840s. Only one of the truly rich of 1810 fell by the wayside and not because of poverty but because of death. In Brooklyn, as in its mighty neighbor, riches achieved by early in the nineteenth century appeared to be the surest guarantee to the possession of wealth a generation later. The many wealthy persons of 1841 who were relative newcomers to the city had achieved their success almost without exception "as a result of a great boost given them at birth by wealthy or comfortably situated parents or relatives."

The pursuit of wealth in Jacksonian America was marked not by fluidity but by stability if not rigidity. Great fortunes earlier accumulated held their own through all manner of vicissitudes. The tax records indicate that the panic of 1837 appeared to have no effect on the minuscule rate by which the mighty fell or the puny rose during the years surrounding that economic convulsion. The Boston tax records disclose that of the owners of the modest property evaluated at between $5,000 and $7,000 prior to the panic of 1837, less than 1 percent became significantly wealthier in its wake, while slightly more than one-third were badly hurt by the cataclysm or compelled to leave the city. In contrast, only 2 of the nearly 100 Bostonians worth $100,000 or more each suffered substantial losses, while about 23 percent of them enjoyed gains of $20,000 or better in the immediate aftermath of the financial crisis.

That the rich typically were wellborn and held on to or increased their wealth does not prove that there was no social mobility during the era. The vast and swelling sociological literature on the related topics of "vertical mobility" and social stratification makes clear that the concept of social mobility is a most complex one, not least because it involves the intangible of status. As has recently been pointed out, "there are a host of different ways of measuring mobility. And mobility has many varied contours." No last word can ever be said concerning a subject so elusive and for which the data are so often imperfect.

If, as Ralf Dahrendorf has written, "the concept of social mobility is too general to be useful," there is much to be said for dealing with specific aspects of it rather than with the concept as a whole. All of which is to say that if no data can measure the immeasurable— social mobility in general—the evidence pointing to the upper-class backgrounds of the Jacksonian era's elite and the tenacity with which they held on to their wealth undermines two of the main supports of the long-popular belief in antebellum mobility.

* * *

During the age of egalitarianism wealth became more unequally distributed with each passing season. Shared less equally, even at the era's beginnings, than it had been a generation or two earlier, in the aftermath of the Revolution, wealth became concentrated in the hands of an ever smaller percentage of the population. The trend persisted through the 1850s, resulting in wider disparities than ever by the time of the Civil War. Far from being an age of equality, the antebellum decades were featured by an inequality that surpasses anything experienced by the United States in the twentieth century.

According to Gerhard Lenski, the central question in studying social stratification is: "Who gets what and why?" For the era of Tocqueville the answer to the first part of this question is clear enough. The few at the top got a share of society's material things that was disproportionate at the start and became more so at the era's end. Why they did is of course more difficult to explain.

It may be, as Lenski has argued, that in a free market system "small inequalities tend to generate greater inequalities and great inequalities still greater ones." Even if Lenski's comment is true, it is more descriptive than analytical, while leaving unanswered the question: Why? The explanation, popular since Karl Marx's time, that it was industrialization that pauperized the masses, in the process transforming a relatively egalitarian social order, appears wanting. Vast disparities between urban rich and poor antedated industrialism. Commercial wealth, as surely as industrial, enabled its fortunate inheritors to command a disproportionate share of society's good things and the children of the fortunate to hold a still greater share. A massive internal migration, above all of younger, marginal persons of little standing, into and out of the nation's cities increased both the power and the share of wealth commanded by more substantial and therefore more stable elements. It is hard to disagree with Robert Gallman's generalization that "there were forces at work in the American economy during the nineteenth century that tended to produce greater inequality in the distribution of wealth over time." A not insignificant task of future scholarship will be to ascertain as precisely as possible the nature of these "forces." I would venture the judgment that the transportation revolution and the de facto single national market it helped create made possible and indeed decisively fostered great increases in profit-making opportunities even before the victory of industrialism, while the system of inheritance and the minimal influence of the non-property-owning classes enabled private accumulators to command a larger share of society's product than they would be able to in a later era of vastly greater absolute productivity and profits. Amid all the hulabaloo about the "common man" during the era, he in fact got what was left over.

It has long been argued that equality of opportunity if not of condition prevailed in antebellum America, the era's numerous success stories testifying to the rule of the former principle. In David Potter's language, in America equality did not mean the possession of uniform wealth so much as "parity in competition." The evidence, however, indicates that if dramatic upward climbs were more fanciful than real in Jacksonian America, competition was also marked by anything but parity. The absence of legal disabilities did not mean that poor men started the race for success on equal terms with their more favored contemporaries.

According to Charles Astor Bristed, the young man who hoped to gain entry into New York's upper 1,000 was one who, possessed of "fair natural abilities, adds to these the advantages of inherited wealth, a liberal education and foreign travel." It need hardly be pointed out that the travel and liberal education mentioned by Bristed were not available to most Americans. Rather, they were accessible to men such as Abram C. Dayton, son of "an opulent merchant" of New York City, who had "all the accomplishments that education, travel and wealth could give." They were available to Andrew Gordon Hamersley, who inherited from his father a fortune, which, by "judicious management," he succeeded in substantially enlarging. Like other of his golden contemporaries he never went into business, owing his success rather to his name, his original possessions, and his "entertaining conversation and courtly manner." They were available to John Collins Warren, Valentine Mott, David Hosack, and Philip Syng Physick, brilliant physicians all, who from childhood had moved in the most rarified circles, attending the greatest universities and studying with the most learned masters at home and abroad, accumulating much wealth largely because they had much to begin with. Means rather than need gave one access to the services of these eminences.

It is of course possible that innate ability or a fortunate genetic inheritance accounted for the success achieved by most of the era's socioeconomic elite. Such traits no doubt played a significant part in some cases. The biographical data indicate, however, that a material inheritance was the great initial advantage that enabled most of those fortunate enough to have it to become worldly successes. Robert A. Dahl has contended that the era was marked by a "cumulative inequality: when one individual was much better off than another in one resource, such as wealth, he was usually better off in almost every other resource," including political influence. It is clear that almost all of the era's successful and wealthy urbanites had initially been much better off than their fellows in possessing the "resource" of wealth.

The race was indeed to the swift, but unfortunately the requisite swiftness was beyond the power of ordinary men to attain. For this swiftness was of a special sort. Unlike the speed of thoroughbred horses, which is a rare but a natural if inbred gift, the ability to cover great ground in the race for human material success appeared to depend less on the possession of innate abilities than on the inheritance of the artificial gifts of wealth and standing. During the "age of the common man" opportunity was hardly more equal than was material condition.

III THE COMPLEX MOBILITY PATTERNS OF THE EARLY INDUSTRIAL ERA, 1860-1900

The decades following the Civil War are often described as the "Era of Big Business." It was an age marked by the completion of the nation's railroad network, the rise of giant corporations—including the nation's first billion-dollar firm, the United States Steel Corporation—at the turn of the century. It was an era of public uproar over "trusts," of powerful industrial magnates— "robber barons," their critics called them—such as John D. Rockefeller and Andrew Carnegie, whose political power seemed as great as their wealth. But as Herbert G. Gutman, Stephan Thernstrom, and Alwyn Barr indicate, there was more to the era than big business.

Most Americans continued to live in rural communities and small towns rather than in great cities. Small business was more common than big; Paterson, Newburyport, and San Antonio were more typical of the country than was New York City.

Fittingly, it was in this era that the Horatio Alger legend was born. The hundreds of novels that seemed to fly off Alger's pen popularized as never before the rags-to-riches theme. Many contemporaries mistook fiction for fact, impressed by the constant trumpeting from press and pulpit that the era's industrial giants had once been little, humble fellows. The studies by Frances W. Gregory, Irene D. Neu, and William Miller indicate that life was very different from myth. Gutman's research, on the other hand, shows that the Alger myth was not totally divorced from reality, at least in certain industries and certain towns. Additional studies of other industries and other places will have to be completed before it is possible to speak with greater assurance of social mobility rates in the late nineteenth century.

Herbert G. Gutman

THE SOCIAL BACKGROUNDS OF ENTREPRENEURS IN PATERSON, NEW JERSEY

Herbert G. Gutman is a versatile scholar who has done important research on the values of American labor, the black family, and social mobility. Here he explores the career paths followed by roughly thirty specialized iron manufacturers in a small American city for the period 1830–1880. His findings indicate that, if not rags to riches, then humble beginnings to fair business success was not unknown in early industrial America. It is possible that in the early phases of certain industries, success required a knowhow that could only come from working in the craft. And, as he notes at the conclusion of the essay, similar studies will be of great importance in determining the typicality of the Paterson pattern.

In recent decades, historians have vigorously disputed the validity of the belief that nineteenth-century American industrialists rose from "rags to riches." A popular literature has been subjected to critical textual analysis, and the promises of popular ideology have been measured by empirical head-counting that involves the collection of data about the social origins of "business leaders." These studies share a common conclusion: very few workers—day laborers, unskilled workers, and skilled artisans—became successful manufacturers. After studying nearly 200 leaders of the largest early twentieth-century corporations, William Miller convincingly concluded that to look for men of "working class or foreign origins" among the most powerful financiers, public utility and railroad executives, and mining and manufacturing corporation officials was "to look almost in vain." Fully 95 percent came from families of upper- or middle-class status. Not more than 3 percent started as poor immigrant boys or even as poor American farm boys. Andrew Carnegie was an important American in 1900, but hardly any men of his

From Herbert G. Gutman, "The Reality of the Rags-to-Riches 'Myth': The Case of the Paterson, New Jersey, Locomotive, Iron, and Machinery Manufacturers, 1830–1880," in Stephan Thernstrom and Richard Sennett, eds., *Nineteenth-Century Cities: Essays in the New Urban History*, pp. 98–122. Copyright © 1969 by Yale University. Footnotes deleted.

economic class or social position shared with him a common career pattern.

Other studies, not as careful in their selection of a representative sample of manufacturers, have tended to validate Miller's findings about the 1900–1910 elite for earlier periods of industrialization. Miller's study carefully explained its limits: his data described " 'career men'—bureaucrats that is . . . all office-holders, many of them [having] *never* organized a business of any kind." The work of C. Wright Mills and his critics Reinhard Bendix and Frank W. Howton ranged over all of American history in an effort to define the changing composition of the "American business elite." Mills drew evidence from biographical sketches of business leaders in the *Dictionary of American Biography.* Bendix and Howton worked primarily from biographical sketches in the *National Cyclopedia of American Biography* to challenge—provocatively but not convincingly—Mills's conclusion that "in the nineteenth century the business elite was composed of significantly more men from the lower classes than was the case previously or than has been the case since." Both Mills and his critics agreed, however, that the "American business elite" always drew its membership predominantly from men born with high status and sired by well-to-do fathers. But Mills and his critics quarreled about the changing social composition of the "business elite" over time. Overall, for the *DAB* entries examined on business leaders born before 1907, Mills found that 9.8 percent were the sons of skilled craftsmen or semiskilled and unskilled workers. The percentage varied from generation to generation but was highest (13.2 percent) among those industrialists, merchants, and financiers born between 1820 and 1849. Using mostly *NCAB* biographies, Bendix and Howton found little change over time in the *percentage* of those industrialists who came from working-class families. The *rates* were consistently low: 2 percent for those born between 1801 and 1830, 1 percent for those born between 1831 and 1860, and 2 percent for those born between 1861 and 1890.

Percentages may be useful for comparative purposes over time, but they are dangerous statistical abstractions and may tell little about a particular moment in history. How representative, for example, was the Bendix and Howton sample for the pre–Civil War generations? They found information about only 56 fathers of "business leaders" born between 1801 and 1830 and 225 born between 1831 and 1860. Translating their findings into absolute numbers, we learn from this sample that only 3 out of 281 business leaders born between 1801 and 1860 came from working-class families. Even cursory knowledge of the history of American manufacturing before 1890 should raise numerous questions about a sampling technique that yields so narrow a base for a historical generalization.

The most detailed study of the early post–Civil War "industrial elite" has been conducted by Frances W. Gregory and Irene D. Neu, who generally confirmed the earlier findings. Gregory and Neu examined the careers of 303 leaders of the railroad, textile (mostly cotton), and steel industries in the 1870s by studying the place of birth, the occupation of the father, the religious affiliation, the educational level attained, and the age on first starting work of the executives of seventy-seven large firms. These included the treasurer and agent of thirty textile mills mostly capitalized at more than $1 million; the president, vice-president, and general manager (or superintendent) of thirty steel mills; and the president, vice-president, and general manager of the seventeen largest railroads. Their careful findings about the occupations of 194 fathers showed that 8 percent (sixteen men) were the sons of "workers." Not one railroad leader rose from the "lower depths"; 15 percent of the textile manufacturers (10 of 67) did, along with 11 percent of the steel manufacturers (6 of 57). In contrast, 64 percent of the entire group came from business or professional backgrounds; 1 of every 4 was born on a farm; 3 percent were the sons of "public officials." The authors asked and answered a critical question: "Was the typical industrial leader of the 1870s, then, a 'new man,' an escapee from the slums of Europe or from the paternal farm? Did he rise by his own efforts from a boyhood of poverty? Was he as innocent of education and of formal training as has often been alleged? He seems to have been none of these things." Combining variables, they described the archetypal industrial leader of the 1870s. He was American by birth, of a New England father, a Protestant in his religion, and distinctly upper class in origin:

> *Urban in early environment, he was ... born and bred in an atmosphere in which business and a relatively high social standing were intimately*

associated with his family life. Only at about eighteen did he take his first regular job, preparing to rise from it, moreover, not by a rigorous apprenticeship begun when he was virtually a child, but by an academic education well above the average for the times.

For the men they studied, Gregory and Neu found little evidence that "the top-level businessman" of the 1870s was "but a generation removed from poverty and anonymity."

More recently, Stephan Thernstrom has brought significant and original insight to the patterns of social mobility in mid-nineteenth-century industrializing America. *Poverty and Progress: Social Mobility in a Nineteenth-Century City* breaks with older studies of social mobility by focusing in close detail on one community: it treats the career patterns of nearly 300 unskilled day laborers in Newburyport, Massachusetts, between 1850 and 1880. Thernstrom finds among them a good deal of geographic mobility out of the city, but for those immigrant and native workers and their sons who remained, substantial material improvement ("property mobility" or the acquisition of personal and real estate) and occupational mobility (from unskilled to semiskilled and skilled work). Their most common form of social advancement was "upward mobility *within* the working class." Thernstrom finds no evidence of spectacular upward mobility: "In the substantial sample of workers and their sons studied for the 1850–1880 period not a single instance of mobility into the ranks of management or even into a foremanship position was discovered." Many workers and their sons improved in these thirty years, some even as small shopkeepers and white-collar workers. But not one met the test of the rags-to-riches ideology. "Few of these men and few of their children," Thernstrom concludes, "rose very far on the social scale; most of the upward occupational shifts they made left them manual workers still, and their property mobility, though strikingly widespread, rarely involved the accumulation of anything approaching real wealth."

The findings of Thernstrom, Gregory and Neu, and Miller, among others, are the work of serious scholars, careful in their methods, deep in their research, and modest in their conclusions. But there is question about the larger inferences to be drawn from these studies about the social origins of the industrial manufacturing class in the decades of prime American industrialization. Hundreds, even thousands, of successful manufacturers—often members of the particular elites in their particular communities but rarely memorialized on the national level—did not meet the criteria for admission to the *Dictionary of American Biography* or the *National Cyclopedia of American Biography.* Gregory and Neu reveal in detail the social origins of "the industrial elite" of the 1870s, but draw heavily in their narrow sample on a well-developed industry (cotton textile manufacturing) and an industry that attracted as its leaders lawyers, merchants, and financiers (the railroads). Thernstrom tells much that is new and significant about the lifestyle and aspirations of mid-nineteenth-century workers, but Newburyport had developed as a manufacturing city before 1850; and although the composition of its population changed between 1855 and 1880, the city underwent little development in the years studied.

What of the manufacturers who founded new firms that involved small outlays of capital at the start? What of the workers, skilled as well as unskilled, who lived in rapidly expanding cities? In these pages, we shall examine a select group of successful local manufacturers in one such city—the locomotive, machinery, tool, and iron manufacturers of Paterson, New Jersey, between 1830 and 1880. Were they as a group a lesser mirror image of the archetypal industrialist described by Gregory and Neu? If there were workers among them, were they unusual and atypical? Information is available only on their occupational careers and their places of birth, but it is sufficient to test the reality of the promise of rags to riches in one important industrial city.

In explaining why Paterson, New Jersey, became a prime nineteenth-century American industrial city, economic and social historians usually have stressed its development as a center of textile, particularly silk manufacture. And with good reason. By 1890, Paterson was the Lyons of America. But the silk industry came quite late in the city's development: not until the Civil War and the decade following did the silk mills and the city become so closely entwined. Yet Paterson had been an industrial city of importance before that time. Its magnificent waterfalls promised potential waterpower, and it early attracted the attention of Alexander Hamilton and other industrial enthusiasts. The story of the ill-fated Society for Establishing Useful Manufacturers in the 1790s is well known. But after it failed, irregular and usually unsuccessful efforts at cotton manufacture

shaped the city's industrial history until 1837 and remained important (although not essential) after that time. However, such uneven
enterprise (only one of nearly twenty cotton "mills" survived intact
the depression in the late 1830s) did not explain Paterson's solid
growth as an industrial city between 1830 and 1880. Early textile
manufacturing mattered mainly because it attracted machinists to
the city to repair and build cotton and other textile machinery. These
men and others who followed them after 1840 were in the city at
the start of a great boom in the manufacture of transportation equipment, machinery, and ironware of all kinds. Between 1830 and 1880,
they sparked the development of Paterson's locomotive, iron goods,
machinery, and machine-tool industries—changes that in turn
spurred the city's growth. In 1850, 11,000 persons lived in Paterson,
and about 1,450 worked in these industries. Ten years later, the city
counted nearly 20,000 residents, and 1 of every 10 was an "iron
worker." A great industrial spurt occurred between 1860 and 1873,
partly the result of the rapid rise of large silk and other textile mills
but also a consequence of the expansion of older industries. By 1870,
the population had risen to 33,581, and the locomotive, iron, and
machinery industries employed 5,300 workers on the eve of the
1873 depression. About 15 percent of the city's entire population
worked in these industries. The invigorated and new textile mills
recruited large numbers of women and children to their factories
so that adult male workers in the Paterson manufacturing industries
after the Civil War found jobs primarily as iron workers and machine,
tool, and locomotive makers.

Although the Paterson iron and machine industries have not yet
found their historian, a quick glance suggests their importance to the
city's development and even to the national economy. In the mid-
1850s, Paterson had four locomotive factories: Rogers, Ketchum &
Grosvenor (probably the second largest such factory in the country,
outdistanced only by the Philadelphia Baldwin Locomotive Works);
the New Jersey Locomotive and Machine Company; the Danforth
Locomotive and Machine Works; and William Swinburne's Locomotive Works. Swinburne's enterprise failed in 1857–1858, but the three
that survived had an annual capacity of 135 locomotives in 1859.
Eighteen years later, their combined capacity had risen to 554, 64
more than the Baldwin Works. In 1837–1838, Rogers, Ketchum &
Grosvenor (renamed the Rogers Locomotive Works in 1858 after

Rogers's death) completed its first 5 locomotives. In the great burst of railroad construction between 1869 and 1873, the factories filled orders for no less than 1,683 locomotives. Overall, between 1837 and 1879, Paterson locomotive workers built 5,167 locomotives and contributed much to the "transportation revolution."

The growth of the Paterson iron, tool, and machinery manufacturers may have been less spectacular than the locomotive manufacture but was just as substantial in different ways. Textile machinery and tools formed an important part of the local manufactured product. The market for Paterson firms after 1850 reached across the continent and even stretched around the globe. The J. C. Todd Machine Works (later Todd & Rafferty) marketed its hemp and twine machinery as far away as England and even in Russia, Latin America, and Asia in the late 1850s. After 1857, the Paterson Iron Works, which specialized in rolling large bars of iron, built heavy forgings used by transoceanic steamship and even sent iron shafts across the continent on order to the Pacific Mail Steamship Company. The Watson Manufacturing Company exported its millwright work and machinery to Mexico and South America, and gained wide attention for its turbine wheels and Corliss steam engines. The huge bevel wheels it constructed helped make the Higgins Carpet Factory one of New York City's great manufacturing establishments. The manufacture of structural iron later allowed the Watson firm to contract to build iron bridges in and near New York City, and its finished iron found place in the city's Museum of Natural History, Metropolitan Museum of Art, Equitable Building, and Lenox Library. In the 1870s and 1880s, the Passaic Rolling Mill also found important customers in the great metropolis nearby: the iron beams that built New York's first elevated trains came from it as did the iron for such projects as the Harlem River bridge, the *New York Post* building, and the massive Seventh Regiment Armory. Finished iron from the Passaic Rolling Mill also helped build the new state capitol in Albany, a widely acclaimed drawbridge over the Mississippi River at St. Paul, an elevated cable car in Hoboken, and the 1876 Centennial Exposition buildings in Philadelphia. These examples are cited merely to illustrate the importance of the Paterson locomotive, iron, and machine factories in the development of industry and transportation and in the building of Victorian American cities.

What were the social origins and career patterns of the men who founded and developed these particular firms between 1830 and 1880? These men or their firms persevered in the turbulent early decades of industrialization. In 1880, some of the pioneer manufacturers were dead, others at the height of their careers, and a few still relatively new to enterprise. Many had failed in comparison to the number that succeeded. Although the printed sources tell little about those who started unsuccessful manufacturing enterprises, there is no reason to doubt that these men differed in social origin from their more favored contemporaries. For the group that succeeded, useful biographical information has been found for nearly all of them. What follows therefore is *not a sample* but a description of the social origins of the most successful Paterson iron, locomotive, and machinery manufacturers.

Scientific American, groping for a simple sociological generalization about these men, praised Paterson's early enterprisers in these words: "In the eastern States [New England], flourishing cities have been built up by corporations of wealthy capitalists. . . . In Paterson, it was different. With few exceptions, almost every manufacturer started, financially, at zero, enlarging his establishment as the quicksilver expanded in his purse." *Scientific American* was not guilty of mouthing abstract rhetoric or just putting forth a paean of traditional tribute to an invisible hero, the "self-made man." Instead, it accurately described the successful locomotive, iron, and machinery manufacturers of the era, and what it wrote applied as well to the group in 1840 and 1880 as in 1859.

One Paterson manufacturer started as a clerk. A second, the son of a farmer, made his way first in railroad construction before turning to iron manufacture. Two others had fathers who were manufacturers. George Van Riper took over a bobbin-pin factory in 1866 that had been started by his grandfather in 1795 as a small shop and then run by his father for thirty-five years. Patrick Maguinnis was the son of an Irish cotton manufacturer who left Dublin after the failure of revolutionary anti-British agitation and manufactured cotton and velveteen first in Baltimore and then in Hudson, New York.

But the social origin of these four manufacturers was not characteristic of the thirty-odd men studied. The typical successful Paterson manufacturer arrived in the city as a skilled ironworker or a skilled craftsman or as a young man who learned his skill by apprenticing in a Paterson machinery works. Individual proprietorship or copartnership allowed him to escape from dependence and start his own firm. Only a small number of Paterson apprentices became manufacturers between 1830 and 1880, but most successful Paterson iron, machinery, and locomotive manufacturers started their careers as workers, apprenticed to learn a skill, and then opened small shops or factories of their own.

With only a few important exceptions, the men who were either Paterson-born or migrants to Paterson before 1830 played an insignificant role in the subsequent development of these industries. In 1825, the Rev. Dr. Samuel Fischer counted seventy-seven ironworkers in eleven blacksmith shops, two millwright shops, and a single iron foundry. Some repaired and built textile machinery. Trumbull lists at least ten machine shops that lasted only a few years. Biographical information is lacking for the men who started these faulted firms, but information is available for four men who pioneered in the development of the Paterson machinery and locomotive industries: John Clark, his son John Clark, Jr., Thomas Rogers, and Charles Danforth. Not one was native to the city. John Clark, Sr., settled there first. Born in Paisley, Scotland, the elder Clark, then aged twenty-one, migrated to Paterson in 1794 with his wife and two children to build machinery for the S.E.U.M. After the society failed, Clark, first with his partner and then alone, used a portion of the idle mill to manufacture textile machinery. One son, John, Jr., followed in his footsteps, and in the early 1820s took two partners, Abram Godwin (a local resident, Godwin's father had served on George Washington's military staff) and Thomas Rogers. A hotel and storekeeper and the father of Parke Godwin, noted later as a journalist and as editor of the *New York Evening Post,* Abram Godwin supplied Clark with capital. Rogers's contribution was of another order.

Born in 1792 in Groton, Connecticut, and, according to Trumbull, descended from a Mayflower Pilgrim, Thomas Rogers apprenticed himself at the age of sixteen to a Connecticut house carpenter. He settled in Paterson as a journeyman house carpenter and built several dwelling houses before a cotton-duck manufacturer hired him to construct wooden loom patterns. Soon Rogers was building wooden looms for John Clark, Sr. After the elder Clark retired, Rogers joined with Godwin and young Clark to expand the firm. The three partners bought an empty cotton mill, purchased a small foundry and a molding shop, and managed, for the first time in Paterson, a machine shop with all branches of the trade under "one roof." The partners prospered in the 1820s, but in 1831 Rogers left the firm to start his own machine works, the Jefferson Works, and to spin cotton yarn. Rogers's early triumphs as a machine builder attracted the attention of Morris Ketchum and Jasper Grosvenor, two New York City merchant capitalists and financiers active as railroad developers. A partnership was founded, called Rogers, Ketchum & Grosvenor. A house carpenter turned skilled machinist and then machine manufacturer thus had as business associates two men whom *Scientific American* called "men of abundant means and decided financial ability."

Charles Danforth replaced Rogers in the machine works of Clark and Godwin. The evidence concerning Danforth's background is unclear. Trumbull records that his father was a Norton, Massachusetts, "cotton manufacturer," but a more detailed biographical sketch in *The History of Bergen and Passaic Counties* notes that Danforth's father was "engaged in agricultural pursuits" and that in 1811, then fourteen, Danforth worked as a throstle-piercer before engaging as an ordinary seaman. After the War of 1812, he taught school near Rochester, New York, and in 1824 superintended a cotton carding room in a Matteawan, New York, factory. Hired to help set up a new cotton mill in Hohokus, New Jersey, he invented an improved spinning frame and settled in Paterson in 1828 to manufacture it as a partner with Godwin and Clark. Financial troubles in the late 1830s caused the dissolution of the partnership, and in 1840 Danforth bought out the entire machine-shop interest and in 1848 formed Charles Danforth and Company. His partner was John Edwards, his foreman. Born in England, Edwards moved to Paterson as a young man and worked in a hotel; he later apprenticed to John Clark and became his foreman, keeping the same supervisory position under Rogers and Danforth. Danforth so valued Edwards's abilities that he gave him a one-tenth interest in the firm.

The career of another workman, William Swinburne, illustrates this same mobility through the possession of technological skills. Born in Brooklyn in 1805, Swinburne first worked as a carpenter before moving to Matteawan as a machine patternmaker. Swinburne then came to Paterson to work as a patternmaker for Rogers and soon found himself draftsman, patternmaker, and superintendent of the new locomotive shops. Here he worked with Watts Cooke, Sr., from County Armagh, Ireland. By trade, Watts Cooke also was a carpenter. He migrated to Montreal in 1822, helped construct Notre Dame Cathedral there, moved to Albany, New York, stayed five years to learn the skill of patternmaking at an Albany furnace, worked for the Matteawan Machine Company, and settled finally in Paterson in 1839. When Swinburne took over the locomotive shops, he hired as his assistant one of Cooke's four sons—the seventeen-year-old John Cooke, an apprentice patternmaker.

In 1845, both Swinburne and young Cooke left Rogers, Ketchum & Grosvenor to become its competitors. Swinburne first joined former iron molder Samuel Smith and cotton manufacturers Patrick Maguinnis and James Jackson to make textile machinery and cotton cloth, but the completion of the Erie Railroad's eastern division directed their attention to locomotives. In 1851–1852, when it incorporated as the New Jersey Locomotive and Machine Company (later renamed the Grant Locomotive Works), Swinburne quit for unexplained reasons and started his own company, the Swinburne Locomotive Works. It was the first large Paterson manufacturer to depend entirely on steam power, and Swinburne soon employed between two and three hundred hands. He prospered until the 1857 depression caused severe financial difficulties that persuaded him to sell this plant to the Bank of New Jersey. Soon his factory was nothing more than an Erie Railroad repair shop.

John Cooke found more fortune than Swinburne. In 1852, Edwin Prall, Danforth's chief bookkeeper, urged his employer to add locomotive manufacturing to his enterprise and suggested John Cooke, then earning $1,800 a year as superintendent of the Rogers locomotive shops, as a partner. When the Danforth works was incorporated in 1865, Danforth, Cooke, and Prall became the principal stockholders. Prall's background differed from that of Cooke, Rogers, Swinburne, and even Danforth. He was born on Staten Island ("of good Knickerbocker-Moravian stock," noted Trumbull) and although orphaned as a child, grew up in a family immersed in entrepreneurial aspirations, surrounded by enterprising relatives. He worked first for a New York City cousin who imported drugs, then for an uncle who manufactured cotton in Haverstraw, New York, and finally for another uncle who was Danforth's bookkeeper. Prall took over when his uncle died.

John Cooke and his brothers, the sons of an immigrant pattern-maker, assumed important roles in the Danforth locomotive shops. Brother William Cooke became chief draftsman, and Watts, Jr., joined the firm under unusual circumstances. Then nineteen years old, he was a bound apprentice to Thomas Rogers and was in Cincinnati installing three engines when John Cooke shifted from Rogers to Danforth. Rogers let him buy the "balance" of this time as an apprentice, and young Cooke became foreman of the Danforth locomotive erecting shops—aged nineteen. Two years later (1854), a customer, the Delaware, Lackawanna & Western Railroad, hired him as Master Mechanic, and Watts Cooke did not return to Paterson until 1868. Significantly, a fellow apprentice at Rogers, James Ayres, took Cooke's place as foreman of the Danforth locomotive erecting shops and held that position for nearly thirty years.

As a group, the developers of the Paterson locomotive industry, except for Ketchum and Grosvenor (and they lived in New York City), experienced enormous occupational mobility in their lives. In one generation—often in a few years—men jumped class lines and rose rapidly in prestige and status. One can argue about Danforth, but Prall had been an orphan and a clerk as a boy, and the others—Clark, Rogers, Swinburne, Watts Cooke, Sr., his sons William, John, and Watts, Jr.—had all started in life as skilled artisans and risen to become factory foreman or superintendents and owners of large, new manufacturing enterprises. The triumphs of these men were only part of the Paterson story. Their locomotive factories became workshops that trained machinists and other skilled ironworkers. Most did not . . . stay within the firm. They struck out on their own as small manufacturers to be swept up and tested by the surge of industrial development after 1843. A few became manufacturers of great wealth; most succeeded in a more modest fashion. All were closely identified with the development of Paterson's iron and machinery and tool industries between 1843 and 1880—a process shaped by the efforts of self-made men entirely different in social origin from the archetypal members of Gregory and Neu's "industrial elite" in the 1870s. None came from professional, mercantile, or manufacturing backgrounds. Only one was born in New England, and almost all of them were British immigrants. These were not "princes" prepared by training and education to become "kings" of industry. Instead, they rose from the lower classes and achieved substantial material rewards in their lifetimes. For those of their contemporaries who sought "proof" about the promise of rags to riches, these men served as model, day-to-day evidence.

Paterson's two most successful machinery works were started by apprentice machinists, one who labored as a child in a cotton factory and the other who grew up on a farm and worked first as a carpenter. William Watson and Joseph Todd learned their machinist skills in the Paterson machine and locomotive shops. In 1844, Joseph Todd and a partner opened a small machine shop in the rear of a cotton mill, a common practice. They started with two lathes (one borrowed), and a few years later one Phillip Rafferty joined them. (The sources tell only that Rafferty was employed to build a black-smith shop in an early textile mill in 1837.) Senior partner Joseph Todd was born on a New Jersey farm and at sixteen apprenticed as a carpenter to his uncle. Three years later, he left for New York City, and then went to Paterson to help construct a Methodist church. He stayed on to work at Godwin, Clark & Company and Rogers, Ketchum & Grosvenor as a machine patternmaker. His successful development of a hemp-spinning machine led him, at twenty-seven, to start his own small machine shop. In 1860, the firm employed 135 workers, and a decade later as many as 350 hands. Its successes rested on the manufacture of the twine machinery, but it also made steam engines and boilers and later manufactured jute bagging.

William Watson was even more successful than Todd. Watson and his younger brother spent their childhood in Lancashire, England, and followed their father to Belleville, New Jersey. At the age of ten he helped his father in a print works. When the family moved to Paterson, the young Watson brothers labored in textile mills. Then William Watson apprenticed to a machinist, studied draftsmanship, and became a foreman. After a few years, Watson left Paterson, worked in a Newburgh mill, and helped run a New York City screw factory. In 1845, then twenty-six, he opened his own Paterson machine shop, employing 10 men in millwrighting work, tool manufacture, and later in structural iron. The firm counted 60 employees in 1860 and no less than 1,100 men and boys in 1873.

Few other manufacturers were as successful as Todd and Watson between 1840 and 1880, but the career patterns of eight lesser manu-facturers and the seven machinists who formed a copartnership called the Machinists' Association paralleled the paths followed by Todd and Watson. Examples from among them show a quite distinct pattern. Samuel Smith left Ireland as a youth and worked for a time for a Nova Scotia clergyman before settling with his family in Paterson and apprenticing as a molder at Rogers, Ketchum & Grosvenor. In later years, he and a copartner started a foundry, opened a machine shop, and manufactured steam boilers.

Benjamin Buckley and a partner began manufacturing spindles and flyers for textile machinery in 1844. Born in Oldham, England, 1808, Buckley came to the United States in 1831, first worked in a Paterson cotton mill, then for Rogers and finally for Danforth. When he opened a small factory of his own he employed six hands. Buckley later failed as a cotton manufacturer, but his spindle works survived more than forty years. He employed twenty workers in 1859 and ran the enterprise with the help of his sons. Buckley also was president of the Passaic County National Bank in the early 1870s.

Three years after Buckley settled in Paterson, John Daggers arrived from Lancashire, England. Born in 1819, he apprenticed at the Rogers factory and then traveled south to construct cotton machinery in Alabama and Georgia. Later he returned to Paterson to manufacture bobbin pins. George Addy and Robert Atherton arrived in Paterson in the late 1840s. Addy, a third-generation Yorkshire blacksmith, borrowed passage fare to cross the Atlantic in 1849, worked two years for Danforth, then for Rogers, and in 1851 started manufacturing bolts and screws. Addy's firm expanded over the years, and in the 1880s made bolts and screws, smut machines, moving machines, and straw cutters. He also earned income from successful urban real-estate investment. Robert Atherton did not rise as rapidly as Addy. Atherton grew up in Westchester County, New York, finished primary school there, moved to New York City, and settled in Paterson in 1848. He labored first in a cotton mill, apprenticed to a roller manufacturer and then to Buckley, failed in a partnership with Samuel Watson (William Watson's son), worked a number of years as a "general machinist," superintended a silk-machinery manufactory, and in 1878 started a machine works with his sons that soon occupied about 7,000 square feet in a cotton mill and employed nearly fifty workers in the manufacture of silk machinery.

Atherton's later success depended in good part on the development of the Paterson silk industry after the Civil War. So did the fortunes of some other Paterson machinists. Among the first to benefit were seven machinists (the *Scientific American* called them "practical mechanics"), most of them former Danforth employees, who formed a copartnership in 1851 called the Machinists' Association. Nothing is known of them as individuals except that each contributed $200 to start the firm. By 1859, with most of their orders coming from Southern textile mills, the firm was assessed at $25,000, clear of all obligations. The Machinists' Association shifted from the manufacture of general textile machinery to silk machinery and soon thereafter employed more than 100 men. By 1876, its machinery had been bought by more than 200 manufacturers.

When he started, Benjamin Eastwood had no partners. In 1872–1873, with an investment of $1,500 and three employees, he began manufacturing silk machinery. Two years later he moved to larger quarters in the rear of a silk mill and hired ten or twelve workers. In 1878, he built his own mill, employed between fifty and sixty men, and was ready to become the city's major manufacturer of silk machinery. Eastwood's career illustrates extensive geographic and occupational mobility. Born in Lancashire, Eastwood benefited from a "common school education" and training in a machine shop before his departure for the United States in 1863. He worked for a time in Paterson, then briefly in Milwaukee, and again in Paterson. A gold-mining venture in Mecklenberg County, North Carolina, took him south to build engines and machinery and to serve as a mine superintendent for two and a half years. The company failed, and Eastwood returned to Paterson to work again as a machinist. He started a small shop but left it to travel to Venezuela as a "mechanical engineer." Illness ("fever") sent him back to Paterson for the fourth time but only to spend a year in a locomotive shop. He then went to a New York City "experimental shop" that hoped to develop ways to use motive power more efficiently on canals. Eastwood remained in New York City for eighteen months. He returned to Paterson again, worked for a year in a sewing-machine factory that soon left the city, and in 1872 or 1873, ten years after he arrived in the country and after having traveled to Milwaukee, North Carolina, Venezuela, and New York City, opened his small silk-machinery factory.

Two other British-born machinists, John Royle and James Jackson, also manufactured textile machinery, but they started at it quite

late in life. Royle was born in Chester, England, migrated to Paterson
with his parents in 1830, worked in a cotton mill as a ten-year-old,
and became an apprentice machinist. Illness forced an early retire-
ment, but he later supervised the construction of turbine water
wheels manufactured by Watson. He remained with Watson until
1860, rented a small machine shop that failed quickly, worked again
for Watson manufacturing flax machinery for two years, left to wan-
der through the West for a time seeking "opportunity," and finally
returned to Paterson in 1863 and started manufacturing textile machinery "on a very limited scale." Royle developed a quality high-
speed routing machine and other valued textile machinery, and the
firm expanded rapidly after 1878. Jackson's career was somewhat
different. Born in Caton, England, he was the son of a silk dresser
and the grandson of a master carder. He did not migrate to the
United States until he was forty. At thirteen, he apprenticed to a
machinist, and at twenty-one he started a ten-year stint as master
mechanic and superintendent of a Caton cotton mill; then he superintended another twelve years at an Oldham mill. Migrating to the
United States in 1869, he spent several months in Philadelphia before
settling in Paterson to work as a machinist at the Rogers Locomotive
Works. In 1873 he started making Jacquard silk machinery. A year
later, he expanded to a larger mill and, like Royle, he took his sons
into the manufacturing business.

Machine and tool shops owned by men like Eastwood, Royle, and
Jackson depended on one or another branch of the textile industry
for customers, but Paterson's two large iron works resulted from
sparks set off by the railroad boom after 1840. Neither the Paterson
Iron Works nor the Passaic Rolling Mill Company was started by apprentices or artisans, but men who had begun their careers as workers soon controlled them. The Paterson Iron Works began in 1853
because of the efforts of two New Hampshire capitalists, cotton
manufacturers in the Granite State drawn to Paterson by the developing locomotive industry. They hoped to manufacture axles, tires, and
shapes for locomotives and heavy engines. A year later, Franklin
Beckwith, a railroad contractor, bought an interest in the firm, and
by 1861 he had purchased the interest of the New Hampshire men
and a local manufacturer. Beckwith dominated the firm until his

death in 1875, when his sons took over the enterprise. Beckwith's career differed from those who ran successful machine shops. Born in Saratoga, New York, one of nine sons of a farmer, he worked on the family farm until aged nineteen and received, at best, a common school education. An older brother who had become chief engineer and contractor in building the Boston & Albany Railroad hired him as a foreman. Beckwith soon became a contractor himself. He settled in Troy, but in 1845 was drawn to Pennsylvania to try iron smelting. Five years later, he was principal contractor on the Delaware division of the Erie Railroad. When the Erie Railroad acquired the old Paterson & Hudson River road, Beckwith went to New Jersey to rebuild its track and its railroad bridges. Paterson attracted his attention, and this farmer turned railroad construction foreman and contractor became an iron manufacturer. In 1860, his firm employed forty workers and built 7,000 railroad tires and forgings for 1,700 locomotives.

Sherman Jaqua [was] one of the men from whom Beckwith purchased an interest in the Paterson Iron Works in 1861 for about $20,000. . . . Soon after, Jaqua received a charter for a new Paterson ironworks that would specialize in making rolled bar iron from scrap. Called the Idaho Iron Company, it failed, and Jaqua sold his machinery to a California company. In 1868, the Cooke brothers, spurred by Watts Cooke, Jr., who returned from Scranton and brought with him some investment capital supplied by the Delaware, Lackawanna & Western Railroad, purchased what remained of the Jaqua property, renamed the firm the Passaic Rolling Mill Company, and in three months turned out rolled iron bar. The firm specialized in making structural iron beams, angels, and teels, and shifted to bridge iron in 1876. William Cooke quit his brothers in 1873 to work in New York City, but W. O. Fayerweather purchased his interest. Watts Cooke, Jr., who had purchased his apprentice contract from Thomas Rogers in 1852, came back to Paterson sixteen years later as president of the Passaic Rolling Mill Company. W. O. Fayerweather, who had left Paterson as a young man to work as an errand boy in the great metropolis nearby, returned in 1873 as treasurer and partner of one of the Northeast's most important iron factories. Like Watts Cooke, Jr., Fayerweather had returned home. Both men traveled different routes, but they followed tracks that moved steadily upward.

Pertinent biographical information to complete this collective portrait is lacking for a number of other Paterson manufacturers of machinery, tools, and textile supplies. Similarly, the social origins of certain small manufacturers of wire hoop, copper and brass castings, files, and weaver's supplies are not recorded. Nevertheless, scattered evidence tells that some of these men and other small manufacturers had careers no different from the dominant pattern uncovered for most Paterson manufacturers. C. C. E. Van Alstine's unusual success resulted from his inventive genius. Van Alstine started as a machinist in Paterson in 1872, worked for a company for a year, took odd jobs repairing optical glasses and sewing machines, and finally invented a machine press that punched "the eye of a lingo" (an important weaving implement) and shaped its head at the same time. Van Alstine became a manufacturer and quickly improved his position. Starting in the mid-seventies with 4 workers, he employed between 175 and 200 in a few years. Other skilled workers and craftsmen began the trek upward in less spectacular ways. When James Walder started manufacturing reeds and heddles in 1866, he hired 2 men and rented factory floor space. He moved several times (always to rented premises) before purchasing a small building and enlarging it to a 20-by-200-foot plant. In the early 1880s, Walder was Paterson's most important reed and heddle manufacturer. Eight other firms followed Walder's path between 1855 and 1880, and the evidence suggests that all were started and developed by skilled workers who opened small shops as individuals or with a partner. Although the data about these men (Charles Moseley, Christian Kohlhaus, James Dunkerley, Robert Brooks, Robert Taylor, Robert McCullough, and Thomas Wrigley and his brother John) is slight, there is enough information to tell that all started as skilled workers, usually machinists, and rose to become manufacturers in a single generation.

Much remains to be written about the Paterson iron, locomotive, and machinery manufacturers who started in life as workers, but their social status, their political role (many held public office), and their labor policies cannot be briefly summarized. What matters for purposes of this study is the fact that the rags-to-riches promise was not a mere myth in Paterson, New Jersey, between 1830 and 1880. So many successful manufacturers who had begun as workers walked the streets of that city then that it is not hard to believe that others less successful or just starting out on the lower rungs of the occupational mobility ladder could be convinced by personal knowledge that "hard work" resulted in spectacular material and social improvement. Thernstrom has argued convincingly that small improvements in material circumstances counted for much in explaining the social stability of Newburyport between 1850 and 1880. What role did the frequent examples of spectacular upward mobility in developing industrial Paterson play vis-à-vis its social structure? Whether the social origin of the Paterson manufacturers was typical of other manufacturers of that era cannot yet be known, but their career pattern was quite different from the one uncovered by other students of the nineteenth-century American "business elite."

Detailed research, however, has not yet been done on the manufacturers of other new industrial cities such as Buffalo, Pittsburgh, Cincinnati, and Chicago. Developing industrial cities and new manufacturing industries offered unusual opportunities to skilled craftsmen and mechanics in the early phases of American industrialization. Such was the case in Paterson, and surely such opportunities existed in other cities. Who took advantage of such opportunities, however, is still a subject for careful inquiry. The detailed examination of other local industrial "elites" will make it possible to learn whether the Paterson manufacturers were a mutant group or mere examples of a pattern of occupational mobility common to early industrializing America. Whatever the final findings, such community-oriented studies will shed unusually important light on one of the many dark corners of the mid-nineteenth-century American economic and social structure.

Stephan Thernstrom

WORKING-CLASS UPWARD MOBILITY IN NEWBURYPORT

Stephan Thernstrom's study of the occupational and property-owning careers of the sons of several hundred mid-nineteenth-century Newburyport workers was the pioneering volume by a historian devoted entirely to the theme of vertical mobility. More than any other work, Thernstrom's book attracted historians' attention to the problem of mobility. The influence of his book rests primarily on its solid research, its clarity, and its refined categorizations and analysis. In Newburyport, as in so many other communities, intergenerational gain was steady but slight. The children of workers improved their lot significantly yet modestly, remaining within their social class of origin.

The laborers of Newburyport have so far been observed from two angles of vision. Hundreds of unskilled workmen and their sons were viewed first in their occupational role; and then in terms of the frequency with which they managed to accumulate savings and to purchase real estate. It was necessary to isolate these two dimensions of social mobility and to consider each separately, but that simplifying device can now be abandoned in order to deal with some of the key relationships between advances in the occupational and property spheres. First, characteristic patterns of working-class family mobility will be identified by surveying some representative cases from the 287 families studied. Then the critical question of whether upwardly mobile fathers customarily succeeded in passing on their gains to their children will be systematically explored. That will lead to an interpretative review of the major findings concerning working-class social mobility in the 1850–1880 period.

Patterns of Family Mobility

A rough classification of Newburyport's laboring families into high mobility, intermediate mobility, and static categories will make it easier to discern typical patterns of family mobility. The high mobility category, which includes a sixth of the 287 families studied, encompasses every family at least one of whose members entered a nonmanual occupation during these three decades. Those families whose male members were all confined to unskilled and semiskilled jobs, and who never came into possession of as much as $300 in property during these years are classed static. The intermediate mobility category covers the range of cases between these two poles.

High Mobility Families. Forty-seven of the 287 laboring families who resided in Newburyport a decade or more between 1850 and 1880 were highly mobile. Twenty-two of these cases involved the mobility of adult laborers into nonmanual occupations; in the other 25 it was the son of the original laborer who first crossed over into the middle-class occupational universe.

The most important avenue of high mobility open to the older generation was, surprisingly, not small business but agriculture. A New England manufacturing city seems an unlikely setting for the fulfillment of Jeffersonian dreams, but sixteen of the twenty-two highly mobile fathers became farm owners, and a good many other laborers did some farming on the side.

Newburyport residents in this period were within reach of a large supply of arable land. Six miles long but only half a mile wide, the city hugged the banks of the Merrimack River; open fields formed its western border. A workman like Thomas Ronan was alert to the possibilities that lay at his doorstep. In 1855, having scraped together a few hundred dollars from his wages, Ronan bought a small house on the western edge of town, and moved his wife and eight children from their cramped working-class dwelling on Beck Street. Ronan reported his occupation as "farmer" on the 1860 census, though he was not yet assessed as the owner of farm equipment or livestock. In 1864 he paid taxes on $900 in real estate, $200 in livestock, and a $100 wagon. By 1867 he had acquired a second house and two more farm lots, and his real property holdings had reached $1,600. The census of 1870 listed Ronan as the owner of $2,000 in real estate and $1,500 in personal property.

Ronan became more affluent than most of his fellow laborers who became farm owners—Dan Creedon's $1,400, William Eustis's $1,800, Ichabod Little's $1,300 were more typical estate values—but the pattern of his ascent was characteristic of the group. The key step was the setting aside of enough money to purchase a lot on the outskirts of the city. Once land had been acquired, the process of becoming a full-fledged farmer was often slow. Ronan claimed his new status very quickly; other laborers continued to live in rented dwellings for years, working as day laborers and farming their plots in their spare time. In many cases it was impossible to distinguish a laborer who owned farm property from a farmer; census and city directory occupational listings for such men were frequently inconsistent. The sixteen farmers placed in the high mobility class here represent a minimum estimate. Some two dozen others who still reported themselves as laborers on the census of 1880 owned small amounts of arable land and livestock, and undoubtedly derived some part of their income from agriculture.

About two-thirds of the common laborers in Newburyport at this time were born in rural Ireland, while a good many others were migrants from the farms of Maine, New Hampshire, and Vermont. They were, in short, no strangers to the soil. It was significant that life in the industrial city did not invariably require a total break from the rural environment to which these men were accustomed. This was the case in Newburyport, and there is evidence that it was true to some degree in even the larger urban centers of the period. A select minority from the laboring class succeeded in becoming full-fledged farmers, and many others became yeomen part-time.

To rank farm ownership and operation a nonmanual occupation is a sociological convention; actually the farmer performed heavy manual labor. The farm owner is classed with the businessman and the professional because he was a proprietor—because he commanded capital, made decisions as to what he would produce, and sold at least part of his product for a profit. The laborers who became farm owners in Newburyport appear to have customarily produced little more than enough to satisfy the wants of their family and to have rarely become significantly involved in farming for the market. Even the exceptionally prosperous Thomas Ronan estimated the value of his produce at only $550 on the census of 1870; most of these men supplied no detailed crop information on the agricultural schedules of the census because they produced less than the $500 minimum specified by the Census Bureau.

The fact that farm work was little different from ordinary labor, and that farms held by mobile laborers were not operated as businesses suggests that the environment in which the children of these mobile laborers grew up was not particularly conducive to success in the middle-class world. The career patterns of the sons of the sixteen farm owners confirm this interpretation. Only two youths from this group entered a white-collar, professional, or business calling: one became a clerk, and eventually an independent grocer; another began his career as a schoolteacher. Several simply stayed home and labored on their fathers' farms; some of these presumably would someday become independent farmers by inheritance. The majority, however, gravitated to simple manual occupations, becoming fishermen, mill operatives, butchers, masons.

Farming was much more accessible to the older generation in our sample than the other nonmanual callings. None of these workmen was able to enter a profession, of course, but it is surprising that only six of the entire group ventured into small business. The security of the farm and the familiarity of its task drew most of these successful laborers, including those with the largest stocks of capital. The few business owners were very small operators: Freeman Greenough's investment as a "provisioner" was a mere $300; William O'Neal's house, the front room of which served as a tavern and liquor store, was valued at $1,000. Whether from insufficiency of capital, incompetence, or bad luck, these small businessmen were much less prosperous than their brethren who purchased farms.

Business pursuits, on the other hand, gave the children of mobile laborers an environment somewhat more favorable to attainment of high-status positions. The experience of the Freeman Greenough family suggests some of the possibilities. The Greenoughs came to the city from Maine sometime in the forties, and the father found work as a day laborer. Freeman and one of his sons were classified as laborers in the census of 1850, while two more of his boys were mill operatives. A few years later, with his small savings, he opened a "provisions" shop at his place of residence. The business returned very little profit, judging from his tax assessments, but Greenough was able to keep it going until his death in 1881. Three of his sons left Newburyport while still youths, one of them with some employment experience as a clerk. A fourth, Joseph, began his career as a hostler. In 1870, at thirty-four, he was still in a humble calling, a driver with no taxable property. His account at the Institution for

Savings must already have contained a substantial capital reserve, however, for in the next decade his rise was meteoric. The 1873 assessments show him with five horses and two carriages, worth $900; in 1876 it was twelve horses, five carriages, four hacks, a stable, and a house, a total investment of $4,800. By 1880 Joseph's livery stable was valued at $11,000; by 1883, $15,000. Joseph's oldest boy was registered in the Latin preparatory section of the high school in 1880; it is very likely that with this much education he entered a nonmanual calling after graduating. Freeman Greenough's fifth son, Henry, had a more erratic career. He was a mill operative as a youth, later a confectioner, then a clerk in a provisions shop. By 1870 he had returned to the mill, and in 1880 he was recorded as a hack driver, probably working for his successful brother. Two of Henry Greenough's sons, however, found white-collar jobs.

In all, twenty-two Newburyport families were ranked in the high mobility category because of the intragenerational mobility of an unskilled manual laborer; another twenty-five families entered that category by virtue of the social advances of their children. The composition of these two groups present sharp contrasts. Three-quarters of the older generation achieved high status by the purchase of a farm; none of the second generation high mobility cases moved into agriculture. Half of these mobile sons found white-collar jobs, a category of occupation entered by none of the older generation of laborers. The other 50 percent of these sons, as opposed to one-quarter of the fathers, became independent small businessmen. Many of these youths had brief experience as factory operatives, but not one made his ascent within the corporate hierarchy. The humble mill hand who struggles to become foreman and ends up chairman of the board, it was shown earlier, was rarely portrayed in the success literature of this period; he was a later creation. In this small way, at least, the mid-nineteenth-century mobility ideology accurately mirrored social reality.

The businesses opened by the sons of Newburyport laborers were precarious ventures. They were neighborhood affairs, requiring only enough capital to buy a small inventory of goods and to pay the rent—five of these sons became retail grocers, three of them were ice dealers, two were fish sellers. Low capital requirements allowed easy entry; members of this group typically worked in some manual job for a few years in order to accumulate savings on which to operate. Profits, not surprisingly, were minimal. Only Stephen Fowle and Joseph Greenough reported a rapid and sustained increase in wealth over the period. The threat of bankruptcy was not negligible. One youth opened a grocery with $500 in 1860 and lost everything in five years; he was forced to find work in a hat factory, where he was still employed in 1880. Had this study been carried past 1880, other instances of downward mobility would have been recorded; several of these tiny enterprises were no longer listed in the 1886 city directory. For fathers and sons alike, then, business ownership was not an unrealizable goal; neither, on the other hand, was it a guarantee of secure prosperity once attained.

A new development was the small white-collar elite group—fourteen clerks, a bookkeeper, and a clerk lawyer—which had come into existence by 1880. Only two of the members of this group had ever worked in a manual occupation. Boys did not begin their careers as laborers or operatives and later edge their way up into white-collar positions. The white-collar and laboring worlds were clearly separated. One entered the white-collar group only after having received considerable schooling, and one entered it directly. The immense growth of the white-collar occupations, just beginning throughout America during this period, was to make the distinction between intergenerational and intragenerational mobility opportunities increasingly sharp; the type of mobility represented by these white-collar workers was to become the chief means of social ascent.

Since the white-collar worker was necessarily an educated man, the family which produced him had to be in a position to forgo the immediate economic benefits of child labor long enough to allow him to attend school longer than his working-class peers, who customarily began work in their early teens. It is not surprising, therefore, that the fourteen families whose sons became clerks and professionals were markedly more prosperous than the families of sons who ventured into business for themselves. Four-fifths of the fathers of the latter group remained propertyless unskilled laborers; fully two-thirds of the fathers of the former group became property owners, and several were occupationally mobile as well. The case of John G. Buckley was representative. Indistinguishable from a hundred other destitute laborers in 1860, Buckley made a respected place for himself in Newburyport during the following two decades, though remaining a laborer. By 1880 Buckley had become the owner of four houses, worth $2,200, and had been appointed a night watchman on the police force. (His younger brother Cornelius accumulated $2,900 in real estate over the same period.) Sending his two sons to school was not an impossible drain on the John Buckley's resources: one attended a seminary and became a priest, the second took a position as a clerk after graduating from high school.

If white-collar workers usually came from families which were able to give special advantages to them, other members of the family should have shared some of the gains. The career patterns of the brothers of these white-collar youths fitted this expectation. The brothers of the laborers mobile into business callings usually found unskilled and semiskilled manual jobs; the siblings of the laborers mobile into white-collar occupations tended to enter skilled or nonmanual occupations. A few took white-collar jobs themselves, and about half chose skilled callings. Thus Pat Moylan's eldest son became a blacksmith, the other two sons obtained clerkships; John Carnes became a barber, James Carnes a clerk; Jeremiah McDonald became a clerk, his younger brother an office boy. The youngest children, as we might expect, were most likely to achieve the highest status; it was often the increment to family income produced by the employment of their elder brothers that paid for their education.

Intermediate Mobility Families. The category "intermediate mobility" designates families whose members remained entirely with the working-class occupational world between 1850 and 1880, but who succeeded in elevating themselves *within* the working class during this period. The 47 families in the high mobility class accounted for all the dramatic interclass mobility achieved by unskilled manual laborers in Newburyport at this time. But the other 240 laboring families included in the survey cannot be indiscriminately characterized as static. Within the broad penumbra of the manual laboring class there were important variations in occupational status and in economic position. Two types of intermediate mobility were distinguished here. A family was placed in this category either if one of its members rose into a skilled occupation, or if it acquired a significant amount of property.

Only one-fifth of the 145 families in the intermediate mobility class achieved occupational mobility into a skilled craft. Thirteen of the older generation of our sample entered skilled positions between 1850 and 1880. They included 4 carpenters, 3 masons, a painter, a tailor, a ropemaker, and an engineer. Wage levels in the skilled trades were well above the prevailing rate for unskilled labor; all but 2 of the 13 came into possession of property worth $500 or more. New security of employment, the relative ease of home ownership and saving, and pride of craft all gave grounds for a feeling of status improvement.

In one important respect, however, the gains of these men were limited. An essential element of the superior status of the traditional artisan was that he was able to transmit craft status to his children. The son of the skilled tradesman was expected to serve an apprenticeship himself, and then to enter a craft, often that of his father. Only two of the twenty sons of these mobile laborers followed this course; fourteen became factory operatives or seamen, and another four became casual laborers. To the extent to which the ability to pass on social and economic advantages to one's children is a criterion of success, the success of these laborers was distinctly qualified.

The skilled trades were a somewhat more important avenue of mobility for the younger generation. In our analysis only sixteen families appear to boast a son in a skilled occupation, but the figure is misleadingly low. To classify families according to the attainments of their most successful member obscures the extent of intermediate mobility of this kind; many of the brothers of youths in white-collar jobs held skilled positions themselves. The analysis in chapter four [of *Poverty and Progress*] provides a better measure of the dimensions of mobility of this kind: laborers' sons who had learned a trade were still a fairly select minority in 1880, but skilled positions were definitely more accessible to them than to their fathers.

Much the largest portion of the intermediate mobility group consisted of families whose members remained in the low-skill, low-pay occupational universe throughout these decades, but who were able to accumulate significant property holdings. The wealth of the 116 occupationally static families in the intermediate mobility category is indicated in Table 1. The variation was wide. A small elite, 21 families, reached the $1,500 mark; a few of these went well above that figure. Jeremiah Long, for instance, already owned a $700

TABLE 1
Maximum Property Holdings of Occupationally Static Laboring Families[a]

Size of Holding	Number of Families	Percentage of Group
$300–599	27	23
$600–899	37	32
$900–1,199	22	19
$1,200–1,499	9	8
$1,500 and over	21	18
Total	116	100

[a] Families are categorized here according to the maximum figure listed in census schedules and assessor's valuation books, 1850–1880.

house in 1850. Two of his sons were employed as mariners. Their wages plus the rent paid by four boarders gave Long an unusually large income. In 1856 he bought another house, increasing his real property holdings to $1,300; in 1860 he paid taxes on property worth $1,700; and by 1870 the census listed him as the owner of $3,000 in real estate and $2,000 in personal property.

A more typical figure from the wealthier stratum of propertied laborers was Tim Marooney. Marooney had scraped together $400 by 1867, when he invested it in a shack on the edge of the city. With two cows, a few chickens, and no rent to pay, Marooney found it possible to save a substantial portion of his wages. By 1870 he paid taxes on $500 in personal property as well as $500 in real estate; during the seventies, with the aid of four mortgages, he built a second house on Railroad Street and a third one on Auburn Street. Marooney was worth $1,900 in 1880. The family of James Barrett eventually arrived at about this economic level too, but its success came in the second generation. Barrett himself, a common laborer on four successive censuses, never acquired any taxable property. Both of his sons took semiskilled positions while in their early teens. One left Newburyport during the Civil War and never returned; the other was at various times a mill operative, a mariner, and a comb factory employee. The 1882 city directory listed the second as a day laborer like his father, yet by this time he had become the owner of two houses valued at $1,800.

These twenty-one relatively wealthy families represented but a small fraction of the total laboring group, of course. The average property-owning laborer in Newburyport accumulated holdings of less than a thousand dollars. The modest progress of the Norton family was characteristic of the dozens of small property holders. The native-born father was a laborer in 1850 and 1860, then a watchman. He saved nothing during those years, so far as can be determined. Three of his four sons as teen-agers worked in the mills. One son moved away in the late sixties. A second became a teamster; he possessed no taxable property by 1880, but did hold an account at the Institution for Savings. The third Norton boy became an operative in a comb factory and was able to purchase a $600 house after two decades of employment there. The fourth, a fisherman, claimed $200 in personal property on the census of 1870 and was a savings bank depositor; despite the fact that three of his young children were employed in 1880, however, as yet he owned no real estate. Not much of a success story, surely, but not a condition of absolute stagnation either. As the Nortons might have viewed it, one member of the family had definitely advanced into the ranks of the respectable, home-owning citizenry, while two others had taken at least a short step in that direction by setting aside some savings.

Static Families.   Two-thirds of the laboring families in Newburyport had advanced themselves at least as much as the Nortons by 1880. The remaining third, ninety-five families, were unable to rise out of the most depressed, impoverished segment of the manual laboring class. A man like John Martin, for instance, was a casual laborer in 1860; he later became a laborer at the local gas works, living with his family in a small building owned by the gas company. An Irish immigrant, Martin was illiterate, and his children saw more of the factory than they did of the schoolhouse. Martin's daughters worked in the cotton mills until marriage; one son became a fisherman, the second an operative in a rope factory. Dennis Sughrue was still an ordinary laborer in 1880; his fourteen-year-old boy was a mill hand, while his older son had graduated to the brickyard. Neither family payed any property taxes at all during this period. The Martins, the Sughrues, and the Lowrys had their names in the newspaper occasionally, when one of them was arrested for drunkenness; heavy drinking on a common laborer's wages was a nearly foolproof way of keeping one's family in dismal poverty. About this substantial segment of the Newburyport working class little more can be said. These men were failures according to the values of the competitive society in which they lived, and the early careers of their children suggested that the habit of failure could easily develop in this environment.

The statement that as many as a third of the laboring families resident in Newburyport at this time achieved neither occupational mobility nor property mobility, however, is in one respect highly misleading. Families which lived in the community for only ten years during the period studied were obviously less likely to accumulate property or climb in the occupational hierarchy than families more firmly rooted in Newburyport. Table 2, which classifies families according to length of residence in the city, shows this clearly. Over 40 percent of the families in Newburyport for ten years remained at the very bottom of the social ladder; only 5 percent of the laboring families who lived there throughout the 1850–1880 period are found in the static category. And, similarly, the proportion of families in the high mobility and intermediate mobility categories rose steadily with increased length of residence in the city. Table 2 provides a simple overview of the cumulative significance of several social processes—selective geographical mobility, occupational mobility, and property mobility—which affected the status of the unskilled laboring families of Newburyport. It reinforces the broad conclusion that the great majority of families who settled in the community for very long were able to make at least a modest social advance.

TABLE 2
Mobility of Laboring Families According to Length of Residence

	Ten Years	Twenty Years	Thirty Years
Number in sample	145	101	41
High mobility	8%	21%	32%
Intermediate mobility			
Occupational skill	8	7	27
Property			
$1000 or more	16	19	12
$300–999	26	22	24
Static	43	32	5

From Generation to Generation: Social Mobility as a Cumulative Process

An important aspect of the social-mobility patterns of working-class families in nineteenth-century Newburyport has only been touched on so far. Was social mobility usually a cumulative process? Was the son of an upwardly mobile laborer likely to emulate his father and continue to climb upward, or were his career prospects no better than those of a youth whose father remained a propertyless unskilled workman?

In Table 3 the occupational achievements of these working-class youths are classified according to the highest occupation attained by their father in the 1850–1880 period, and the results are rather surprising. No consistent positive relationship between the occupational mobility of fathers and sons is revealed. The children of laborers mobile into a semiskilled occupation were more successful than the sons of static laborers in both the semiskilled and skilled callings, as we would expect. But workmen who climbed into a skilled trade were unable to transfer higher status to their children; their sons found skilled jobs less often than the sons of semiskilled men, and were the least successful of all the groups at penetrating the nonmanual occupations. And the sons of the small elite of laborers who rose into a nonmanual occupation during this period, paradoxically, clustered in unskilled laboring jobs more heavily than the sons of men still at the bottom of the occupational

TABLE 3
Occupational Status Attained by Laborers' Sons According to the Highest Occupation of Their Fathers

Son's Occupation at the Last Census on Which He Was Listed in the 1850–1880 Period	Father's Highest Occupation in the 1850–1880 Period			
	Unskilled	Semi-skilled	Skilled	Non-Manual
Number in sample	234	38	23	24
Unskilled	26%	3%	9%	29%
Semiskilled	54	63	70	29
Skilled	13	24	17	8
Monmanual	8	10	4	33

scale. The children of these highly mobile fathers, it is true, obtained nonmanual positions more often than did men in the other groups. But even so, only a third of them attained middle-class occupational status, and this is a liberal estimate, since it includes youths working on a farm owned by their father as nonmanual employees. Table 3 provides no support for the belief that occupationally mobile men imparted exceptionally high mobility aspirations to their children, nor for the hypothesis that a mobile father was able to ease his sons' entry into a higher status occupation.

If the occupational mobility of working-class fathers did little to further their children's career prospects, perhaps property mobility had a more positive effect. Common sense suggests that youths from the thrifty, respectable, home-owning segment of the working class would develop higher ambitions than the children of laborers living at the bare subsistence level, and that they would possess superior resources in the contest for better jobs. The evidence, however, does not confirm this plausible hypothesis. Property mobility and intergenerational occupational mobility were not necessarily complementary forms of social mobility; indeed, Table 4 indicates that in some instances they were mutually exclusive. The sons of property-owning workmen entered skilled manual callings more often than the sons of propertyless laborers, but they remained dis-

TABLE 4
Occupational Status Attained by Laborers' Sons According to the Property Holdings of Their Fathers

Son's Occupation at the Last Census on Which He Was Listed in the 1850–1880 Period	Father's Maximum Property Holding in the 1850–1880 Period		
	Less than $300	*$300–$899*	*$900 or more*
Number in sample[a]	121	65	48
Unskilled	24%	22%	35%
Semiskilled	59	57	38
Skilled	7	18	21
Nonmanual	11	3	6

[a] The numbers here are smaller than on Table 3, because property data was analyzed only for families resident in Newburyport for a decade or more during the period.

proportionately concentrated in unskilled positions and, most surprising, somewhat underrepresented in nonmanual occupations.

This striking discovery recalls an aspect of working-class property mobility about which the prophets of the mobility ideology were understandably silent. The ordinary workman of nineteenth-century Newburyport could rarely build up a savings account and purchase a home without making severe sacrifices. To cut family consumption expenditures to the bone was one such sacrifice. To withdraw the children from school and to put them to work at the age of ten or twelve was another. As Table 4 shows, the sons of exceptionally prosperous laborers did *not* enjoy generally superior career opportunities; the sacrifice of their education and the constriction of their occupational opportunities, in fact, was often a prime cause of the family's property mobility.

This pattern was particularly characteristic of Irish working-class families in Newburyport.... immigrants and their children moved upwards on the occupational scale with greater difficulty than their Yankee counterparts. When we consider property mobility, however, the roles of the two groups are reversed. In Table 5, which reveals ethnic differences in family mobility patterns, the occupational advantages of the native are again evident. But within the large group of laboring families whose members remained in unskilled and semiskilled jobs, the immigrants were notably more successful in ac-

TABLE 5
Mobility of Native-born and Foreign-born Laboring Families by Length of Residence

	Ten Years		Twenty Years		Thirty Years	
	Native	*Foreign*	*Native*	*Foreign*	*Native*	*Foreign*
Number in sample	36	109	27	74	16	25
High mobility	8%	8%	30%	18%	31%	32%
Intermediate mobility						
Occupational skill	8	7	15	4	38	20
Property						
$1,000 or more	8	18	4	24	6	16
$300–999	17	28	19	23	13	32
Static	58	38	33	31	13	0

cumulating property. Of those who had been in Newburyport for ten years nearly 60 percent of the native families but less than 40 percent of the foreign families failed to accumulate significant property holdings. Thirteen percent of the native families in residence for thirty years but none of the foreign families in this group were completely immobile in both the property and occupational hierarchies. In each of the three groups close to 50 percent of the immigrant families obtained a property stake in the community while remaining near the bottom of the occupational ladder; the comparable figure for native families was only half that.

That Irish working-class families were especially successful in accumulating property but especially unsuccessful in climbing out of the low-status manual occupations was hardly a coincidence. The immigrant laborer received wages no higher than those of the Yankee workman, but he had a greater determination to save and to own. Perhaps the land hunger displayed by the Irish laborers of Newburyport was a manifestation of older peasant values. In any case, it was a hunger which could be satisfied to a remarkable extent by even the lowliest laborer—but only at a price. The price was not only ruthless economy; equally necessary was the employment of every able-bodied member of the family at the earliest possible age. The cotton mill or the shoe factory was not to provide the teen-agers of the second generation with the education made increasingly necessary by a rapidly industrializing economy, as the exceptionally low mobility of Irish youths into nonmanual occupations so plainly reveals.

For the working-class families of nineteenth-century Newburyport, therefore, social mobility was not a cumulative process. The varying kinds of social advances made by laboring families were not complementary aspects of a smooth natural progression out of the working-class occupational world. Property mobility did not usually facilitate intergenerational occupational mobility; often it was achieved by sacrificing the education of the younger generation. Nor did the movement of a laboring father into a higher-status occupation seem to improve the career prospects of his children very much. The upward advances of these ordinary laboring families remain impressive, but the facile assumption of progress from generation to generation must be abandoned.

The Meaning of Mobility: A Trial Balance

If nineteenth-century Newburyport was to develop a permanent proletarian class, the families dealt with in this study should have
formed it. These unskilled workmen began at the very bottom of the
community occupational ladder in the 1850–1880 period. Their situation seemed anything but promising. They lacked both vocational
skills and financial resources. Many were illiterate, and few had the
means to see that their children received more than a primitive education. Most were relative strangers in the city, migrants from New
England farms or Irish villages. Few inhabitants of Newburyport at
mid-century were more likely candidates for membership in a per-
manently depressed caste.

That these working-class families did not remain in a uniformly
degraded social position throughout the 1850–1880 period is by now
abundantly clear. If the Newburyport laboring class gave birth to no
self-made millionaires during these years, the social advances registered by many of its members were nonetheless impressive. A brief
review of the findings on geographical, occupational, and property
mobility will clarify the significance of these social gains and provide
a fresh perspective on social stratification in the nineteenth-century
city.

By 1880 the undifferentiated mass of poverty-stricken laboring
families, the "lack-alls" who seemed at mid-century to be forming a
permanent class, had separated into three layers. On top was a small
but significant elite of laboring families who had gained a foothold in
the lower fringes of the middle-class occupational world. Below them
was the large body of families who had attained property mobility
while remaining in manual occupations, most often of the unskilled
or semiskilled variety; these families constituted the stable, respectable, home-owning stratum of the Newburyport working class. At the
very bottom of the social ladder was the impoverished, floating lower
class, large in number but so transient as to be formless and power-
less.

The composition of the Newburyport manual labor force in the
latter half of the nineteenth century, we have seen, was extraordinar-
ily volatile. A minority of the laboring families who came to the city

in those years settled for as long as a decade. Most did not, and it was these floating families whose depressed position most resembled the classic European proletariat. Recurrently unemployed, often on relief, they rarely accumulated property or advanced themselves occupationally. Substantial numbers of these impoverished unskilled workmen, men who "had no interest in the country except the interest of breathing," were always to be found in Newburyport during this period, but this stratum had remarkably little continuity of membership. Members of this floating group naturally had no capacity to act in concert against an employer or to assert themselves politically; stable organization based on a consciousness of common grievances was obviously impossible. The pressure to migrate operated selectively to remove the least successful from the community; a mere 5 percent of the laboring families present in Newburyport throughout this entire thirty-year period found both occupational mobility and property mobility beyond their grasp.

The floating laborers who made up this large, ever renewed transient class occupied the lowest social stratum in nineteenth-century Newburyport. A notch above it was the settled, property-owning sector of the working class; above that was the lower middle class, the highest social level attained by members of any of these laboring families. To obtain middle-class status required entry into a non-manual occupation and the adoption of a new style of life; this was an uncommon feat for either unskilled laborers or their children. Five-sixths of the laboring families resident in Newburyport for a decade or more during this period found the middle-class occupational world completely closed to them. And among the remaining sixth, the high mobility families, were many which remained partially dependent on manual employment for their support. It is doubtful that many of the elite high mobility families developed the attitudes and behavior patterns associated with the middle-class style of life. This seems particularly unlikely in the case of laborers who became the operators of small farms, whose sons rarely entered middle-class occupations. Nor did a marginal business or a menial clerkship necessarily provide the economic security and inspire the commitment to education needed to insure the transmission of middle-class status to the next generation. The importance of the small group of laborers and laborers' sons who purchased shops and farms or found white-collar jobs should not be minimized: these men did provide proof to their less successful brethren that class barriers could be hurdled by men of talent, however lowly their origin. But it should be emphasized that many of these upwardly mobile workmen obtained only a precarious hold on middle-class status, and that their social milieu often differed little from the milieu of the propertied sector of the working class.

By far the most common form of social advance for members of laboring families in Newburyport in this period was upward movement *within* the working class, mobility into the stratum between the lower middle class and the floating group of destitute unskilled families. A few men from these intermediate mobility families became skilled craftsmen; this was extremely rare for the older generation but less unusual as an intergenerational move. Most often, however, these families advanced themselves by accumulating significant amounts of property while remaining in unskilled or semiskilled occupations. Here were men who offered the market little more than two hands and a strong back, but who succeeded in becoming respectable home owners and savings bank depositors.

What was the social significance of these modest advances? Nineteenth-century propagandists took a simple view. The property-owning laborer was "a capitalist." If there was a working class in America, as soon as "a man has saved something he ceases to belong to this class"; "the laborers have become the capitalists in this new world." Accumulated funds, however small, were capital, and the possession of capital determined the psychological orientation of the workman. It was the nature of capital to multiply itself; he who possessed capital necessarily hungered for further expansion of his holdings. To save and to invest was the first step in the process of mobility; investment inspired a risk-taking, speculative mentality conducive to further mobility. The distinction between the "petty capitalist" workman and the rich merchant was one of degree. To move from the former status to the latter was natural; it happened "every day." Similar assumptions lie behind the still-popular view that "the typical American worker" has been "an expectant entrepreneur."

This was sheer fantasy. A mere handful of the property-owning laborers of Newburyport ventured into business for themselves. More surprising, the property mobility of a laboring man did not even heighten his children's prospects for mobility into a business or professional calling. Indeed, the working-class family which abided by the injunction "spend less than you earn" could usually do so only by sacrificing the children's education for an extra paycheck, and thereby restricting their opportunities for intergenerational occupational mobility.

Furthermore, the use these laborers made of their savings testifies to their search for maximum security rather than for mobility out of the working class. An economically rational investor in nineteenth-century Newburyport would not have let his precious stock of capital languish in a savings bank for long, and he certainly would not have tied it up in the kind of real estate purchased by these laborers. The social environment of the middle-class American encouraged such investment for rising profits, but the working-class milieu did not. The earning capacity of the merchant, professional, or entrepreneur rose steadily as his career unfolded—the very term "career" connotes this. The middle-class family head was ordinarily its sole source of support, and the family was able both to accumulate wealth and to improve its standard of living out of normal increments in the salary (or net profits) accruing to him over the years.

Ordinary workmen did not have "careers" in this sense. Their earning capacity did not increase with age; in unskilled and semi-skilled occupations a forty-year-old man was paid no more than a boy of seventeen. Substantial saving by a working-class family thus tended to be confined to the years when the children were old enough to bring in a supplementary income but too young to have married and established households of their own.

The tiny lots, the humble homes, and the painfully accumulated savings accounts were the fruits of those years. They gave a man dignity, and a slender margin of security against unpredictable, uncontrollable economic forces which could deprive him of his job at any time. Once the mortgage was finally discharged, home ownership reduced the family's necessary expenses by $60 to $100 a year, and a few hundred dollars in the savings bank meant some protection against illness, old age, or a sluggish labor market. A cynical observer would have noted the possibility that home ownership served also to confine the workman to the local labor market and to strengthen the hand of local employers, who were thus assured of a docile permanent work force, but few laborers of nineteenth-century Newburyport were disposed to think in these terms.

Families belonging to the propertied stratum of the working class, in short, were socially mobile in the sense that they had climbed a rung higher on the social ladder, and had established themselves as decent, respectable, hard-working, churchgoing members of the community. They had not, however, set their feet upon an escalator which was to draw them up into the class of merchants, professionals, and entrepreneurs.

The contrast between the literal claims of the rags-to-riches mythology and the actual social experience of these families thus appears glaring. A few dozen farmers, small shopkeepers, and clerks, a large body of home-owning families unable to escape a grinding regimen of manual labor: this was the sum of the social mobility achieved by Newburyport's unskilled laborers by 1880. Could men like these have felt that the mobility ideology was at all relevant to their lives?

I think so. True, many of the optimistic assertions of popular writers and speakers were demonstrably false. Class differences in opportunities were deep and pervasive; a large majority of the unskilled laborers in Newburyport and a large majority of their sons remained in the working class throughout the 1850–1880 period. Not one rose from rags to genuine riches. Whoever seeks a Newburyport version of Andrew Carnegie must settle for Joseph Greenough, keeper of a livery stable worth $15,000, and Stephen Fowle, proprietor of a small newsstand. But we err if we take the mobility creed too literally. The rapt attention nineteenth-century Americans gave Russell Conwell did not mean that his listeners literally believed that they soon would acquire riches equivalent to "an acre of diamonds." One ingredient of the appeal of mobility literature and oratory was that pleasant fantasies of sudden wealth and a vicarious sharing in the spectacular successes of other ordinary men provided a means of escaping the tedious realities of daily existence. Fantasies of this sort are not likely to flourish among men who have no hope at all of individual economic or social betterment. And indeed the laborers of Newburyport had abundant evidence that self-improvement was possible. To practice the virtues exalted by the mobility creed rarely brought middle-class status to the laborer, or even to his children. But hard work and incessant economy did bring tangible rewards—money in the bank, a house to call his own, a new sense of security and dignity. "The man who owns the roof that is over his head and the earth under his dwelling can't help thinking that he's more of a man than though he had nothing, with poverty upon his back and want at home; and if he don't think so, other people will."

The ordinary workmen of Newburyport, in short, could view America as a land of opportunity despite the fact that the class realities which governed their life chances confined most of them to the working class. These newcomers to urban life arrived with a low horizon of expectations, it seems likely. If it is true that "in the last analysis the status of the worker is not a physical but a mental one, and is affected as much by comparisons with past conditions and with the status of other groups in the community as by the facts in themselves," the typical unskilled laborer who settled in New-buryport could feel proud of his achievements and optimistic about the future. Most of the social gains registered by laborers and their sons during these years were decidedly modest—a move one notch up the occupational scale, the acquisition of a small amount of property. Yet *in their eyes* these accomplishments must have loomed large. The contradiction between an ideology of limitless oppor-tunity and the realities of working-class existence is unlikely to have dismayed men whose aspirations and expectations were shaped in the Irish village or the New England subsistence farm. The "dream of success" certainly affected these laboring families, but the per-sonal measure of success was modest. By this measure, the great majority of them had indeed "gotten ahead."

Alwyn Barr

OCCUPATIONAL AND GEOGRAPHICAL MOBILITY IN SAN ANTONIO

Adding to the value of Alwyn Barr's study of social mobility is its focus on the Southwest, a region whose social patterns have not been heavily re-searched by scholars. Together with the essays by Herbert G. Gutman and Stephan Thernstrom and the work done by Carolyn T. and Gordon W. Kirk,

From Alwyn Barr, "Occupational and Geographic Mobility in San Antonio, 1870–1900," *Social Science Quarterly* 51 (September 1970): 396–403. Reprinted by permis-sion of author and publisher. Footnotes deleted.

Jr., on Holland, Michigan, Howard Chudacoff on Omaha, and Richard J. Hopkins on Atlanta, it helps piece together an invaluable mosaic on the mobility patterns of small, and therefore representative, American cities in the late nineteenth century.

In recent years a few historians have begun to test the validity of the popular assumption that extensive socioeconomic mobility has existed in the United States throughout its history. From the limited number of studies now available it appears that great geographical mobility existed in the nineteenth century, especially at the lowest levels of society. It also seems that most persons remained in the same occupational class throughout their lives, but that few fell below their original class status, while a larger number advanced within their class or to a higher one—especially from the working class to the middle class. Only one study has been conducted of a Southern city, Atlanta, with a smaller immigrant and larger Negro population than in most urban areas. It produced similar findings for native whites and immigrants, but indicated little upward mobility and less geographic mobility for Negroes.

Additional mobility studies seem warranted simply because "The evidence available today is regrettably scanty." San Antonio, Texas, appears particularly attractive as the subject for such consideration because it provides the possibility of comparing not only native white, immigrant and Negro mobility, but also that of Mexican-Americans in the Southwest, an area not yet represented in the existing studies. In the period from 1870 to 1900 San Antonio grew from a population of 12,256 to 53,321. It served as the major shipping point for the cattle and sheep industries and for imported goods in southwest Texas. For Sam Houston, a permanent Army post, also contributed to the local economy.

Method

To determine mobility from 1870 to 1900 a basic sample of every fourth male wage earner for each ethnic group was taken from the manuscript returns of the United States Census of 1870 for San Antonio. This produces samples of 156 native whites, 296 European immigrants, 189 Mexican-Americans, and 129 Negroes. These groups were then divided into seven occupational-status categories: unskilled, semiskilled, skilled, sales and clerical, proprietorial, managerial, and professional. After the job categories were further divided into age groups, the number in each category for the 1870 sample who remained in 1880, 1890, and 1900 was tabulated. For that purpose the San Antonio city directories for 1879–1880, 1881–1882, 1889–1890, 1891, 1897–1898, and 1899–1900 were used. The resulting statistics appear in Table 1.

To delineate career occupational mobility the job categories were then divided into manual (unskilled, semiskilled, and skilled) and nonmanual (sales and clerical, proprietorial, managerial, and professional) classes. A member of the manual class gave evidence of upward mobility by advancement to the skilled category from the unskilled or semiskilled or into the nonmanual class. A fall from the skilled into the semiskilled or unskilled categories showed downward mobility. For the nonmanual class a rise from the sales and clerical to other nonmanual categories represented upward mobility. A move from the proprietorial, managerial, or professional to the sales and clerical category or from the nonmanual to the manual class indicated downward mobility. Table 2 shows the percentages of occupational mobility for both classes.

Geographical mobility is suggested by the persistence rate, or percentage, of individuals in the job categories for the 1870 sample who reappear in 1880, 1890, or 1900. These persistence rates are shown in Table 3.

Findings

An analysis of the tables indicates that, as in Atlanta, the unskilled in 1870 formed a higher percentage among Negroes (67 percent) than in any other group. Unskilled Mexican-Americans barely trailed at 61 percent, however, followed by unskilled native whites (24 percent) and European immigrants (21 percent). Since most of the remaining Negroes fell into the semiskilled (11 percent) and skilled (18 percent) categories, 96 percent of all Negro wage earners in San Antonio could be classified as manual laborers. Mexican-Americans again followed closely with 90 percent manual laborers (14 percent semiskilled and 15 percent skilled), while 69 percent of the European immigrants (11 percent semiskilled and 37 percent skilled) and 61 percent of the native whites (7 percent semiskilled and 30 percent skilled) could be placed in that class. European immigrants, because they formed the largest single ethnic group, dominated the skilled category even more than the percentages indicate, for they provided 53 percent of all skilled laborers in San Antonio. Thirty-nine percent of native whites fell in the nonmanual class, followed by European immigrants with 31 percent, Mexican-Americans with 10 percent, and Negroes with 4 percent. Yet the European immigrants, because of their numbers, provided a larger group of nonmanual workers (92) than the other three groups combined (84). European immigrants also included the highest percentage of persons in the proprietorial, managerial, and professional categories (23 percent, compared to 21 percent for native whites, 8 percent for Mexican-Americans, and 4 percent for Negroes).

Occupational mobility statistics indicate that of those remaining in 1880, 26 percent of the European immigrants, 24 percent of the native whites, 17 percent of the Mexican-Americans, and 9 percent of the Negroes classified as manual laborers in 1870 had shown some significant degree of upward mobility. In the same period only 3 percent of the remaining European immigrants, 4 percent of the remaining Negroes, and 6 percent of the remaining Mexican-Americans in the manual class had suffered downward mobility. Of those in the manual class of 1880 who remained in 1890 native whites led with 25 percent upwardly mobile, compared to 21 percent for European immigrants, 19 percent for Mexican-Americans, and 13 percent for Negroes. At the same time remaining Mexican-Americans showed 5 percent downward mobility in the manual class, remaining Negroes and native whites 6 percent, and remaining European immigrants 7 percent. Of those in the manual class of 1890 who remained in 1900 native whites evinced no upward mobility while European immigrants led with 19 percent, followed by Mexican-Americans with 14 percent, and Negroes with 7 percent. During that time remaining Negroes in the manual class suffered 4 percent downward mobility while remaining Mexican-Americans showed 5 percent. For the entire thirty-year period European immigrants in the manual class had the highest rate of upward mobility with an average of 19 percent, followed by native whites with 14 percent, Mexican-Americans with 11 percent, and Negroes with 5 percent.

Figures for nonmanual workers of 1870 who remained in 1880 indicate 12 percent upward mobility among native whites offset by

TABLE 1
Population Samples

Occupational Category	Base Year	Remaining in Year	Native-Born Whites Age						European Immigrants Age					
			20 & under	21–39	40–49	50–59	60 & over	Total	20 & under	21–39	40–49	50–59	60 & over	Total
Unskilled	1870		17	14	4	—	2	37	9	21	11	13	7	61
		1880	2	1	—	—	—	3	1	3	5	1	1	11
		1890	—	1	—	—	—	1	—	1	1	1	—	3
		1900	—	1	—	—	—	1	—	—	1	—	2	1
Semiskilled	1870		2	5	2	2	—	11	2	15	8	6	2	33
		1880	1	5	2	—	—	8	1	6	4	2	—	13
		1890	—	2	2	—	—	4	—	3	4	1	—	8
		1900	—	2	2	—	—	4	1	1	1	—	—	3
Skilled	1870		19	12	12	4	0	47	4	52	29	19	6	110
		1880	8	5	4	1	—	18	3	16	12	7	3	41
		1890	6	4	1	1	—	12	1	12	11	2	1	27
		1900	6	4	1	1	—	12	1	7	5	2	1	16
Sales and clerical	1870		14	10	3	1	—	28	4	16	2	2	—	24
		1880	—	3	—	—	—	3	2	5	2	—	—	9
		1890	—	2	—	—	—	2	2	4	2	1	—	9
		1900	—	3	—	—	—	3	3	2	3	—	—	8
Proprietorial	1870		—	7	4	2	1	14	—	11	14	7	4	36
		1880	4	4	4	1	—	13	1	5	8	6	1	21
		1890	6	3	3	1	—	13	1	3	6	1	1	12
		1900	6	1	3	—	—	10	—	6	3	—	—	9

Mexican-Americans / Negroes — Occupational persistence (continued from preceding page)

Occupational Category	Base Year	Remaining in Year	Mexican-Americans Age 20 & under	21–39	40–49	50–59	60 & over	Total	Negroes Age 20 & under	21–39	40–49	50–59	60 & over	Total
Managerial	1870		—	4	4	—	—	8	—	7	1	5	1	14
		1880	—	1	2	1	—	4	—	7	—	1	—	8
		1890	—	3	2	—	—	5	1	6	—	—	—	7
		1900	—	1	1	—	—	2	—	5	2	—	—	7
Professional	1870		—	7	3	—	1	11	4	10	—	3	1	18
		1880	—	3	2	—	—	5	—	4	—	1	—	5
		1890	—	2	2	—	—	4	—	2	—	1	—	3
		1900	—	2	2	—	—	4	—	2	—	—	—	2
Total	*1870*		*52*	*59*	*32*	*9*	*4*	*156*	*19*	*132*	*69*	*55*	*21*	*296*
		1880	*16*	*20*	*16*	*2*	*—*	*54*	*8*	*46*	*31*	*18*	*5*	*108*
		1890	*12*	*17*	*10*	*2*	*—*	*41*	*5*	*31*	*24*	*7*	*2*	*69*
		1900	*12*	*14*	*9*	*1*	*—*	*36*	*5*	*23*	*15*	*2*	*1*	*46*

Occupational Category	Base Year	Remaining in Year	Mexican-Americans Age 20 & under	21–39	40–49	50–59	60 & over	Total	Negroes Age 20 & under	21–39	40–49	50–59	60 & over	Total
Unskilled	1870		29	45	15	13	13	115	24	44	12	4	3	87
		1880	2	9	3	1	1	16	4	18	4	3	2	31
		1890	1	10	2	—	—	13	3	15	3	2	—	23
		1900	2	5	1	—	—	8	5	10	1	2	—	18
Semiskilled	1870		5	13	6	2	1	27	2	8	3	1	—	14
		1880	2	2	2	—	—	6	3	4	—	2	—	9
		1890	1	1	1	—	—	3	3	3	—	1	—	7
		1900	—	1	1	—	—	2	1	4	—	—	—	5

(Continued)

TABLE 1 (cont.)
Population Samples

Occupational Category	Base Year	Remaining in Year	Mexican-Americans Age						Negroes Age					
			20 & under	21–39	40–49	50–59	60 & over	Total	20 & under	21–39	40–49	50–59	60 & over	Total
Skilled	1870		7	12	6	4	—	29	3	11	5	3	1	23
		1880	2	3	1	1	—	7	2	1	2	—	—	5
		1890	3	3	1	—	—	7	1	1	—	—	—	2
		1900	2	4	2	—	—	8	—	2	—	—	—	2
Sales and clerical	1870		1	1	1	1	—	4	—	—	—	—	—	—
		1880	1	—	—	—	—	1	—	—	—	—	—	—
		1890	—	—	—	—	—	—	—	—	—	—	—	—
		1900	—	—	—	—	—	—	—	—	—	—	—	—
Proprietorial	1870		—	6	3	2	1	12	—	3	—	—	—	3
		1880	—	4	—	—	—	4	—	—	—	—	—	—
		1890	1	—	1	—	—	2	—	—	—	—	—	—
		1900	1	1	1	—	—	3	—	—	—	—	—	—
Managerial	1870		—	—	—	—	—	—	—	—	—	—	—	—
		1880	1	—	—	—	—	1	—	—	—	—	—	—
		1890	—	2	1	—	—	3	—	—	—	—	—	—
		1900	—	1	1	—	—	2	—	—	—	—	—	—
Professional	1870		—	—	—	—	—	—	—	1	—	1	—	2
		1880	—	2	—	—	—	2	1	1	—	—	—	2
		1890	—	2	—	—	—	2	1	—	—	—	—	1
		1900	1	—	1	—	—	2	1	1	—	—	—	2
Total	*1870*		*42*	*77*	*32*	*22*	*16*	*189*	*29*	*67*	*20*	*9*	*4*	*129*
		1880	*7*	*20*	*6*	*2*	*1*	*37*	*10*	*24*	*6*	*5*	*2*	*47*
		1890	*6*	*18*	*6*	*—*	*—*	*30*	*8*	*19*	*3*	*3*	*—*	*33*
		1900	*6*	*12*	*5*	*—*	*—*	*23*	*7*	*17*	*1*	*2*	*—*	*27*

TABLE 2
Occupational Mobility in Percentages

	Manual Laborers				Nonmanual Workers			
	Native whites	European immigrants	Mexican-Americans	Negroes	Native whites	European immigrants	Mexican-Americans	Negroes
1870–1880								
Upward mobility	24	26	17	9	12	—	—	—
No significant mobility	76	71	77	87	76	98	87	100
Downward mobility	—	3	6	4	12	2	13	—
Total Percent	100	100	100	100	100	100	100	100
(N)	(29)	(65)	(29)	(45)	(25)	(43)	(8)	(2)
1870–1890								
Upward mobility	25	21	19	13	4	4	—	—
No significant mobility	69	72	76	81	92	83	49	50
Downward mobility	6	7	5	6	4	13	51	50
Total Percent	100	100	100	100	100	100	100	100
(N)	(17)	(38)	(23)	(32)	(24)	(31)	(7)	(2)
1870–1900								
Upward mobility	—	19	14	7	—	—	20	—
No significant mobility	100	81	81	89	94	96	80	100
Downward mobility	—	—	5	4	6	4	—	—
Total Percent	100	100	100	100	100	100	100	100
(N)	(17)	(20)	(18)	(25)	(17)	(26)	(5)	(2)

TABLE 3
Persistence Rates for 1870 Occupations in Percentages[a]

Occupational Category	Native Whites		European Americans		Mexican Americans		Negroes	
1870–1880								
Unskilled	8	(37)	15	(61)	14	(115)	36	(87)
Semiskilled	73	(11)	39	(33)	22	(27)	64	(14)
Skilled	38	(47)	37	(110)	24	(29)	22	(23)
Sales and clerical	12	(28)	37	(24)	25	(4)	—	(—)
Proprietorial	93	(14)	58	(36)	33	(12)	—	(3)
Managerial	50	(8)	57	(14)	200	(—)	—	(—)
Professional	46	(11)	28	(18)	100	(2)	100	(2)
(Total Sample)		(156)		(296)		(189)		(129)
1880–1890								
Unskilled	33	(3)	27	(11)	81	(16)	74	(31)
Semiskilled	50	(8)	61	(13)	50	(6)	78	(9)
Skilled	67	(18)	66	(41)	100	(7)	40	(5)
Sales and clerical	67	(3)	100	(9)	—	(1)	—	(—)
Proprietorial	100	(13)	52	(21)	50	(4)	—	(—)
Managerial	123	(4)	88	(8)	300	(1)	—	(—)
Professional	80	(5)	60	(5)	100	(2)	50	(2)
(Total Sample)		(54)		(108)		(37)		(47)
1890–1900								
Unskilled	100	(1)	—	(3)	61	(13)	78	(23)
Semiskilled	100	(4)	38	(8)	67	(3)	71	(7)
Skilled	92	(12)	59	(27)	114	(7)	100	(2)
Sales and clerical	150	(2)	89	(9)	—	(—)	—	(—)
Proprietorial	77	(13)	75	(12)	150	(2)	—	(—)
Managerial	40	(5)	100	(7)	67	(3)	—	(—)
Professional	100	(4)	67	(3)		(2)	200	(1)
(Total Sample)		(41)		(69)		(30)		(33)
1870–1900								
Unskilled	3	(37)	—	(61)	7	(115)	21	(87)
Semiskilled	36	(11)	9	(33)	7	(27)	34	(14)
Skilled	26	(47)	15	(110)	28	(29)	9	(23)
Sales and clerical	12	(28)	33	(24)	—	(4)	—	(—)
Proprietorial	71	(14)	25	(36)	25	(12)	—	(3)
Managerial	25	(8)	50	(14)	200	(—)	—	(—)
Professional	36	(11)	11	(18)	—	(2)	100	(2)
(Total Sample)		(156)		(296)		(189)		(129)

[a] N's in parentheses.

12 percent downward mobility for the same group, while European immigrants suffered 2 percent downward mobility and Mexican-Americans 13 percent. Of those in the nonmanual class in 1880 who remained in 1890 native whites and European immigrants showed 4 percent upward mobility, offset by 4 percent downward mobility for native whites and 13 percent for European immigrants. In the same period remaining Negroes suffered 50 percent downward mobility and remaining Mexican-Americans 51 percent. Of those in the non-manual class in 1890 who remained in 1900 Mexican-Americans evinced 20 percent upward mobility, while European immigrants showed 4 percent downward mobility and native whites 6 percent. For the thirty-year period each group suffered overall downward mobility ranging from a 2 percent average for native whites to 5 percent for European immigrants, 14 percent for Mexican-Americans, and 17 percent for Negroes. Unlike Atlanta, the European immigrant manual laborers in San Antonio achieved greater upward mobility than native whites, though both groups ranked ahead of Mexican-Americans and Negroes. Thus it appears that race played an important role in the socioeconomic mobility of those in the manual labor class which included large numbers of Mexican-Americans and Negroes. But in the nonmanual class that contained few members of those groups, nativity of whites apparently played a greater role since European immigrants suffered greater downward mobility than native whites. Yet European immigrants in San Antonio achieved occupational and mobility rates virtually equal to those of native whites. Their larger proportion in San Antonio's overall population may in part account for their better position in comparison to their immigrant counterparts in Atlanta. Yet their success seems to bear out the conclusion that European immigrants could expect more favorable occupational opportunities in areas such as the South or Southwest where far more distinctive ethnic minorities formed a laboring-class base and served as focal points for racial prejudice. The number of immigrants in a city seemed to have had little impact on racial prejudice, since they formed the largest single group in San Antonio and the smallest in Atlanta.

The geographical mobility statistics in Table 3, without considering the impact of mortality rates, indicate an exodus of 50 percent or more in most occupational categories during the 1870s, with the lowest persistence rate among unskilled laborers. Persistence rates increased, not only among skilled manual laborers and nonmanual workers but also with each succeeding decade. This suggests that once established in San Antonio individuals tended to be much less likely to leave. By projecting the available mortality rates for 1890 and 1900 (about 2.5 percent for whites and 2.3 percent for Negroes) back to 1870, European immigrants showed the highest persistence rate in 1880 (47 percent), compared to 46 percent for native whites and Negroes, and 25 percent for Mexican-Americans. By projecting these mortality rates over the entire thirty-year period native whites showed a persistence rate of 49 percent, Negroes 44 percent, European immigrants 33 percent, and Mexican-Americans 26 percent. These figures again support two findings from the Atlanta study. First, men who had moved from one nation to another—all European immigrants and two-thirds of the Mexican-Americans—showed a greater willingness to move once more. Second, Negroes showed a high persistence rather than the high rate of instability attributed to them by some historians of the postwar period.

Conclusions

This study of occupational and geographical mobility in San Antonio for 1870–1900 seems to reinforce the developing concept of extensive geographical mobility in the late nineteenth-century United States, especially at the lowest levels of society. Yet it also supports the view that Negroes showed less urge to migrate than most of their white counterparts. San Antonio statistics in addition lend support for the idea that most Americans remained in the same occupational class throughout their lives, but that more showed upward rather than downward mobility in the manual labor class. The study again suggests that Negroes provided a marked variation, however, with their extremely limited rate of upward mobility. Moreover it suggests that Mexican-Americans also fell significantly below the native white and European immigrant rates of upward mobility though above that for Negroes. Finally figures for San Antonio reinforce the view that the presence of more distinct ethnic groups such as Negroes and Mexican-Americans apparently enhanced the chances for occupational advance by European immigrants and reduced the level of prejudice against them.

Along with the existence of its Mexican-American population San

Antonio differed from Atlanta in two other ways. First, European immigrants achieved occupational and mobility levels equal to native whites and numerically dominated some occupational categories at least in part because they formed the largest group in the San Antonio population. Thus European immigrants in the city showed a clear if limited advantage over their counterparts in Atlanta. Second, Mexican-Americans and Negroes both achieved slightly higher occupational and mobility levels than Negroes in Atlanta. Because the two groups represented only about 36 percent of the San Antonio population, while Negroes formed 46 percent of the Atlanta population, their advantages lend at least limited support to the assumption that employment and advancement problems for these minority groups in the United States increase in proportion to their percentage of the population in a given area.

Frances W. Gregory and Irene D. Neu

THE INDUSTRIAL ELITE OF THE 1870s: THEIR SOCIAL ORIGINS

For a long time social mobility studies seemed to mean studies of the social origins of successful businessmen. The following essay is one of the most comprehensive and accessible examples of this kind of research. Choosing their population from the top leadership of the textile, steel, and railroad industries, Gregory and Neu trace the backgrounds of the men who held leadership positions immediately after the Civil War—that time when an industrial revolution had truly transformed the American economy. Their findings were starkly clear: the business elite of the 1870s were born into great advantages.

Despite the importance of business in the United States, as elsewhere, the social origins of business leaders, the social sources of

Frances W. Gregory and Irene D. Neu, "The American Industrial Elite in the 1870s: Their Social Origins," pp. 193–204. Footnotes deleted. Reprinted by permission of the publishers from William Miller, *Men and Business: Essays in the Historical Role of the Entrepreneur,* Cambridge, Mass.: Harvard University Press. Copyright, 1952, by the President and Fellows of Harvard College.

business leadership, have received but little attention from scholars. A few biographies and autobiographies have tended to point up the spectacular and the unusual, with the result that the origins of a handful have been attributed to the many, though the grounds of attribution have remained vague. What have been the actual origins of American business leaders? And what have been the consequences, for the business community and for society at large, of the actual process of recruitment? These are questions of great magnitude and are not to be resolved by the findings of a single study. It is felt, however, that the information presented [here] is a contribution toward the eventual answers.

The characteristics of the industrial leader in the United States, as tradition had sketched him, reflect the idealism of the American heritage. Specifically, his was the Carnegie story. A poor immigrant boy arrived on the shores of a new nation which abounded in endless opportunity. As the boy was the son of a workingman, he had little or no formal education and was forced by circumstances to seek employment at a tender age. His first job was a lowly one, but in short order he rose to prominence, usually as a result of cleverness, diligence, or luck. In this manner, the top-level businessman was but a generation removed from poverty and anonymity.

This story was not unheard of before the golden age of American industrial expansion that followed the Civil War. It was already frequently told in the early decades of the nineteenth century when the merchant was at the apex of the business ladder. It is the theme of the short biography of Amos Lawrence, suggestively entitled *The Poor Boy and Merchant Prince.* Nathan Appleton, the Boston textile magnate and backer of Webster, also voiced this thesis of freedom of ascent to financial success and industrial prominence, and always projected himself, indeed with more or less accuracy, as an example of this fluidity of social and economic structure. It was only with the appearance on the American scene of such businessmen as Carnegie, Vanderbilt, and Rockefeller, however, that this thesis found its major exemplars, and in the history books and biographies of succeeding generations their lives continue to be used to buttress the tradition.

Only within the last twenty years has this tradition been seriously questioned. F. W. Taussig and C. S. Joslyn in *American Business Leaders: A Study in Social Origins and Social Stratification,* published in 1932, cast doubt upon the widely held belief in the easy ascent of the poor boy to business prestige and financial power. They showed that the way was considerably more accessible to the sons of the middle and upper classes, and advanced the hypothesis that the absence of representation of the lower classes among business leaders was chiefly the result of a lack of innate ability not lack of opportunity. Studies of this subject by other scholars have appeared from time to time in learned journals. For the most part, these have been concerned with but small groups of businessmen or with but one or two characteristics of larger groups, and their value has been limited for these reasons.

Recently William Miller published two essays in which he analyzed the backgrounds of 190 American business leaders of the first decade of the twentieth century and compared their social characteristics with those of the population generally. In these essays he set forth the conclusion that the men who held the top positions—essentially presidencies or board chairmanships—in the largest industrial and financial institutions in the United States during this period were recruited, in great part, from a highly select segment of the population. Typical of these magnates in the early twentieth century was the son of a professional or business man of colonial American heritage, born in some American city or town of more than 2,500 persons. This executive very likely had attended high school and had had a 40 percent chance of reaching college. Moreover, he certainly was over sixteen and was likely to be over nineteen before going to work. In all probability, he was a member of the middle or upper class. Unlike Taussig and Joslyn, who offer no acceptable evidence for their thesis of innate ability among the business elite, Miller presents verifiable data to support his contention that certain social characteristics marked a man as good material for the leading business positions.

These findings prompted the Research Center in Entrepreneurial History at Harvard University to conduct an investigation into the origins of a group of business leaders of an earlier period and to compare the findings with Miller's for the period 1901–1910. This is the first report of that investigation.

II

At the outset it was decided that the period for study should be the decade 1870–1879, one recent enough to assure adequate biographical information for a considerable number of men, yet not too close to that of 1901–1910 for purposes of comparison and contrast. To keep the number of business leaders within manageable limits, men were chosen from three major fields only: textiles, steel, and railroads. Textiles and steel were selected because the first was the oldest large-scale industry in America and the second was then the newest. Railroads were an obvious choice for they represented by far the largest agglomeration of capital in the period.

Once these three industries had been decided upon, the next step was to ascertain the key top jobs in the major companies. In textiles the treasurer and agent of each establishment were used. The treasurer was the chief executive officer and had charge of the financial end of the business, including the purchase of cotton from the South. The agent was the local authority on the job and supervised the construction of the factory, the manufacture of cloth, and the employment of labor. In steel corporations the top men were taken to be the president, the vice-president, and the general manager or superintendent. This industry, however, was still organized largely on a partnership basis, and since there was no general way of determining the relative interests of the several partners in an establishment, all known partners were included. The top men in the railroads were taken to be presidents, vice-presidents, and general managers.

The men in textiles represented all cotton manufacturing concerns having an authorized capital of more than $1 million and a spindlage of at least 70,000; all wool manufacturing companies with an authorized capital of $600,000 or more and at least 49 sets of cards; and the single American silk company which had a capital of $1 million. The men in steel covered all eleven Bessemer and all fifteen open-hearth plants in the United States in 1878, as well as the six crucible plants which produced 10,000 tons or more that year, or were attached to ironworks having a combined production of iron and steel in excess of 10,000 tons. The railroaders represented all companies in their field capitalized in excess of $24 million and having construction and equipment accounts in excess of $38 million, according to the census of 1880.

In all, seventy-seven companies supplied men for the list. These were the thirty largest textile companies, the thirty largest steel manufacturers, and the seventeen largest railroads in the country. The names of the leaders themselves were found, for the most part, in industrial directories. The final aggregate of 303 men includes 102 from textiles, 100 from steel, and 101 from railroads. No men known to have held the positions named above in any of these companies were omitted from the list, though, of course, for some not all the information sought could be found. . . .

III

Though the men with whom this study is concerned were all industrialists and represented but three industries in an economy which was already highly diversified, these three industries were among the four largest in the United States. Since the results of this study will be compared with Miller's for the period 1901–1910, other things should also be noted here. While about 20 percent of Miller's men were bankers and life insurance executives, and an additional 15 percent were in public utilities, these activities are represented in the present study only by executives who were also in textiles, steel, or railroads. Further, it must be remembered that Miller writes largely of the bureaucratic business hierarchies which had become common by 1910, while the present essay is concerned with an age when even some of the topmost companies were still organized as family concerns. This certainly was largely the case in steel but much less so in textiles in which most firms were already incorporated and career lines of a professional, managerial type could be found. A bureaucracy, it is true, was emerging in railroads by the 1870s but even here its organization was far from complete.

Whether bureaucrats or family-made men or general entrepreneurs, however, it is clear that the men both in Miller's sample and our own were among the topmost business leaders of their time.

IV

The businessmen in Miller's group, averaging approximately fifty years of age in 1900, were considerably younger than men in similar positions today. The men of the 1870s, in turn, were younger still; their average age, brought down, to be sure, by the sizable representation of men other than those at the very top, was 45. But even these men were already in the prime of life, nor had they, as the tradition would have it, spent much of their time in becoming accustomed to a strange culture in a strange land. Some, of course, like English-born John Fallon in textiles, and Scotsman Thomas Carnegie in steel, were born abroad. That these men, however, were exceptional, not typical, among the industrial elite of the 1870s, as among the business leaders of the later decade, Table 1 attests.

Besides Fallon, five other textile men are known to have been born abroad. Two were the Cumnock brothers (a third brother was born in America) whose father, a freeholder of Glasgow, was "a man

TABLE 1
American Industrial Leaders of the 1870s by Industry and Region of Birthplace[a]

Birthplace	Textiles	Railroads	Steel	Total	Miller Totals[b] (1901–1910)
New England	90%	39%	24%	51%	18%
Middle Atlantic	1	40	50	29	37
East North Central	1	4	7	4	22
South	1	6	1	3	9
West	—	1	—	1	4
U. S., unspecified	—	—	4	2	—
United States	93%	90%	86%	90%	90%
Foreign	7	10	14	10	10
Total Cases[c] (= 100%)	87	80	80	247	187

[a] These are census regions. Combined in "South" are south Atlantic, south central, west south central; in "West" west north central, mountain, Pacific.
[b] Statistics in this column, in all the tables, are taken from Miller's "American Historians and the Business Elite," unless otherwise credited.
[c] As stated in the text, the total number of men in the 1870s group is 303: 102 in textiles, 101 in railroads, and 100 in steel. The number in the Miller group is 190. In this and all succeeding tables where total cases are fewer than just stated, the difference indicates the number of men about whom information was unavailable.

of fair estate." Andrew F. Swapp, another immigrant, like Fallon, was from a working-class family. Of all those born abroad, only Alexander G. Cumnock ever reached the treasurership and he, of a company too small to be included in this study. The others were agents only. In steel, ten men in addition to Carnegie were born outside the United States. At least six of these—the three Chisholms, Reginald H. Bulley, William Butcher, and Otto Wuth—appear to have come from substantial middle-class backgrounds. In the railroad group there is not a single instance of a "poor immigrant" working his way up the ladder. Of the eight men known to have been born in foreign countries, Jacob D. Cox, John Murray Forbes, and Azariah Boody were the children of American parents and therefore could hardly be called "immigrants." Of the five men who may properly be so labeled, James B. Hodgskin, James McHenry, and Gustavus A. Nicolls were the sons of well-established professional men, Alexander Mitchell was the son of a "well-to-do" farmer, and Peter H. Watson apparently had been trained in the law before the time at which he arrived in the United States, after having been forced to leave Canada for his part in the rebellion of 1837.

Not only were few of these business leaders immigrants; but few were the sons of immigrants. Of the native-born in the group about whom information is available, only 3 percent were the sons of foreign-born fathers.

It would seem, therefore, that the top-level leadership in American industry in the 1870s, as in the 1900s, was native-born and of native families. Indeed, the immigrant ancestors of these families, in all likelihood, had come over to America in the seventeenth century. Not John Fallon, therefore, who came to this country as an expert in calico-printing, but George Atkinson, Edmund Dwight, or Augustus Lowell, men born in New England whose fathers and grandfathers were also born there, would seem to be characteristic of the topmost men in textiles. In steel the typical leader was not Thomas Carnegie, but such a man as James I. Bennett or William Sellers, both born in Pennsylvania to fathers who were native Pennsylvanians. A typical railroader might be John H. Devereux, who was born in Boston, and whose father was a native of Massachusetts; or Charles E. Perkins, who was born in Cincinnati of New England parents and whose relatives were still prominent Bostonians.

Perkins's history, moreover, illustrates the shift in the geographic origins of American business leaders away from storied New England, a shift that took place, perhaps, a good deal earlier than has commonly been supposed. By the 1900s, indeed, as Miller's totals show (see Table 1), fewer than two in ten of the men studied were themselves born in New England; more striking, fewer than three in ten of their fathers had been born there (Table 2). For the 1870s, of course, the proportions of New Englanders are considerably greater; but even so, including the almost 100 percent representation of the textile sample, about half the whole group was born there; and of those not in the textile group, considerably less than half had New England-born fathers.

The decline of New England as a source of business leadership is paralleled by the falling off between the 1870s and the 1900s in men of British but especially of English origins. Even so, such men continued to be represented at the top of American business far out of proportion to their representation in the population generally.

Most of the leaders of the 1870s had been reared in a period of religious ferment and fragmentation of some of the older established

TABLE 2
American-born Industrial Leaders of the 1870s by Industry and Region of Father's Birthplace

Father's Birthplace	Textiles	Railroads	Steel	Total	Miller Totals[a] (1901–1910)
New England	98%	49%	36%	65%	29%
Middle Atlantic	1	32	42	22	34
East North Central	—	—	—	—	5
South	—	4	2	2	13
West	—	—	—	—	—
U. S., unspecified	—	13	12	8	8
United States	99%	98%	92%	97%	89%
Foreign	1	2	8	3	11
Total Cases (= 100%)	72	53	50	175	158

[a] These totals, which do not include the father's birthplace in the case of men who were themselves foreign-born, were compiled by Miller especially for this table, and are not the same as those which appear in Table III of "American Historians and the Business Elite," where fathers of foreign-born leaders were included.

TABLE 3
American Industrial Leaders of the 1870s by Industry and Paternal Family's Origin

Family Origin	Textiles	Railroads	Steel	Totals	Miller Totals[a] (1901–1910)
England and Wales	80%	59%	69%	71%	53%
Ireland	9	10	13	11	14
Scotland	9	13	2	7	7
Canada	—	1	5	2	3
British Empire, other or unspecified	—	—	—	—	5
British Empire	98%	83%	89%	91%	82%
Germany[b]	2	4	9	4	12
Other countries	—	13	2	5	6
Total Cases (= 100%)	65	52	58	175	162

[a] Or country of leader's own origin, if he was the first in the family to settle in America. In either case, *last country* before settlement in America.
[b] In this category are included those states which in 1871 were united to form the German Empire.

sects. Aside from the Unitarians, however, most of whom must either have embraced this faith themselves or been the sons of men who did, only fourteen of the group are known to have shifted from one denomination to another, and among these it was more often a shift to the older elite Episcopal church than to any one of the more zealous or more intellectual ones. This, as Table 4 shows, served to bring those who shifted into closer conformity with their associates in the business community.

V

There is in American literature considerable evidence of the view that the business leader, if not a refugee from abroad, was at any rate a refugee from the farm. Nor is this theme confined to fiction. Andrew Carnegie, himself the son of a city worker, was but stating a popular belief when he wrote in 1886, "Most great men, it is true, have been born and brought up in the country...." In speaking of

TABLE 4
American Industrial Leaders of the 1870s by Industry and Religious Background[a]

Denomination	Textiles	Railroads	Steel	Total	Miller Totals[b] (1901–1910)
Episcopal	24%	21%	29%	25%	25%
Presbyterian	—	16	26	14	21
Congregational	42	18	6	22	—[c]
Unitarian	20	9	2	10	6
Methodist	4	5	8	6	9
Baptist	—	5	8	4	5
Quaker	4	7	13	8	—[c]
Other Protestant	—	12	6	6	8
Protestant, unspecified	6	7	2	5	16
Protestant	100%	100%	100%	100%	90%
Catholic	—	—	—	—	7
Jewish	—	—	—	—	3
Total Cases (= 100%)	50	43	51	144	174

[a] In almost all instances this is the religion of the leader himself and probably of his family as well. In instances where a shift of religion is known to have occurred, only the religion in which the subject was reared is counted.
[b] Statistics in this column are taken from Miller, "The Recruitment of the American Business Elite," p. 249.
[c] An insignificant number included in "other Protestant."

the 1870s, one of the outstanding historians of our own day has said, "The cities were full of wealthy newcomers of rural antecedents. . . ."; but he cites as his only reference William Dean Howells's *Silas Lapham*, a fictional Boston capitalist who was born and reared on a Vermont farm. Certainly there were such cases in real life, too, in the 1870s as in all periods of American history, but the statistics in Table 5 show that these cases were hardly representative in our period, and this at a time, be it remembered, when by far the larger part of the nation's population was composed of farm dwellers.

According to the table, half the industrial leaders of 1870–1879 were born in places with more than 2,500 persons as compared with 59 percent of the business leaders of 1901–1910. But even the remaining half in the 1870s was not necessarily of rural origin. A population

TABLE 5
**American-born Industrial Leaders by Industry and
Size of Birthplace[a]**

Size of Birthplace	Textiles	Railroads	Steel	Total	Miller Totals (1901–1910)
Under 2,500	38%	59%	57%	50%	41%
2,500–8,000	26	21	20	23	19
Over 8,000	36	20	23	27	40
Total Cases *(= 100%)*	80	71	66	217	174

[a] Population is from the census nearest each man's date of birth. The Miller totals include a few instances in which the place where a man was reared, rather than his birthplace, was used.

below 2,500 is roughly the measure used by the Bureau of the Census, both in designating modern rural areas and in going back into the past for purposes of comparison. Yet it is scarcely sound to suggest, on that account, that every community having a population of less than 2,500 in 1825 (the year in which the "average" industrial leader of 1870–1879 was born), was essentially rural. Take, for instance, St. Albans, Vermont, which even as late as 1830 falls into our "rural" category populationwise, but which, when J. Gregory Smith, the railroad man, was born there in 1818, was already a flourishing community with many of the refinements of the urban life of the time. Smith's father was a lawyer and businessman, and of Smith himself it has been said, "established position and affluence were his birthright." Another example is Erie, Pennsylvania, in which railroad man John F. Tracy was born in 1827. With a population of 1,465 in 1830, Erie was a bustling lake port, and a rapidly expanding business center. Tracy's father was a railroad contractor; the academy which the boy attended had been a feature of Erie life since 1806.

Nor are Erie and St. Albans the only examples. It is perhaps a fairer measure, therefore, to count as having been brought up in rural surroundings only those men actually born on farms. When this is done, the rural classification in the 1870s, as shown in Table 6, drops from 50 to 25 percent, and the farm boy who becomes a successful businessman appears a much less frequent phenomenon.

TABLE 6
**American Industrial Leaders of the 1870s by Industry and
Father's Occupation[a]**

Occupation	Textiles	Railroads	Steel	Total	Miller Totals[b] (1901–1910)
Businessman	57%	49%	48%	51%	55%
Professional	7	16	16	13	22
Farmer	19	31	27	25	14
Public official	2	4	—	3	7
Worker	15	—	11	8	2
Total Cases (= 100%)	67	70	57	194	167

[a] Some fathers engaged in more than one occupation. The one used here was dominant in the period in which each leader was reared.
[b] These figures adjusted by Miller, in line with the criteria used for the 1870 study. The adjustments result in but very slight changes.

The prevalence of businessmen among the fathers of the leaders in our group is noteworthy. While the term "businessman" is interpreted to include such widely separated occupations as bank president and peddler, only two fathers fit into the first category and but one in the second. One-third of the fathers designated as businessmen were merchants; another third were manufacturers. Among the remaining third were three contractors or builders, two sea captains, a supercargo, a river captain, a railroad superintendent, a gristmill operator, the owner of a country store, a newspaper publisher, and a bookseller. The fathers of seventeen textile leaders were themselves textile men, while the fathers of a like number in the steel industry had preceded their sons as iron and steel manufacturers. Only seven railroaders were the sons of men who had engaged in railroading.

Such crude occupational categories as we have used are not necessarily precise criteria of social status in any of its various meanings. "Farmer" may include men who were able to afford education for their children, while some petty businessmen could not do so. And if, at one end of the scale among business and professional men we find those who could not give their children higher education, at the other end are fathers who were already at the top in their respective fields and men of more than local power and prestige. Precise calculations of class or status do not seem feasible, but every effort to take all known factors into account reemphasizes the general impression that most—perhaps 90 percent—of the industrial leaders in our group were reared in a middle- or upper-class milieu.

That the education of most of these men was not limited to what the little red schoolhouse had to offer is indicated by Table 7, which shows that the large majority at least attained the equivalent of high school training, while a sizable number also had a taste of college. This is particularly apparent in the textile group, almost half the men whose education is known having attended college. Among the railroad men, moreover, while not as many had gone to college, almost half had had professional training, usually in law or engineering.

A natural consequence of a longer education period is delay in starting to earn a living. Table 8 shows that almost half the men for whom data were to be had did not go to work before they had reached their nineteenth birthday. Less than one-quarter were set to work when they were younger than sixteen. These figures and Miller's for the later decade point up the fact that in the earlier

TABLE 7
American Industrial Leaders of the 1870s by Industry and Highest Educational Level Attained[a]

Education	Textiles	Railroads	Steel	Total	Miller Totals (1901–1910)
Grammar school	25%	22%	43%	30%	22%
High school	31	48	20	33	37
College	44	30	37	37	41
Total Cases (= 100%)	59	64	60	183	183

[a] The many types of older schools have been reduced to modern terminology. Included in "grammar school" are institutions called by that name, as well as district, public, common, and similar schools. In "high school" are included academies and other institutions of similar rank. Counted among grammar-school boys are those who had little or no formal education as well as graduates; among high-school boys, all those who attended whether graduates or not. The same rule was followed for college men. A few leaders who had private tutors well into their teens but did not attend college are with the high-school group.

period, as in the later, we are dealing with a favored segment of the population.

TABLE 8
American Industrial Leaders of the 1870s by Industry and Age on Going to Work[a]

Age	Textiles	Railroads	Steel	Totals	Miller Totals (1901–1910)
15 or under	30%	23%	18%	23%	20%
16–18	21	35	38	32	35
19 and over	49	42	44	45	45
Total Cases (= 100%)	57	62	57	176	179

[a] This is age on taking first regular business, professional, or other job (except work on father's or other relative's farm) after leaving school.

VI

Was the typical industrial leader of the 1870s, then, a "new man," an escapee from the slums of Europe or from the paternal farm? Did he rise by his own efforts from a boyhood of poverty? Was he as innocent of education and of formal training as has often been alleged? He seems to have been none of these things. American by birth, of a New England father, English in national origin, Congregational, Presbyterian, or Episcopal in religion, urban in early environment, he was rather born and bred in an atmosphere in which business and a relatively high social standing were intimately associated with his family life. Only at about eighteen did he take his first regular job, prepared to rise from it, moreover, not by a rigorous apprenticeship begun when he was virtually a child, but by an academic education well above average for the times.

William Miller

AMERICAN HISTORIANS AND THE INDUSTRIAL ELITE OF 1900

William Miller is one of the outstanding traditional economic historians of the United States. An important feature of his essay is its critical survey of the uncritical attitudes of so many scholarly historians who preceded him, historians who simply accepted the Horatio Alger version of success or relied on biographical data on a few men to account for the backgrounds of the nation's greatest business leaders at the turn of the century. Drawing his wealthy population of 200 from a broader range of industries than had Gregory and Neu, Miller found the backgrounds of the business elite of 1900 to be as narrow as those of the previous generation had been.

One might have supposed that historians, largely occupied as they have been with the activities of ruling classes, would have been among the first to study systematically the problem of the recruitment and tenure of elites. This problem is an especially interesting one in a country such as the United States which has had no official caste systems and no legally established hereditary hierarchies. Yet most American historians have shied away from it. Few of them have even raised questions about the locus and transmission of power or status in modern times. Moreover, those who have discussed in particular the ascent of nineteenth- and early twentieth-century business leaders have tended to attribute their success simply to the possession of more shrewdness or trickiness or more pluck or luck or other private qualities than competitors who failed to rise; the very few historians who have considered social determinants such as family background or work experience have, by stressing the alleged values of poverty or of starting business in boyhood, placed their emphasis, as we shall see, quite at the opposite pole from where it belongs.

The present study of 190 business leaders of the first decade of the twentieth century and of 188 contemporary political leaders on whom data are presented for comparison aims to call historians'

From William Miller, "American Historians and the Business Elite," *Journal of Economic History* 9 (November 1949): 184–208. Reprinted by permission of the author and publisher. Footnotes deleted.

attention to the critical but neglected field of elite recruitment, to suggest a method by which data may be collected and analyzed, and to present some of the results of applying this method to a particular area in which a few historians have speculated to strikingly misleading effect.

II

This essay is not wholly a pioneer effort to analyze the social characteristics of the American business elite, and a word should be said about the work already done in this field. I am not concerned with full-length biographies of business leaders, of which there are very few of value, nor with popular studies of groups of businessmen, such as Matthew Josephson's *The Robber Barons* or Frederick Lewis Allen's *The Lords of Creation.* Of somewhat greater interest, at least methodologically, are two books by Fritz Redlich—*History of American Business Leaders* and *The Molding of American Banking: Men and Ideas.* These discuss certain "entrepreneurial" characteristics of *sizable numbers* of business leaders; the first, leaders in the iron and steel industry in England, Germany, and the United States, largely in the nineteenth century; the second, American bankers and related politicos, 1781–1840. Unlike the more popular books, Redlich's are long on theory; but, like them, his are short on synthesis. Systematic summaries of his data can be made, but he has not made them.

Most germane to the field of the present essay are the following *statistical* studies of American business leaders: Pitirim Sorokin, "American Millionaires and Multi-Millionaires"; Chester M. Destler, "Entrepreneurial Leadership among the 'Robber Barons': A Trial Balance"; C. Wright Mills, "The American Business Elite: A Collective Portrait"; and, the only full-length book, F. W. Taussig and C. S. Joslyn, *American Business Leaders: A Study in Social Origins and Social Sratification.*

The first two, by Sorokin and Destler, are suggestive, but certain internal weaknesses reduce their scientific value. Sorokin lumps many kinds of millionaires and near millionaires; his 668 persons selected haphazardly (but not, statistically speaking, at random), over a period of some 200 years, include actors, preachers, statesmen, and physicians as well as businessmen, and in his tables he seldom distinguishes the last group from the rest. The difficulty with Destler's work lies mainly in the vagueness of some of his categories, though the small number of businessmen studied by him (43) also diminishes confidence in his results.

The essay by Mills and the book by Taussig and Joslyn, while satisfactory as starting points for additional studies, present their own problems, the first mainly because of the nature of its sample, the second partly because of the nature of its questionnaire. Mills selected his men only from the *Dictionary of American Biography,* the subjects for which were named on grounds that made some businessmen eligible for reasons that had little to do with their business achievements and others ineligible however eminent they may have been in the business community of their time. Taussig and Joslyn, in turn, setting out to prove that heredity is more important than environment in business success, asked their respondents for so little information that, as William F. Ogburn said in a review of their book, they have "such a small fraction of the environment measured that they, in the nature of the case, cannot do much toward a solution of the problem." Yet Taussig and Joslyn's initial data were carefully gathered and as presented in some of the tables in their book are available for more scholarly and scientific use.

III

The present study is focused upon "career men"—bureaucrats, that is—who often must have been as occupied with getting and staying ahead in their companies as with keeping their companies ahead of the field. In studying the so-called robber barons, Destler was impelled to consider also a few early "career men," an odd-sounding designation for "semipiratical entrepreneurs who roamed the United States virtually unchecked before 1903." I, in turn, have had to include some atavistic captains of industry. Nevertheless, except for a few partners in unincorporated investment-banking houses, the men discussed in these pages were all officeholders; many of them *never* organized a business of any kind.

Yet the dull titles by which these men are called and the bureaucratic maneuvering in which they must often have engaged should not suggest that these were petty men exercising small powers in petty domains. The mere fact that they were bureaucrats should suggest the contrary, for while there are many examples of petty bureaucracies, generally speaking only large enterprises operating in large theaters need hierarchical structures. The fact is, the men discussed in this essay were at the apex of some of the mightiest organizations the world up to then had seen. In the vernacular of their times, their bureaucratic structures were among the first great industrial, commercial, and financial "trusts."

As late as 1896, except for some railroads, there were probably fewer than a dozen American corporations capitalized at more than $10 million. By 1903, again excepting railroads, there were more than 300 corporations capitalized at $10 million or more, approximately 50 at $50 million or more, and 17 at $100 million or more. A similar change may be traced in the modern history of other capitalist nations in which, as in the United States, the startling upward curve in the productivity of workers, attributable in part to the new technology of electricity and alloys, helped bring about an unprecedented speeding up in the accumulation of money and power and in the combination of business firms.

In this period one after another of the key segments of the world's economy was engrossed by the world's business leaders, Americans not least among them. And in the United States as elsewhere it became possible in regard to scores of commodities and key services such as transportation, communication, and the granting of credit to name the corporations or clusters of corporations that dictated the quantities which could be produced or employed and the prices and places at which they could be sold. Such fateful decisions were in the domain of tne early business bureaucrats studied here and were communicated to and carried out by the bureaucracies they controlled—organizations that would scarcely have been understood by early nineteenth-century entrepreneurs or by those Jacksonian politicians who had sought, in the name of equal entrepreneurial opportunity, to make the establishment of corporations so easy.

IV

At the start of this work I had decided that 200 men were all that an individual could study in a reasonable time and that from that number (various contingencies reduced the final group to 190) statistically reliable results could be obtained. If these men were selected from the largest companies regardless of field, the bulk of them would have come from the railroads; if, on the other hand, an equal number were taken from each major business field, representatives of small insurance companies and banks would have mingled with the elite while many from great railroads would have been excluded. This dilemma could be solved only arbitrarily.

The companies from which men were chosen were taken from the following major fields: (1) manufacturing and mining, (2) steam railroads, (3) public utilities, (4) finance (commercial banking, life insurance, investment banking). Companies in the first three fields were ranked by capitalization, the commercial banks by deposits, and the life-insurance companies (no other types of insurance companies approach the life companies in size) by assets. From the *Statistical Abstract of the United States* and other sources summarizing census information, I then took the capitalization of the entire manufacturing and mining, steam railroad, and public-utilities industries in the United States in or near 1910, the total deposits of the national banks, and the assets of the life-insurance companies. These I simply added together and distributed the leaders among the four fields more or less according to the proportion of the total represented by the figure used for each. This total of capital, deposits, and assets came to $57 billion. Table 1 shows how the leaders would have been distributed had the proportions been followed exactly, and how they actually are distributed in this study.

The next step was to choose the topmost positions from which these men should be selected. Should directors be included, or chairmen and members of key panels such as finance or executive committees? What of executive vice-presidents, general managers, or cashiers of banks? Investigation of the locus of different types of power in large corporations has only just begun; for the period of this work it may fairly be said that there are no studies. The decision to limit this work to presidents and board chairmen of corporations and some partners of unincorporated investment-banking houses permitted me to choose men from a larger group of companies than would have been possible had men from more positions been selected; it may have caused some persons of great importance to be excluded, but all of those included, at any rate, were bound to be men of first rank. . . .

One hundred and seventy-four of these men (information on this

TABLE 1
Distribution of Business Leaders by Type of Industry

Industry	Number of Men from Each Industry if Representation Were Proportionate to "Size" of Industry	Actual Number of Men from Each Industry
Manufacturing and mining	65	64
Steam railroads	58	58
Public utilities	29	31
National banking ⎫ Finance	16 ⎱ 29	19 ⎱ 28
Life insurance ⎭	13 ⎰	9 ⎰
Total	181 [a]	181 [a]

[a] The nine investment bankers, selected on a different basis, are excluded from this table. See n. 20 [in original article].

score is lacking for sixteen) held approximately 2,720 business directorships. A few held more than 100 each; the average was about 16. Clearly, these men were leaders not only in their own companies but in the entire business community.

V

As stated earlier in this essay, some general American historians have made enough casual remarks about the recruitment of modern business leaders to form a rough explanatory model. I want now to point out some of the facets of this model and then to introduce some of my own findings to show how obsolete it had become by the first decade of this century, if, indeed, it ever fitted the facts.

Virtually all the generalizations that go to make up this model are based upon a few remarkable life histories from the "robber baron" period; thus in most of the books that are at all concerned with the recruitment of business leaders one finds accounts of Andrew Carnegie, John D. Rockefeller, J. Pierpont Morgan, James J. Hill, and Edward H. Harriman. In *The Growth of the American People 1865–1940,* Arthur M. Schlesinger, Sr., cites in addition such older heroes as Cornelius Vanderbilt and Gustavus F. Swift but not later ones. Charles A. and Mary R. Beard, in *The Rise of American Civili-*

zation, add to the ubiquitous five Jay Gould, William H. Vanderbilt, Collis P. Huntington, Jay Cooke, William A. Clark, and Philip D. Armour. Few general historians discuss a greater number of men than do the Beards; but much more significant, practically none discusses any *later* men.

The last extended discussion of the "typical" business leader by Samuel Eliot Morison and Henry Steele Commager in *The Growth of the American Republic*—a widely used textbook—follows (emphasis mine):

> *The* most typical figure *of the industrial age was undoubtedly Andrew Carnegie. A* poor immigrant boy *from Scotland, he followed and helped to* perpetuate *the American tradition of rising* from poverty to riches, *and his success he ascribed entirely to the political and economic democracy which obtained in this country. By dint of unflagging industry and unrivalled business acumen and resourcefulness and especially through his extraordinary ability to choose as associates such men as Charles Schwab, Henry Frick, and Henry Phipps, and to command the devotion of his workmen, Carnegie built up the greatest steel business in the world, and retired in 1901 to chant the glories of "Triumphant Democracy" and to give away his enormous fortune of three and a half hundred millions.*

Arthur Schlesinger says vaguely of the latest group of business leaders he discusses that they arose "in most cases from obscure origins and unhindered by moral scruples, they were fired by a passionate will to succeed." In the last discussion of business leaders in *The American Nation,* John D. Hicks says: "Typical of the railroad builders was James J. Hill," who, he points out, was an immigrant from Canada. The Beards' analysis of the life histories of American business leaders ends with the eleven men named above, of whom they write:

> *Of the group here brought under examination only two, Morgan and Vanderbilt, built their fortunes on the solid basis of family inheritances while only one had what may be called by courtesy a higher education: Morgan spent two years in the University of Göttingen. Carnegie began life as a stationary engineer; Jay Cooke as a clerk in a general store in Sandusky; Jay Gould as a surveyor and tanner; Huntington, Armour, and Clark as husky lads on their fathers' farms; Hill as a clerk for a St. Paul steamboat company; Harriman as an office boy in a New York broker's establishment; Rockefeller as a bookkeeper in Cleveland.*

The Beards' inference is that these men, starting from the lowliest jobs as exemplars of the tradition, rose from the most humble origins to the very top. This may actually have been so, not only of these few men but of the large majority of business leaders whom they are taken to represent. But, it may be asked, how many in modern times start much higher than these men did, even among the well-born, college-trained young men who, as *Fortune* put it, spend a few years in "the mummery of 'working in the plant' " before ascending to the highest executive levels? Surely, of itself, an initial low-status job does not necessarily imply lowly origins.

It is instructive to note that even the more perspicacious historians, when they err on the origins of business leaders, do so on the side of the tradition. Thus the Beards describe Rockefeller, the son of a "Barnumesque" itinerant entrepreneur, as "the son of a farmer"; and Henry B. Parkes writes of F. Augustus Heinze, the copper magnate who was born in Brooklyn, New York, into a comfortable business family, as a "young German immigrant."

Though most historians say little about it, there has been in the United States for well over a century a sizable and growing working class, propertyless, segregated, often remarkably apathetic to the alleged opportunities of American business and political life. Into this class most immigrants, starting with the Irish in the 1840s, have been channeled. Historians generally imply by the individuals they select as examples that this class and (for so little is said in this connection of rich men's business-bred, college-educated sons) this class alone has supplied our business leaders, that their school, to quote Carnegie himself, was "the sternest of all schools—poverty," that they were graduated from it early in life into apprenticeships as "mechanics" or "poor clerks," and that "against the boy who swept the office, or who begins as a shipping clerk at fourteen," the college graduate "has little chance, starting at twenty."

Yet to read the lives of business leaders, even of those who presumably are the pillars of this tradition, is to look almost in vain for working-class or foreign origins, and even poor and unschooled farm boys are not conspicuous among such leaders. Of Rockefeller and Heinze I have already spoken. The historians themselves have accounted for J. Pierpont Morgan and William H. Vanderbilt. Jay Cooke's father, Eleutheros, was "a lawyer who was sent to Congress." Harriman's father, Orlando, was an Episcopal clergyman, "the one exception of his generation in a family of several brothers" who followed the family tradition of successful "trading and commercial pursuits." Harriman himself married the daughter of a banker and railroad president who started him on his railroad career. Even a farm boy such as Elbert H. Gary, who "experienced early in life the arduous regimen of work on a pioneer farm, an experience which endowed him with excellent health and a robust physique," was raised in a settlement named after his forebears and in a house that "was a large one for the time—the largest in the settlement . . . 'the big white house on the hill' it came to be called."

Doubtless examples can be found in the period emphasized by the historians of men whose life histories more fully substantiate the tradition. What of the men in the later period to which the historians tacitly allow their explanations of origins and ascent to apply and which is the subject of this essay?

VI

Had the "typical" American business leader of the first decade of the twentieth century been an immigrant? Was he best represented in manufacturing, for example, by Franz A. Assmann, the German-born president of the American Can Company; or in railroading by Edward T. Jeffery, the English-born president of the Denver and Rio Grande; or in insurance by Alexander E. Orr, the Irish-born president of the New York Life; or in banking by Jacob H. Schiff, the German-born Jew who became senior partner of Kuhn, Loeb and Co.?

Simply to ask the question is to answer it. Of the 187 businessmen studied here whose birthplaces are known, only 18, or less than 10 percent, were born abroad. Surely these men were less "typical" of the topmost business leaders of their time than the 55 percent who were born in the eastern part of the United States, in New England and the Middle Atlantic states.

Of the eighteen business leaders who were foreign-born, moreover, scarcely two or three fit the historians' concepts of the *poor* immigrant who made good, and even these men had been brought to the United States at such an early age that they may be said to have been bred if not borne here. Two of the eighteen men were of rich, colonial American business families who happened to be residing temporarily in Canada when they were born. Four more, rich and

TABLE 2
American Business and Political Leaders by Region of Birthplace[a]

Birthplace	Business Leaders	Political Leaders
New England	18 ⎱ 55%	22%
Middle Atlantic	37 ⎰	27
East North Central	22	27
South	9	11
West	4	7
United States	90%	94%
Foreign	10	6
Total Cases (= 100%)	187	188

[a] These are census regions. Combined in "South" are South Atlantic, South Central, West South Central; in "West" West North Central, Mountain, Pacific.

highly placed abroad, either settled here as representatives of big foreign business firms or were brought over by fathers who represented such firms. At least two others had letters of introduction from their fathers or other relatives abroad to American bankers and merchants who helped to establish them here. Thus it appears to be unsafe in writing of elites to associate immigrant status, even where that fits, with the idea of poverty.

If not typically poor immigrants, were these business and political leaders the sons of foreigners? More of them were, surely, but Table 3 shows that the typical leader in each field was born into an American family.

Moreover, these families themselves had, in most instances, been in America for many generations. Almost three-fourths of the business and political leaders were at least of the fourth generation of their paternal lines to reside in America; many were of the seventh and even the eighth generations. Colonial families were represented by 73 percent of the business leaders and 79 percent of those in politics. Fifty-six percent of the former and 47 percent of the latter were of families that had settled in America in the seventeenth century.

Even were they not of colonial ancestry, most of these leaders could point to British, and many to English, forebears.

They could claim Protestant, and often Episcopal or Presbyterian backgrounds.

TABLE 3
**American Business and Political Leaders by Region of
Father's Birthplace**

Father's Birthplace	Business Leaders	Political Leaders
New England	27%	33%
Middle Atlantic	31	28
East North Central	4	5
South	12	17
United States, unspecified [a]	7	4
United States	81%	87%
Foreign	19	13
Total Cases (= 100%)	176	176

[a] Fathers of none of these men were known to have been born in the "West" as defined in Table 2. All those known to have been born in the United States, the exact region being unknown, are counted here.

TABLE 4
**American Business and Political Leaders by
Paternal Family's Origin[a]**

Family Origin	Business Leaders	Political Leaders
England and Wales	53%	56%
Ireland	14	13
Scotland	7	8
Canada	3	1
British Empire, other, or unspecified	5	5
British Empire	82%	83%
Germany	12	8
Other countries	6	9
Total cases (= 100%)	162	162

[a] Or country of leader's own origin if he was the first in the family to settle in America. In either case, *last country* before settlement in America.

If not of recent foreign origin, was the typical American business leader of the early twentieth century a migrant from a farm?

Table 6 shows that the political leaders far more frequently than those in business came from rural areas, that almost 60 percent of the latter were recruited from the larger towns and cities. Indeed,

TABLE 5
American Business and Political Leaders by Religious Background[a]

Denomination	Business Leaders	Political Leaders
Episcopal	25%	12%
Presbyterian	21	17
Methodist	9	13
Baptist	5	7
Other Protestant	14	20
Protestant, unspecified	16	25
Protestant	90%	▲ 94%
Catholic	7	4
Jewish	3	2
Total Cases (= 100%)	174	165

[a] In almost all instances this is the religion of the leader himself and most likely of his family as well. In a few instances where a shift in religion is known to have occurred, only the old religion is counted.

TABLE 6
American Business and Political Leaders by Size of Birthplace[a]

Size of Birthplace	Business Leaders	Political Leaders
Rural (under 2,500)	41%	75%
Town (2,500–8,000)	19 ⎫ 59	9
City (over 8,000)	40 ⎭	16
Total Cases (= 100%)	164	180

[a] Population is from the census nearest each man's date of birth. In a few instances of men raised in places (that is, moved there before reaching the age of 7) sufficiently larger or smaller than their birthplaces to alter their classification in the scale used in the table, that place, not the birthplace, was used.

more than 20 percent of them were born in cities that around the middle of the nineteenth century had populations of 100,000 or more. Upon these men rural influences even in a predominantly rural society must have been at a minimum.

Yet more significant in answering the question are the occupations of the fathers of these business leaders. Here we find that even of those born in rural areas fewer than one-third (and only 12 percent of the whole group) had fathers who were mainly farmers. Fifty-six percent of all the business leaders, on the other hand, had fathers who had been in business—often big business—before them; eight of ten, indeed, came from business or professional families.

TABLE 7
American Business and Political Leaders by Father's Occupation[a]

Occupation	Business Leaders		Political Leaders
Businessman	56	79%	33%
Professional	23		18
Farmer	12		38
Public Official	7		9
Worker	2		2
Total Cases (= 100%)	167		167

[a] Some fathers engaged in more than one occupation. The one used here was dominant in the period in which each man was raised. In a few instances this was not clear so a choice was made more or less arbitrarily (considering our lack of knowledge of income and status factors in the early nineteenth century) by which business (including higher company positions as well as company ownership) took precedence over farming and professional or public-official positions over both. This conforms roughly to the ascending order of status used in classifying occupations today. In no instance was there a problem of a father who was a worker (including wage as well as salaried occupations). About one-third of the professionals were lawyers or engineers who might have been called businessmen, given the nature of their professional work; the others were clergymen, doctors, writers, etc. "Public official" includes professional politicians (even if not officeholders) and lawyers who were chiefly public men.

Darwin P. Kingsley, who was president of the New York Life Insurance Company from 1907 to 1931 and chairman of the board from 1931 to his death two years later, once said of his impoverished early years:

On the 40-acre farm, in Vermont, where I was born, everything we wore and everything we ate was grown on the farm, except a little sugar once in a while in place of maple sugar, which was indigenous, and a little tea. From a dozen sheep came wool which was first spun and then woven by hand into winter clothing. Our garden supplied flax which was made into summer garments. . . . I well remember the first time my father took his wool and swapped it for fulled cloth. We all regarded that as an epochal advance into a higher state of civilization.

> *At Alburg, where I was born, there were not then (1857) enough houses to form even a hamlet. In the summer I attended the old "deestrict" school, a primitive affair innocent of any suggestion of higher education. In our home were very few books. Life there was clean through and through, self-respecting, and full of moral and religious discipline. But it was extremely narrow, uninspiring, and unimaginative. There was little or nothing to fire a boy with ambition or enthusiasm or to acquaint him with the world that lay beyond his "cabined, cribbed, and confined" sphere.*

Yet it was not this kind of poverty that Carnegie had in mind when he recommended his "sternest of all schools"; this kind of spiritual and intellectual poverty was probably most prevalent among the poor, but this much at least they shared with large segments of the population at all levels, including those born and raised among the very rich. Call Kingsley's family poor in material things as well; but compared with the sons of many urban and rural wage workers even in the 1850s he and other farmers' sons like him were not worse off.

Nevertheless, in Table 8, showing the social status of the families of these business and political leaders, Kingsley and a few others with apparently similar or poorer backgrounds were classified as lower class. Men were classified as of the upper class when it was clear that their fathers, like those of August Belmont, Cornelius K. G. Billings, or Charles Deering, were themselves big businessmen, or where their families, like those of Robert Todd Lincoln or Winslow Shelby Pierce, were politically eminent. Generally speaking, those in between—including some businessmen with no special claims to wealth or power or professionals like the average clergyman, doctor, or lawyer—were ranked as of middle-class origins. This does not mean that their fathers were not of help to them. James B. Duke, for example, rose to wealth and power with a company

TABLE 8
American Business and Political Leaders by Family Status

Status	Business Leaders	Political Leaders
Upper	50%	36%
Middle	45	50
Lower	5	14
Total Cases (= 100%)	179	180

founded by his father; George W. Perkins moved to a partnership in the House of Morgan—probably the acting head of the house at one stage—from a vice-presidency in the New York Life Insurance Company in which his father, a minor executive there, had given him his business start.

Not all the men ranked in the upper class, of course, had fathers as rich and powerful as those of Belmont or Billings, or families as well connected as those of Lincoln or Pierce. Many in the middle bracket, likewise, probably were not as fortunate in their upbringing as Elbert H. Gary, whose family is classified there; probably few so classified were as poor in material things as the Harrimans.

Poor boys, as Carnegie rightly said, usually go to work early in life. Clearly few of these business and political leaders were poor boys. And, as Table 9 shows, few of them went to work at an early age.

TABLE 9
American Business and Political Leaders by Age on Going to Work[a]

Age	Business Leaders	Political Leaders
15 or under	20%	13%
16–18	35	10
19 and over	45	77
Total Cases (= 100%)	179	182

[a] This is age on taking first regular business, professional, or other job (except work on father's or other relative's farm) after leaving school or, in a very few instances, after leaving the Union or Confederate armies.

Only one in five of these business leaders had a job before he was sixteen; slightly more than half of them had jobs before they were nineteen. Delaying the business debuts of most of the others—their late start, according to the tradition, being itself a handicap—was the pursuit of higher education, an undertaking that should so have altered their characters as to make them even poorer prospects for business success. The educational levels attained by all the leaders studied here are shown in Table 10.

Of the business leaders who did not go to work until they were

TABLE 10
American Business and Political Leaders by Highest
Education Level Attained[a]

Education	Business Leaders	Political Leaders
Grammar school	22%	18%
High school	37	27
Some college	12 ⎱ 41	11 ⎱ 55
College graduate	29 ⎰	44 ⎰
Total Cases (= 100%)	183	188

[a] I have reduced the many types of older schools to this modern terminology, including in "grammar school" institutions called by that name, as well as district, public, common and similar schools; in "high school," academies and others of similar rank. Counted among grammar-school boys are those who had little or no formal education as well as graduates; among high-school boys, all those who attended whether graduates or not. A few who had private tutors well into their teens but did not attend college are counted with the high-school group.

nineteen or older, 76 percent had gone to college. Four out of five of these, in turn, were of the upper class. No group, if the traditional account of the origins and ascent pattern of the American business elite truly represented the facts, could have been worse off than this one in the competition for business eminence. Yet about 28 percent of the business leaders are found in it. These men shared *all* the alleged handicaps: upper-class upbringing, college education, a late business start; yet, if speed of ascent be taken as the measure of the *greatest* attainment, these men were actually the most successful of all. Not only did they spend less time after starting to work in getting to the top, but, as Table 11 shows, they got there on the whole earlier in life than those allegedly most favored. This table shows the ages at which the two polar groups attained the high positions that made them eligible for this study.

Still, one has to stretch a point to attribute to more than two or three general American historians *any* discussion of the speed of ascent of the business elite. More of them stress this elite's typically lower-class, foreign, or farm *origins* and speculate on the forces that impelled men upward from such insalubrious environs. Yet poor immigrant boys and poor farm boys together actually make up no

TABLE 11
American Business Leaders by Age on Becoming President or Partner of Major Company[a]

Age	Late-Starting, Upper-Class, College Men	Early-Starting, Middle- and Lower-Class Noncollege Men
Under 45	43⎱ 66%	26⎱ 48%
45–49	23⎰	22⎰
50 and over	34	52
Total Cases (= 100%)	40	53

[a] Board chairmen are a special case in regard to age on attaining the position and were omitted from this table.

more than 3 percent of the business leaders who are the subject of this essay. If men with such backgrounds had been in fact representative of the great entrepreneurs of the later nineteenth century, they must have been supplanted with extraordinary rapidity by the higher status, more highly educated bureaucrats of the following generation. More likely, poor immigrant and poor farm boys who become business leaders have always been more conspicuous in American history books than in American history.

IV THE TWENTIETH CENTURY: NEW DIMENSIONS, NEW APPROACHES, INCONCLUSIVE MOBILITY PATTERNS

In 1958 Gerhard Lenski wrote that sociologists "still lack the data required to answer with any assurance the question of whether the rate of vertical movement in [American] society has increased, decreased, or remained constant." The problem, in addition to inadequate evidence, was that mobility studies were not commensurate with one another. And yet an amazing quantity of data has been accumulated, before and after 1958, on social mobility in twentieth-century America. The origins of business leaders have been examined in a half-dozen major studies. The backgrounds of cross-sections of the populations of such cities as Indianapolis, Norristown, San Jose, and Oakland have been intensively researched, as have been the social origins of such diverse groups as factory managers, doctors, lawyers, and engineers, Jews and Italians, and in one famous occupational study, the careers of a "representative sample of over 20,000 Americans between the ages of 20 and 64." While the results point in many directions, a close examination of all these studies leads one inescapably to the conclusion that despite the effects of twentieth-century structural change—which increases "opportunity" by replacing manual labor and agricultural jobs of low prestige with more highly regarded white-collar work—social mobility rates and opportunities have remained remarkably static.

In one of the most admired of these studies, Natalie Rogoff found that "the processes by which men were selected for occupations were more closely related to social origins in 1940 than in 1910." Most of the other students, as a matter of fact, also found slight decline in opportunity, a few found a very slight increase, but the burden of almost every one of the two dozen or so major studies is the essential continuation of earlier patterns. The successful continue to descend inordinately from the successful; changes made in occupations are typically to occupations of similar standing; men starting out low, say as manual workers, in the words of Otis D. Duncan and Peter M. Blau, "ended up as adults in the aggregate [in occupations] little different from their fathers'."

Gordon F. Lewis

THE BACKGROUNDS AND CAREERS OF SMALL BUSINESSMEN IN LEXINGTON, KENTUCKY

Special interest adheres to two aspects of Gordon F. Lewis's study. Breaking with the emphasis on elite business leaders, Lewis studies modest, and therefore more typical, businessmen. And the locale of a small, Southern community enables him to make fruitful comparisons with studies of larger urban centers. The reader should note too that Lewis, who is a sociologist, uses different analytical categories than Miller or Gregory and Neu. One of the great obstacles to synthesizing the results of these and other mobility studies stems precisely from their diverse schemes of categorization.

Inquiry into small business has centered mainly on its economic significance. Considerable attention has been directed also to the question of "free entry" into it. In general, however, studies have focused on the firms themselves rather than on the men who run them. The sociologist is interested in the latter because entry into any social group is decisive in stratification and mobility. The few sociological analyses have been confined mainly to the "big" businessmen; the characteristics of the operators of smaller and more typical firms are almost entirely unknown.

This [essay] reports part of a larger study of the occupational mobility and career patterns of small businessmen in Lexington, Kentucky. Certain characteristics and aspects of the careers of big business leaders will be compared with those of Lexington businessmen and, where possible, with data from one or two other studies.

All business firms in Lexington, irrespective of size, were included in this study; in fact, nearly all the firms would be "small" businesses as defined by Kaplan and other writers: over nine-tenths of all businesses in the United States are "small." Data on managers in

From Gordon F. Lewis, "A Comparison of Some Aspects of the Backgrounds and Careers of Small Businessmen and American Business Leaders," *American Journal of Sociology* 65 (January 1960): 348–355. Copyright © 1960 by the University of Chicago Press. Reprinted by permission of the author and publisher. Footnotes deleted.

Lexington firms, regardless of business size, were included also because of the functional similarity of owners and managers. A questionnaire was mailed to the proprietor or chief executive of every business firm in Lexington excepting those operated by Negroes. Firm names were taken from the 1952 *Lexington City Directory,* which specified 1,673 establishments. Follow-up letters and cards were used in an attempt to obtain maximum response. A 10 percent systematic sample of the nonrespondents was taken, and these people were interviewed. Information thus gained was weighted and combined with the mail replies.

The Lexington population of small businessmen cited here varies in age and length of time engaged in business. The mortality rate is generally high in small business, and any given population of small businessmen includes both people who have reached occupational stability and success and those new to the field, a high proportion of whom will fail to survive. No attempt has been made here to distinguish or compare the veterans and the neophytes in the Lexington sample.

Age. The mean age of the small businessmen of Lexington is forty-nine years, compared with fifty-two years for the small businessmen in the Oxenfeldts' study and fifty-four years for the big business leaders in Warner and Abegglen's study. Eleven percent of Lexington's small businessmen were age thirty-two or younger. While identical age breakdowns are not available in the two studies of business leaders cited, only 5 percent of Taussig and Joslyn's men and 1 percent of Warner and Abegglen's were age thirty-four or less.

Region of Birth. Lexington businessmen are much more homogeneous as regards region of birth than the business leaders reported by Warner and Abegglen. This is to be expected in view of the geographical dispersion of the latter's sample; hence, comparisons between the two are irrelevant except at one point: the percentage of foreign-born. There were more foreign-born in Warner and Abegglen's group (5 percent) than in the Lexington group (3 percent); 5 percent of Warner and Abegglen's national sample were foreign-born as compared with 6.7 percent of all males in 1950. In Newcomer's study of executives 6 percent were foreign-born. Though Lexington's businessmen were predominantly native Kentuckians, 5 percent were foreign-born, compared with 0.5 percent of Kentucky's population in 1950, indicating, in contrast to Warner and Abegglen's group, an overrepresentation of foreign-born.

Education. Businessmen are, in general, better educated than the adult male population as a whole (Table 1). Business leaders in six national studies are better educated than their minor counterparts in three communities. Among the latter, the Lexington businessmen are the best educated, surpassing in a few instances the national samples of big businessmen. Small business apparently provides more opportunity for the man with the modest education than does big business. The data in the table also indicate a greater similarity between the educational attainments of Lexington businessmen and Lexington white males than between the several groups of business leaders cited and all United States white males. However, this is attributable more to the greater educational achievement of Lexington white males as compared with all United States white males than to the meagerness of the Lexington businessmen's education. Both they and other small businessmen seem to be a segment of the population which is better educated than are males in general, and this educational advantage undoubtedly served as a differentiating factor in their achievement of status.

Occupation of Father. In Lexington the small businessmen came disproportionately from certain backgrounds, chiefly the business and professional classes (Table 2). Other studies are consistent generally with this conclusion, although the degree of occupational inheritance has varied. The small businessmen of Lexington are more mobile occupationally in some respects than the various business-leader groups; for example, the percentage of them coming from business-owner or executive families (37 percent) is considerably lower than that of men in any of the other groups cited. Possibly the Oxenfeldts' study of small businessmen has a similar percentage, or approximately so, but, since its data are for business owners only, precise comparison is impossible.

The Lexington group includes from two to three times as many farmers' sons (35 percent) as do the business leaders; this figure takes on less significance, however, when compared with the percentage of farmers among the total employed people in the state, for approximately 40 percent of the employed males in Kentucky in 1920 were farm operators. A slight underrepresentation of farmers' sons in the small business group is evident. Among Warner and

TABLE 1
Education of Nine Groups of Businessmen and the General Population in 1950, Expressed as Percentages

Education	U.S. White Males (1950) (Age 25 b)	Taussig & Joslyn (1928)	Warner & Abegglen (1952)	Miller, "Elite"	Shannon & Shaw, Leaders	Newcomer, "Older" Execs. (1950)	Pearson, Execs.a	Anderson & Davidson, "Props," etc.b	Oxenfeldt, Businessmen	Lexington, Businessmen (1954)	Lexington, White Males (Age 25 b) (1950)
Less than high school	46	27	4	22	15	7	7	44	31	20	29
Some high school	17	28	9		14	24	10	35		18	11
High-school graduation	19	13	11	37	15	12	17		19	27	16
Some college	7		19	12				21	16	15	15
College graduation	8	32	57	29	56	57	62		15	20	17
Unreported	3										12
Total	100	100	100	100	100	100	96	100	100	100	100

a Figures for this group do not include 4 percent who attended "business college, trade, or technical school."

b In the Anderson and Davidson study businessmen were included in the category of "Proprietors, Managers, and Officials." This category also included farmowners and tenants and hence is a poor group with which to compare the more rigidly defined businessmen from the other studies. However, it is one of the few studies concentrating on a single community, as does the present study, and was included for this reason. The reader will have to take the broad composition of this group into account when interpreting the figures; for example, it probably accounts for their comparatively low educational level.

TABLE 2
Occupation of Fathers of Nine Groups of Businessmen, Expressed as Percentages

Occupation of Father	Lexington, Business-men	Oxenfeldt, Business-men[a]	Center, Small Business-men	Anderson & Davidson	Wagner & Abegglen	Taussig & Joslyn	Newcomer (1950)	Miller, "Elite"	Keller, "Leaders" (1950)
Business owner	30	34	55	73	26	34	56	56	58
Business executive	7	28			22	24			
Farmowner	28	—	—	—	9	12	13	12	15
Farm tenant	7	—	8	2		13	18	23	14
Professional	4	—	—	—	14	13	18	23	14
Service worker	1	—							
Clerical worker	3	—	9	5	8	5	6[b]	2	12
Foreman, crafts, skilled	16	—	18	11	13	9	5		
Unskilled and semiskilled	3	—	10	9	5	2	2		
Other, incl. "No answer"	1	—	—	—	3	1	—	7	1
Total	100	—	100	100	100	100	100	100	100

[a] Only occupations of owners and managers were reported in the Oxenfeldts' study.

[b] Includes "Minor Administrative and Sales (1.9%)."

Abegglen's leaders the disparity is much the same, using the national figures as a basis of comparison. Nine percent of Warner and Abegglen's leaders had fathers who were farmers, while farmers comprised 15 percent of the total United States white male employed population in 1920. In the Oxenfeldts' study of small businessmen 28 percent of the men were reported to be sons of farmowners. How many more were sons of farm managers or tenants is not known.

The recent study by Warner and Abegglen indicates the greatest mobility among leaders. A smaller percentage of men in this study are sons of business owners, or executives, and a larger percentage of manual workers than are men in the other studies. Warner and Abegglen indicate increasing mobility into big business in America —a tendency which will bring big business slightly more in line with small business. To be sure, upward mobility into big business seems to require greater education than is necessary for small business. However, Warner and Abegglen's and Newcomer's studies show that the father's occupation is of less significance now than formerly in determining the son's education and hence his chances for advancement.

Because somewhat dissimilar age categories were used in classifying age at initial employment, it is impossible to compare precisely the several studies of the businessmen. However, the Lexington businessmen started their first regular jobs, in general, at a considerably earlier age than did the business leaders (Table 3). The one possible exception is the group of leaders of the generation of 1900 described by Keller, 80 percent of whom started work before twenty-one, as compared with 61 percent of the Lexington men who started at nineteen or younger. However, the situation has changed considerably since 1900, and, of the 1950 generation of business leaders in Keller's study, only 50 percent started work by age twenty-one. The increase in education and particularly the growing force of advanced education to maximize opportunities induce the businessman of today, especially the big businessman, more frequently to postpone full-time employment in favor of further education. In Newcomer's study, for example, the percentage of big businessmen starting their first jobs at the age of twenty decreased by more than half between the 1900 and 1950 generations.

TABLE 3
Age at First Regular Job of Six Groups of Businessmen, Expressed as Percentages

Group	Age at First Regular Job						Total
	21 or less	Over 21	20 or less	Over 20	19 or less	Over 19	
Keller's leaders							
1900 generation	80	20	—	—	—	—	100
1950 generation	50	50	—	—	—	—	100
Pearson's leaders[a]	—	—	29	71	—	—	100
Newcomer's leaders							
1900 generation	—	—	40	60	—	—	100
1925 generation	—	—	35	65	—	—	100
1950 generation	—	—	17	83	—	—	100
Miller's leaders[b]	—	—	—	—	55	45	100
Anderson & Davidson's "proprietors, etc."	—	—	—	—	78	22	100
Lexington businessmen	—	—	—	—	61	39	100

[a] Judson B. Pearson, "American Business Leaders: Social Characteristics and Occupational Ascent" (unpublished Ph.D. dissertation, University of Washington, 1953).

[b] William Miller, "American Historians and the Business Elite," *Journal of Economic History*, IX (November, 1949), 84 ff.

The greater mobility of the small businessmen is seen in a comparison of the first regular jobs with which they and the leaders embarked on their careers. The first regular job of the Lexington businessman was typically that of unskilled, semiskilled, or clerical worker. The same is true of the heterogeneous group of "proprietors, managers, and officials" of Anderson and Davidson's study of small businessmen. Big business leaders studied by Warner and Abegglen, Pearson, and Newcomer, however, often began at the clerical or professional level. Clerical jobs, indeed, provided a common starting place for a large percentage of men in all studies.

The big businessmen start at jobs above the unskilled or semiskilled level, regardless of their education, and here they have an advantage at the outset over small businessmen. Lexington businessmen with only a grade school education started in unskilled or semiskilled occupations more frequently than did the leaders with a similar education studied by Warner and Abegglen. Over two-thirds of the Lexington men with a grade school education began in jobs of this sort, as compared with slightly over a fourth of the similarly educated in the Warner and Abegglen sample. Also, over two-fifths of the Lexington men with a high school education started as unskilled or semiskilled workers, as compared with less than a sixth of Warner and Abegglen's leaders, the majority of which, at each educational level, started as clerical workers. Slightly less than two-fifths at each educational level in Lexington started thus.

The small businessmen of Lexington achieved their present positions at a considerably earlier age, in general, than did the business leaders in Keller's or Newcomer's studies—the only two studies with comparable data. The percentage of leaders achieving their positions before fifty has declined considerably since 1900, being 14 percent less for the generation of 1950 than for that of 1900. Thus, while in small business younger men can achieve headship of a firm, the leadership of big business is becoming increasingly age-graded, with the majority of top positions going to men who have attained at least their fiftieth birthday. Perhaps this indicates that the vehicles of economic expansion, the corporation and the bureaucracy, inhibit the rise of all except those who progress steadily through the various levels of management. Small business may be a profitable and satisfying outlet for the talents of those who are poorly equipped to compete in the managerial class of big business and for those temperamentally unsuited to climbing patiently up the organizational ladder.

Lack of a college education was little or no hindrance to achievement of an important position before forty-five by the small businessmen in the Lexington study but seemed a drawback for big business men. Keller found approximately one-fifth of both college and noncollege men achieved their positions by this age, as did three-fourths of the noncollege men in Lexington and one-fourth of the noncollege men Miller studied.

A fifth of the Lexington businessmen had their first regular jobs in firms in which their parents or kinsmen were owners, executives, or holders of a major block of the voting stock. Of the generation of 1950 of the Newcomer group of business leaders, approximately one-eighth had relatives in their first regular jobs, but the comparable figure for Warner and Abegglen's leaders was less than one-twentieth, and it was one-sixth in the Oxenfeldts' sample. The dissimilarity between the business leaders and the small businessmen in this regard vanishes, however, if we consider the present business of the respondent: here the percentage is very .similar for both groups. Fourteen percent of both the Lexington and the Warner and Abegglen samples have relatives in their present firms, as do 15 percent of Newcomer's leaders.

In general, businessmen in all the studies surveyed came up the hard way—without financial aid from relatives or friends. Where aid was received, the small businessmen led their fellows who were in big business. Almost a third of the Lexington group received some sort of aid from kin and nonkin. A fifth received financial aid from parents or kin, while slightly over a tenth received other kinds of aid (nonfinancial) from kin and nonkin. Warner and Abegglen found that only 6 percent received financial assistance in their business venture, approximately half by inheritance and half from relatives. In the Newcomer group, approximately 8 percent of the generation of 1900, 7 percent of the generation of 1925, and 2 percent of the generation of 1950 received financial aid.

There is a notable association between the size of the respondent's business and the extent of his education for the Lexington sample. In the Taussig and Joslyn (1928) and Warner and Abegglen (1952) samples, however, the relationship is very slight. Figures for the Newcomer (1950) executives are given only for college and noncollege education and show that a higher percentage of men in the largest firms have a college education than do men in the next-to-largest category.

In Lexington the percentage of men with only a grade school education declines, while the percentage with a college education increases with size of business; the percentage of college-trained men ranges from 4 in the smallest firms to 54 in the largest. In the Warner and Abegglen study the percentage of men with a grade school, high school, or college education remains generally the same as size of business increases: approximately three-fourths of the men in each category of size are college trained. The percentage of those in Taussig and Joslyn's study with only a grade school education is more similar to that of the Lexington group in most categories of size than it is to Warner and Abegglen's. The one exception is in the biggest business, where 21 percent of Taussig and Joslyn's leaders had only a grade school education, as compared with 6 percent reported by Warner and Abegglen and 9 percent found in Lexington; the difference is perhaps testimony to the greater difficulty of getting into the largest firms today with only a grade school education. In general, it seems that the extent to which each increment of education serves as entry to successively larger firms in small business today is more similar to the situation existing in big business in 1928 than in 1952. Warner and Abegglen's leaders are a much more homogeneous group as regards education than Lexington's small businessmen; there are minimal educational requirements for entrance into the world of big business, and education serves more as a test of admittance than as an instrument of upward mobility.

The percentage whose fathers were business owners or executives increases as size of business increases in Lexington, while in the Warner and Abegglen and Taussig and Joslyn samples of leaders the percentage of such fathers declines slightly as size increases. In the Lexington group there is roughly an inverse relationship between size of business and being a farmer's son, while for the two groups of business leaders the percentage of farmers' sons is approximately the same for each size, as is the percentage of sons of professional men. For the Lexington group the greatest percentage of sons of professional men is found in the largest firms (ten times that of the smallest).

Among the leaders in Lexington, those associated with parents or kin in their present businesses are more often affiliated with the largest firms than with the middle-sized or smallest: over half of these men are in the largest firms, while approximately one-eighth are in the smallest firms. In the Warner and Abegglen sample, however, men with relatives in the business are rarely found in the largest firms: less than one-tenth are in the largest firms, approximately three-fifths in the middle-sized firms, and the remaining one-third in the smallest.

Comparison of son's education and paternal occupation seems to demonstrate a selective educational floor for entry into big business firms not found in small businesses. Variation in the education of the son with paternal occupation is more noticeable in the case of the small businessmen of Lexington than in the two groups of business leaders cited (Table 4). Evidently, those who have achieved business leadership, however, have been able to overcome any adverse effect their father's occupation might have had on their education.

Sons of business owners and executives are the best-educated men in the Lexington, Warner and Abegglen, and Keller studies. The

TABLE 4
Education of Businessman and Occupation of His Father,
Expressed as Percentages

Occupation of Father	Education of Respondent (Years)			
	1–8	*9–12*	*13* [b]	*Total*
Business owner and executive				
Lexington businessman	12	42	46	100
Warner and Abegglen[a]	4	23	73	100
Keller[b]	—	27	73	100
Farmowner or tenant				
Lexington businessman	29	51	20	100
Warner and Abegglen	5	23	72	100
Keller	—	42	58	100
Foreman, craftsmen, etc.				
Lexington businessman	22	43	35	100
Warner and Abegglen	10	35	55	100

[a] Figures of Warner and Abegglen are for small business owners only.
[b] Keller's figures includes "high school or less."

distribution among the three levels—grade, high school, and college —of the sons of business owners and executives is practically identical in both Keller's and Warner and Abegglen's business leaders. The small businessmen in Lexington from this occupational background, however, include a smaller percentage of college-trained men and a higher percentage of grade- or high-school-educated men than is true for the two groups of leaders.

Sons of farmers are the most poorly educated of the Lexington group, a significant fact in view of their large number. The educational standing of farmers' sons among the business leaders is much better, however, especially in Warner and Abegglen's study, where there is only a very slight difference in percentage distribution among the three educational levels between them and the sons of owners or executives.

Data on sons of foremen, craftsmen, or skilled workers are available only for Lexington and the Warner and Abegglen sample: in the latter, leaders who are sons of foremen, craftsmen, or skilled workers are considerably better educated than their counterparts in Lexington.

In each of the three studies which had data on this subject, a higher percentage of sons of businessmen received aid in their business venture from parents or kin than did sons of farmers or of men in other occupations. Small businessmen received it more frequently than the business leaders. Half of the small businessmen in the Oxenfeldts' study who were sons of businessmen received aid from relatives, as did at least 29 percent of the sons of businessmen in the Lexington study and 6 percent of such men in Warner and Abegglen's study. Sons of farmers in the Oxenfeldts' group fared better than those in the other studies, with a third of them receiving aid from their families as compared with at least a sixth of the Lexington sample and a meager 3 percent of Warner and Abegglen's.

Considering all backgrounds together, over a third of the Oxenfeldts', a fifth of the Lexington, and less than one-twentieth of Warner and Abegglen's leaders received aid from their families in their first business. While small businessmen from the occupational backgrounds cited were so helped more often than the business leaders in the Warner and Abegglen study, the occupation of the father seems more closely associated with financial aid among the business leaders than among either of the two groups of small businessmen.

The highest percentage receiving financial assistance in the Warner and Abegglen group (the sons of business owners or executives) is over six times as great as the smallest percentage (the sons of farmers or "other" workers). However, for Lexington, the difference is less than three times as great, and for the Oxenfeldts' group it is less than twice (i.e., 29 versus 11 percent and 50 versus 28 percent).

Finally, although the data provide some clues as to the relative openness of two important sectors of American business, definitive statements regarding the mobility of small businessmen are impossible, obviously, solely on the basis of material from Lexington, Kentucky, and the Oxenfeldts' Colorado study. From other cities of the United States and from the country as a whole, data on small businessmen comparable to those on big businessmen would serve to put the data on small businessmen discussed here in perspective. They would provide, also, a basis for going beyond description to an analytical interpretation. In view of the importance of the business enterprise in our society, both as an economic institution and an avenue of upward social mobility, such study should command more attention than it has thus far.

Glen H. Elder, Jr.

APPEARANCE AND EDUCATION IN MARRIAGE MOBILITY OF WOMEN

Glen H. Elder's study is an excellent example of the varied approaches taken in recent vertical mobility research. It assumes that there is more to the issue of mobility than finding out what kind of men sit at the top or the routes they took to get there. Elder's essay goes beyond the patterns to the causes of mobility, in this case to the causal roles played by "looks and learning" in the marriages made by women of different social class. The article may appear to confirm the obvious; but as many studies have shown, what people— scholars included—often think is obvious often turns out to be untrue.

From Glen H. Elder, Jr., "Appearance and Education in Marriage Mobility," *American Sociological Review* 34 (August 1969): 519–533. Reprinted by permission of the author and publisher. References and footnotes deleted.

Marriage between persons of similar class-origin is partly an un-
conscious result of a process in which many individuals attempt to
achieve the best possible bargain for themselves or their children
by weighing marital resources and alternatives. Whether mates are
selected by the young or not, conditions supporting class endogamy
for high-status daughters are sought by parents with an interest in
preserving family lineage and status. A girl from the lower classes,
on the other hand, has much to gain by marriage to a man of high
social-standing or mobility potential, including higher status for
herself and her children and vicarious rewards for her parents.

The social advantages of hypergamy for the low-status girl—in
which she achieves higher status through marriage—appear as
status costs for the man, though what he loses in social rank may be
surpassed by gains in other forms of status. Equity in this type of
exchange would require the woman to be exceptional in other qualities which are defined as desirable in the culture. A sizable groom-
price might be added by parents to enhance their daughter's marriage prospects in a traditional society. Depending on the society,
the status-determining qualities of women include shade of skin
color, facial and morphological features, and relative age. As yet, we
do not know the preferential value (or utility) of these qualities within
differing cultures, when compared to each other or to the weight
attributed to other commodities of exchange, such as temperament,
interests, values, wealth, and social origin. Nevertheless, throughout
human history some women have been able to exchange their physical beauty for a young man's family lineage, accomplishments, or
mobility potential. Typically, "a woman is expected to use her attractiveness to gain certain legitimate ends such as recognition,
status, and a husband. The family stands back of her and helps her
to make a respectable bargain."

As suitors, men determine to a large extent the value of physical
attraction in the marriage market. American men, for instance, rank
physical attractiveness at or near the top among the qualities they
desire in women, and this seems to be especially true of the upward
mobile or strongly ambitious. Since the upper class is generally the
guardian and embodiment of symbols indicating beauty, the com-
panionship of an attractive woman has utility for the status climber.
Such women, in Veblen's words, enable "... successful men to put

their prowess in evidence by exhibiting some durable result of their exploits."

An exchange between the man's social rank and the woman's beauty is facilitated by culturally defined differences in the primary status-conferring qualities of each sex. The American male is expected to achieve status through his occupation, while the woman he marries assumes his status and name in exchange for her social rank and personal qualities. American society generally disapproves of a marital exchange in which the ownership of these attributes is reversed, such as when the woman has the intelligence and talent, and the man has youth or beauty. Within the upper classes, however, physical attractiveness appropriate to each sex may be a primary commodity in marital exchange.

In developmental formulations of dating, courtship, and marriage, the point at which physical attractiveness has its primary effect on movement from one phase to another has not been clearly determined. Kerckhoff and Davis suggest that a sequence of "filtering factors" is operative in mate selection, from social status determinants in the initial stage, to value consensus, and finally to need complementarity. It is probable that physical beauty serves as a screening device or a commodity for exchange on the initial contact. The degree of equity achieved at this stage would determine whether contact is maintained.

The actual influence of a girl's attractiveness on her bargaining position in mate selection has been most firmly documented by evidence showing a strong relationship between lightness of skin color and mobility among Negro women. There are few regions of the world where the maiden of fair skin is not considered more desirable for marriage than a girl with dark skin. Assuming that height is associated with a slender, feminine build among Western women, there is some evidence relevant to the attractivness-mobility relationship in a study of women in Aberdeen, Scotland. Lower-strata women who married men of high status were taller and healthier than their non-mobile counterparts. And in a sample of female students at an American university, facial attractiveness was found to be predictive of married status at the time of a follow-up several years after college. Overall, these data provide some evidence of a relationship between a woman's attractiveness and her chances for achieving higher status through marriage. Although class differences in this association have not been reported in the literature, we have reason to expect that attractiveness has the strongest influence on marriage mobility among women from the working class. This attribute, as well as the others, would be needed to compensate for low class-origin in marital exchange with a man of higher social rank.

Women in modern societies may surpass their family's status by their own educational attainment and by the accomplishments of their husbands. The sequence of high intelligence, a desire to excel, and entrance into college is a common path to high adult status among women as well as men, and some evidence suggests that ambitious women are most likely to use their physical assets to impress or charm high-status men. Although a woman's intelligence or ambition may indirectly influence her marital prospects through higher education, they are apt to have less *direct* relevance for her marriageability than physical attractiveness.

If intelligence and ambition are not a woman's most valued resources for marital exchange, at least two pathways could be followed to marriage mobility: exchange between the attractiveness of the woman and the higher social rank or potential of the man, and movement through the educational system—resulting from intelligence, ambition, and successful academic performance—which eventually provides contact with high-status men. These paths intersect in the life course of an attractive girl who enters college, while the marital prospects of an attractive, working-class girl with only a high school education depend partly on her access to middle-class work settings.

The primary objective of this study is to assess these two modes of achieving higher status through marriage—an attractive appearance and educational attainment—in a longitudinal sample of women from middle- and working-class families. Educational attainment was viewed as most influential among women from the middle class, while the effect of physical attractiveness was hypothesized as strongest among women of working-class origin. These hypotheses were tested with data from the Oakland Growth Study, whose subjects were born in the early twenties and were studied intensively during the 1930s; most have participated in at least one adult follow-up.

Sample and Methods

The Oakland Growth Study was initiated in 1932 to assess the physical, mental, and social development of a sample of boys and girls selected from fifth and sixth grade children in five elementary schools. Intention to remain in the area and willingness to cooperate were the primary criteria for selection of the subjects. Eighty-three girls were selected for the present analysis on the basis of the continuous participation in the research program from 1932 to 1939: all were white, most were Protestant, and slightly less than half came from middle-class families. Three-fourths of the families were intact and were headed by native-born parents. The median intelligence quotient, based on average scores on Stanford-Binet tests administered in 1933 and 1938, was 110.

Data collected during the thirties include annual ratings of social and emotional behavior made by staff members from observations of the children in natural situations, a series of self-report inventories on the adolescents, and ratings by teachers and mothers. A complete description of the instruments and data collection procedures employed during the 1930s is provided in an early report by Harold Jones (1939).

The five elementary schools attended by the subjects were situated in contiguous residential areas in the northwestern sector of Oakland, California. The family background of enrolled students showed that two of the schools were largely working class, one was lower middle class, and the other two were middle class. From these schools, the children entered the same junior high school, and all but a few later attended the same high school. Cross-sectional samples of students in these two schools during the mid-thirties showed that from 55 to 60 percent were from middle-class families. The high school was primarily a college preparatory institution and maintained high academic standards. Approximately 1,900 students were enrolled at the time the subjects were in high school. Among residents in the community, the high school enjoyed a favorable reputation for placing qualified students in the nearby state university. These features of the educational setting indicate that ambitious, capable girls from low-status homes were offered opportunities for mobility through education and marriage.

Seventy-six members of the adolescent sample were contacted
in at least one of the three adult follow-ups. Information on occupation, education and marital status was available up to 1958 for all
women in the sample. A comparison of the adolescent *and* adult
samples disclosed no differences in family social-class (as of 1929),
ethnicity, household structure, or IQ. Measurement of attractiveness,
aspirations, academic aptitude, and mobility through marriage is
described below. The levels of educational attainment used in the
analysis are described later in the text.

Attractiveness. Information on the girls' appearance was obtained from observational ratings made by staff members in a play-
ground setting during semiannual visits to the Institute of Human
Development. The two or more staff members in attendance were
well known by the girls and related to them as interested, friendly
adults. Observations made during these sessions were recorded
afterwards on comment sheets and on seven-point scales (interrater
reliabilities were above .90 on the appearance scales listed below).
To increase the stability of the judgments, scores on selected
scales were averaged for the senior high school period. The following scales were selected as measures of appearance: good physique, well-groomed, sex appeal, and an overall index of appearance.
This last index represents an average of scores on the following
scales: attractive coloring, good features, good physique, thin-to-fat,
femininity of behavior and physique, pleasing expression, and sex
appeal.

Status Aspirations. The status aspirations of women have been
defined by particular goals—such as their own education, material
possessions, and the prestige of their future husband's job—and by
the strength of their orientation toward high status. Although more
refined measures of ambition would have been desirable, the lack
of requisite data necessitated the use of two general indexes of
status aspiration: a five-point rating of the desire for social dominance (defined as the "desire to control one's human environment by
suggestion, persuasion, or command) and a nine-point rating of
aspiration for high status. Scores on the former index represent an
average of the ratings made by three judges on the basis of qualitative observations obtained during the subjects' high school years
(interrater reliability = .76). Although the rating was based on observed behavior in peer interaction, subtle indirect cues as well as

overt features of behavior were used to infer the underlying motive. According to these data, the rating is primarily an index of the desire for status or mastery within the high school or peer environment.

The second index—a measure of the aspiration for high status—was obtained from the 104-item California Q set, which provided ratings for the high school period. Three psychologists were first presented with the same set of data on each subject—including parental interviews, self-reports from the subjects, classmate impressions of each other, and staff observations—and were asked to sort independently the 104 items into nine ordered categories, ranging from one (uncharacteristic) to nine (characteristic). The three judgments on each item were then averaged to obtain each subject's score. From item descriptions given to the judges, it is clear that the "aspiration" rating refers to the girls' orientation toward future status rather than to status within the high school setting.

Intelligence and Academic Aptitude. As noted earlier, IQ scores of girls in the sample were obtained by averaging scores on Stanford-Binets administered in 1933 and 1938. The girls' academic aptitude in high school was measured by the average value of two seven-point ratings on academic interest and performance that were made by three teachers. This rating was used in lieu of grade-point average since the latter was not available on all of the girls. The two indices are, however, highly intercorrelated ($r = .85$) in the subsample of girls for whom both measures were available.

Mobility through Marriage. As a measure of mobility through marriage, we chose to compare father's social position and husband's occupational status at approximately the same point in the life cycle. The qualities ambitious women desire in a prospective husband presumably include those which promise future achievements. Such qualities may be more important to the girl than the social status and accomplishments of her fiancé, especially since marriage often occurs during or before the man's completion of formal education and selective service requirements. A majority of women in the sample married shortly before or during World War II —more than half were married by the age of twenty-two. Since most of their husbands either were in the armed forces or were enrolled in an institution of higher education, matrimony involved marriage to a man with a given potential rather than to a person with an occupation.

Two methods were employed to identify patterns of mobility through marriage. One involved the delineation of groups of women by cross-tabulating father's and husband's occupational status (1929 and 1958), indicated in each case by Hollingshead's seven-level index. The second procedure—correlational and path techniques—will enable the identification of direct and indirect paths to high status.

Findings

A woman's attractiveness of physique and grooming was hypothesized as a valued resource for marital exchange involving a man of high social standing or mobility potential, while her intelligence, academic aptitude, and aspirations facilitate entry into college settings which provide opportunities to meet socially desirable men. As the first step in the analysis, then, middle- and working-class girls were compared on measures of both attractiveness and achievement orientation in order to describe their socioeconomic context in marriage mobility.

Class Variations in Attractiveness. Girls from the working class are likely to have been ranked lower on attractiveness of physique than middle-class girls. Since the heritability coefficient for morphological characteristics is relatively high (for instance, r's between the height of parents and offspring vary between .50 and .60), the social ascent of attractive women could produce class-linked genetic differences in morphology which favor middle-class girls on physical appearance. Available data show only a slight positive correlation between the physical characteristics of marital partners, aside from constitutional types. The nutritional advantages of a middle-class background or a measurement bias on the part of observers which favored middle-class girls could also produce this expected class difference in physical appearance.

There may also be a relationship between family status and a well-groomed appearance since middle-class families were characterized by higher appearance standards and economic resources than families in the working class. Mothers in the working class, for instance, were judged significantly more unkempt than mothers from the middle-class on an interviewer rating, and their daughters differed from middle-class girls to a similar extent on the adequacy of their standards regarding cleanliness and the selection of clothes.

The data generally support these expectations, although the differences are not large (Table 1). As a group, middle-class girls were judged more attractive than girls from the working class on physique, sex appeal, grooming, and on overall appearance. Since attractive girls were characterized as popular with both sexes and were described as self-assured (not shown in the table), it is not surprising that the popularity and self-assurance of girls in the sample were significantly correlated with their family status.

TABLE 1
Social-Class Variations in the Appearance of Girls in High School: Staff Ratings

Senior High Staff Ratings	Means and Standard Deviations				Level of Statistical Significance
	Middle Class		Working Class		
	x̄	s	x̄	s	
Appearance	N=35		N=43		
Good Physique	56.6	13.5	48.6	14.2	b
Well-groomed	57.8	13.4	49.0	13.5	c
Sex Appeal	56.2	15.1	48.9	15.0	b
Appearance—General rating	55.8	11.3	46.3	14.3	c

[a] $p < .10$ (two-tailed t test).
[b] $p < .05$.
[c] $p < .01$.

Intelligence, Aspirations, and Academic Aptitude.   Whatever marital advantage middle-class girls derived from their appearance might well have been enhanced by their greater access to educational opportunities. Their parents read more magazines and books, and held higher educational expectations than did parents from the working class. All of these influences suggest that middle-class girls were higher in IQ, aspirations, and academic aptitude than girls with a working-class background. The data generally show differences in the expected direction, but they are very small, with the exception of IQ (112.8 vs. 107.2, $p < .05$). The middle-class climate of the high school may have contributed to the similarity of girls in the two social classes on measures of achievement motivation. Exposure to academic models and ambitious students very likely increased the aspirations and school performance of girls from low-status families.

Attractive girls were generally ambitious within the context of social relationships in the high school, as indicated by a desire for social dominance ($r = .32$). However, they were not more likely to aspire to high status in the future, nor were they brighter or more achievement-oriented than their less attractive classmates.

According to these data, a large number of girls are likely to be ranked differently on intelligence and appearance. In a culture which values beauty more than intellect in women, girls who possess high intelligence but lack desired physical characteristics may elicit negative responses and conflicting perceptions from their agemates. Whether these girls hide or display their intellectual talents may depend on their self-concept and upbringing.

Development of a "meritocratic" utopia is complicated by the relative independence of attractiveness and intelligence in women, as noted in Michael Young's humorous description of feminist dissatisfaction with intelligence as a primary basis of mate selection. By the emphasizing on romantic values and beauty, the feminists "... have echoed the lower classes who esteem bodily prowess and give a heightened value, a symbolic value, to a superficial quality not at all related to intelligence, that is, to appearance." Although a popular slogan of the feminists portrayed beauty as an achievable goal for all, this claim is questioned by data in the present study; on the average, working-class girls were ranked lower on physical appearance than their classmates from the middle class.

Mobility through Marriage. Before we examine the effects of attractiveness and educational achievement on mobility through marriage, attention must be given first to differences between mobility from the working class and status change within the middle-class. Mobility from the working class usually represents a sharper disjuncture in life circumstances and reference sets than movement from the lower to the upper middle class. Other things being equal, working-class girls can of course achieve a larger status gain than their higher-status counterparts. In view of these considerations, one might prefer to restrict the term "mobility" to the process of moving into the middle class through marriage, and define marriage to a high-status man within the middle class as high achievement. For purposes of the present study, however, an intergenerational increase in status through marriage was defined as upward mobility, regardless of family origin. We assumed that the hypothesized qualities and accomplishments which enable a girl to marry a man with high potential or rank (and which are not conterminous with a middle-class upbringing, such as a well-groomed appearance) would predict mobility among women from both social classes.

Upwardly mobile and nonmobile groups were defined in each of the two social classes. Among women from the middle class, the mobile group was composed of women who achieved higher status through marriage; those who had married up one or more occupational levels, as well as eight women whose husbands were in the same upper-middle-class stratum as the subjects' fathers. Although the indices show no intergenerational change in status for these latter women, work history information indicated that the husbands were above the status of their fathers-in-law in terms of status in the work setting and/or on education.

The second group of middle-class women—defined as nonmobile—had husbands who were either on the same relatively low-status level as their fathers, or were one or more levels below their fathers in occupational status. Sixty-two percent of the women from middle-class families were classified as having married high-status men.

The primary criterion used to define upward mobility among women from the working class was ascent into the middle class. Thirty-six percent of the women were in this category; all of their husbands were two or more occupational levels above the status of the subjects' fathers (most were in the managerial-professional group). The nonmobile group included fourteen women who were stable in occupational status, three who lost status through marriage, and six women who married up one level but remained in the working class.

Attractiveness. The dynamics of an equitable exchange in mate selection and marriage suggest the following proposition: the more a man's social rank exceeds his wife's premarital social rank, the more likely is his wife to possess exceptional personal qualities, such as appearance.

Mobile women from the middle and working class were rated significantly higher in adolescence on attractiveness of physique, sex appeal, and overall appearance than nonmobile women of similar class origin (Table 2). Mobile women of working-class origin were clearly exceptional in appearance relative to nonmobile women, and in this respect they resembled women from the middle class who achieved higher status through marriage. The overall rating of attractiveness was more strongly related to husband's occupational status among women from the working class than among women of middle-class background (r = .46 vs. .35).

TABLE 2
Mobility Through Marriage by Appearance in Adolescence

Staff Ratings of Appearance in Senior High School	Mean Scores by Mobility and Childhood Social Class			
	Middle Class		Working Class	
	Upwardly mobile	Nonmobile	Upwardly mobile	Nonmobile
	N=19	N=13	N=13	N=23
Good physique	59.5 [b]	49.4 [b]	56.2 [b]	47.0 [b]
Well-groomed	60.0	57.9	60.1 [c]	46.3 [c]
Sex appeal	57.9 [a]	52.4 [a]	59.3 [c]	46.5 [c]
Appearance—General rating	57.9 [b]	52.4 [b]	57.2 [c]	42.5 [c]

[a] p<.10 (two-tailed t test).
[b] p<.05.
[c] p<.01.

In adolescence, mobile women from the working class were also more likely to be seen as well-groomed than their less successful counterparts. The adoption of middle-class standards of grooming by lower-status girls in the premarital years seems likely to reflect both social ambition and anticipatory socialization toward higher status. Since a well-groomed appearance is traditionally a middle-class expectation, and was most prevalent in this stratum, its negligible effect on the marital prospects of women from this social class is not surprising.

As a resource in heterosexual relationships, personal attractiveness provides some clues to the social process by which pretty girls from the working class achieved mobility through marriage. According to Waller's principle of least interest, a low-status girl's prospect for achieving a desirable marital exchange with a higher-status male depends on her bargaining position or possession of valued personal qualities. In this respect, an attractive girl would be less vulnerable to his sexual claims than a less appealing girl. With more to offer in such a relationship, she could well afford to be more selective regarding suitors and their demands. In addition, relatively pretty girls elicit social responses that enhance their self-image; in the sample, these girls were likely to feel secure and self-confident in the presence of others. In reference to the interests of American fashion models, Campbell observes that they "... are pretty, they know it, and they prefer activities that allow them to take advantage of their beauty." The rewards associated with feminine attractiveness suggest that pretty girls are conditioned to employ their bargaining advantage in dating and mate selection.

Exploration of the adolescent heterosexual experience of mobile and attractive women from the working class provided evidence which is generally consistent with the above interpretation. As summarized, the analysis showed that the upwardly mobile were less likely than nonmobile women to go "steady" with one boy. Though they spent similar time with boys, the mobile women appear to have been more guarded and selective in relations with the opposite sex than the nonmobile.

This difference in behavior is also suggested by data on adolescent sexual experiences, obtained retrospectively in the 1958 interview. Coitus during high school was much less frequently reported by mobile than by nonmobile women from the working class (10 vs. 70 percent), and a similar difference was obtained on petting. The social risks associated with sexual experience, especially a damaged reputation, undoubtedly contributed to this negative relationship between degree of coitus and marriage mobility. Findings from studies by Kinsey, Reiss, and Lindenfeld also show a moderate relationship between sexual restraint among women and their mobility (mainly through education). Among women from the middle class, the only meaningful variation in social patterns occurred on steady dating, which was negatively associated with marriage to a high-status husband.

Class Origin, Appearance, and Status Aspirations. In family resources, middle-class girls have a bargaining advantage over their lower-status counterparts, and a large percentage succeed in marrying men who closely resemble them in background. A selective, demanding attitude toward suitors is an appropriate expression of social advantage. Scott describes this attitude as "class-specific vanity," and suggests in his research on upper-middle-class sorority girls that it is a generalized consequence of an indulgent upbringing, consisting of the expectation that they should ". . . receive in courtship the same extravagant favors and attention that their well-situated parents have made for them." Although the class origin of women in the sample influenced their chances of marrying high-status men, this relationship was not as strong as that between attractiveness and husband's status ($r_s = .27$ vs. .43). However, class origin is but one aspect of the family's overall influence on status placement.

Women from the middle and working class resembled each other on status aspiration in adolescence—in desire for social dominance among agemates and high status in the future, and these measures were significantly correlated with marriage mobility in each stratum (Table 3). In the total sample, husband's status was more highly correlated with status aspirations (as measured by the two indexes, both ($r_s = .38$) than with class origin.

One of the more significant contributions of family status to mobility through marriage may have occurred through related contexts and opportunities. For instance, class-linked barriers to higher education might increase reliance on modes of achievement through marriage which are unrelated to academic performance and intelligence, such as physical attractiveness. This adaptation could explain why attractiveness and husband's status were more highly related among women from the working class than among women from higher status families. Only 20 percent of the women from the working class achieved any college education, in contrast to nearly two-thirds of the women from middle-class families. From these findings, it appears that nonacademic resources in mate selection are more important to women from the working class, and a college education is relatively more influential in the marital careers of women from the middle class. According to regression analyses within each social class, attractiveness, social dominance, and aspiration for high status explained a larger proportion of the variance in husband's status in the working class than in the middle class (43 vs. 28 percent).

Education and Marriage Mobility. The relatively more important

TABLE 3
Mobility through Marriage by Social Motivation and Aspirations in Adolescence[a]

Ratings of Social Motivations and Aspirations	Mean Scores[b] by Mobility through Marriage and Childhood Social Class[b]			
	Middle Class		Working Class	
	Upwardly mobile	Nonmobile	Upwardly mobile	Nonmobile
Desire for social dominance	(18)	(11)	(11)	(15)
(1=low; 5=high)	2.4 [e]	1.8 [e]	2.7 [e]	1.7 [e]
Aspiration level	(15)	(9)	(10)	(11)
(1=low; 9=high)	5.4 [d]	4.0 [d]	4.5 [d]	3.3 [d]

[a] The number enclosed within each parenthesis represents the total N on which the mean is based.
[b] On the original social dominance scale, the highest rating was a score of one. Scores on the scale were reversed in order to make them consistent with the direction of other scales in the analysis. A strong desire for social dominance is thus indicated by a score of five.
[c] $p < .10$ (two-tailed t-test).
[d] $p < .05$.
[e] $p < .01$.

role of education in the marital achievement of women from the middle class is most clearly expressed in college attendance and its relation to husband's status. Women from the middle class were more likely to have had at least some college, and, in the college group, a larger proportion of these women than those from the working class were upwardly mobile (72 vs. 50 percent). In the noncollege group, 45 and 35 percent of the women with middle- and working-class origins were upwardly mobile. This class difference may be partly a consequence of the qualitatively better schools attended by women from the middle class, e.g., Stanford vs. the state colleges.

In both social classes, higher education and the marital opportunities it provides are most likely to be available to girls who are above average in mental ability and academic aptitude. Consistent with research findings on the careers of men, we expected these attributes to affect marriage mobility primarily through the educational system, although they may also contribute directly to social sophistication and marriageability. In a recent study of men, academic ability was associated with occupational achievement, but its effects occurred mainly within the school system.

Upwardly mobile women from the middle and working class were not brighter than the nonmobile (less than two point differences between group means). Even without controlling for social origin, the correlation between the women's IQ in adolescence and their husbands' occupational status was only .14. There is also no evidence of markedly different marital achievement between women who were rated high and low on academic aptitude by their high school teachers (r with husband's status = .14). Although one might conclude from these results that intellectual talents have little bearing on the status achieved by the women through marriage, this ignores their effect on educational attainment and its relation to the social standing of their husbands. The significance of this indirect path to a high-status marriage is indicated by the substantial relationship of educational level to IQ and academic aptitude in adolescence (r_s = .30 and .47 respectively).

The direct and indirect effects of academic aptitude and mental ability on husband's status are more appropriately assessed by the path technique, as recently described by Duncan. Path coefficients for linear, asymmetric relationships represent estimates of the main or direct effects of independent variables on the dependent variable. A pictorial representation of paths is not an essential feature of the technique, although it does facilitate their interpretation, since it requires an explicit statement of assumptions, especially regarding the time order of the variables, and clearly shows the indirect effects of antecedent factors on the dependent variable, such as the path from academic aptitude through education after high school to husband's status.

In a diagram, the path connecting two variables whose relationship is asymmetric and linear is described by a one-way arrow and a path coefficient. The relationship between variables that are given, or, in other words, whose relationship is not to be explained, is represented by a curved two-way arrow and a correlation coefficient. Since path analysis requires that each dependent variable be completely determined by variables within the system, a residual factor—assumed to be uncorrelated with the antecedent or other residual factors—must be introduced to account for the unexplained variance.

In order to assess the indirect educational path to a high-status marriage, and to compare it with the effects of attractiveness, we defined both childhood social class and attractiveness as given. Academic aptitude and educational attainment were defined as intervening between class origin and attractiveness, on the one hand, and husband's status, on the other. Since academic aptitude is a product of intellect and motivation, we chose to include it in the analysis instead of IQ. Although the effects of educational attainment and attractiveness on marriage mobility vary by class origin, the small proportion of women from the working class who entered college made within-class analyses impractical. Use of the total sample, however, does enable us to compare the influence of class origin with the above factors on mobility through marriage. This model of the mobility process is shown in Figure 1.

Elements in the educational path to a high-status marriage clearly differ from attributes (such as attractiveness) which are directly involved in mate selection. Both class origin and academic aptitude influenced the status achieved by women in marriage primarily through the educational system. In fact, the path coefficient for the relationship between academic aptitude and husband's status is slightly negative. A similar result was obtained with IQ. Attractiveness, on the other hand, directly influenced the likelihood of marriage to a man of high status and was relatively independent of educational attainment and its determinants. Only two main sources of husband's status are shown in the diagram, but the results suggest that there are alternative ways in which different women can achieve the same status through mate selection and marriage. To ignore this diversity is to overlook or obscure the potentially different implications of social conditions and attributes for each pathway and their interrelations. The present analysis is a mere beginning since many relevant factors and settings were not examined. For instance, work settings in the premarital period were undoubtedly important in determining the marital opportunities of women who did not attend college.

Since two of the variables in Figure 1—class origin and academic aptitude—show very little relationship to husband's occupational status, it is not surprising that most of the variance in the dependent

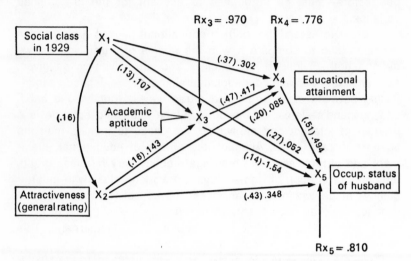

FIGURE 1. Diagram showing paths relating subject's educational attainment and husband's occupational status to pre-adult academic aptitude, appearance, and social class. (Zero-order correlation coefficients in parentheses alongside path coefficients.)

variable is unexplained. However, the most predictive variables in the study—educational attainment, the two measures of status aspiration, and attractiveness—account for approximately 47 percent of the variance in husband's status. The addition of class origin to the regression analysis did not increase this percentage.

Although intelligence and academic aptitude had little direct bearing on marital achievement, this effect may vary according to the woman's appearance. For instance, the attractive girl who is also bright would have the advantage, relative to her less able counterpart, of the social skills and mating opportunities in college which are associated with intellectual competence. Such ability could lead to similar opportunities among the less attractive, but it would not be embedded in physical qualities which are valuable in mate selection. To explore these potential interactions the women were sorted into four subgroups according to whether they were above or below average on both IQ and physical attractiveness, and mean values on the index of husband's occupational status (range = 1, high, to 7, low) were computed. The only positive effect of IQ on husband's status occurred among women who were above average in attractiveness (high vs. low IQ, $\overline{X}s = 2.1$ vs. 3.0), a difference which was slightly larger among women from the working class. Although IQ influenced husband's status through marital opportunities in the college environment, the above result was not dissimilar among women who did not attend college. Across all four groups, bright, attractive women were most likely to achieve a higher status through marriage, and their class origin did not alter this outcome. Comparable results were obtained with academic aptitude substituted for IQ, and neither attribute modified the relationship between appearance and husband's status.

The divergent implications of scholastic excellence and heterosexual status are evident in the culture of high schools, where girls, rewarded more for their social than academic skills, must nevertheless achieve satisfactory grades in order to qualify for college and its marital opportunities. Social skills also elicit more immediate social rewards than effort applied to a distant goal such as higher education which, in effect, generally postpones marriage. Adolescent girls' concern (to the degree it exists) with physical appearance, grooming, and clothes—frequently surpassing overt interest in the academic role—becomes more than simply a consequence of coeducational youth culture when viewed within the exchange framework of courtship and marriage. One could restructure the academic process to make it more exciting and rewarding, while downgrading competing social influences, but this does not alter criteria directly operative in assortative mating, such as the girl's appearance.

In a marital exchange which is truly reciprocal, the man and woman may exchange similar personal and social characteristics, or they may contribute different resources which are generally equivalent in value. Resemblance between marital partners or homogamy is well documented with respect to social characteristics, but much less is known about the conditions under which homogamy on education or on other attributes is greatest or least. Contextual factors, such as the proximate availability of marriageable persons with similar social characteristics, are known to influence both the prevalence and degree of social homogamy. Within a particular context, however, variation among couples in social homogamy is likely to require an explanation based on the personal qualities of each spouse. For instance, when a woman marries a man with more education, qualities of the woman, such as her appearance, may provide equity in the exchange. The absence of such resources, on the other hand, is likely to increase the prospect of educational homogamy or even hypogamy. Particularly, we would expect educational homogamy to increase as the attractiveness of women decreases. This relationship was tested by correlating the educational level of husband and wife (with the woman's class origin controlled) among women who were above and below the median on appearance. The results do show a slightly higher degree of educational homogamy in the marriages of women in the unattractive group than in the attractive (r_s=.32 vs. .20). Educational variations between marital partners are also consistent with "equity" in marital exchange; wives with more education than their husbands were more prevalent in the low attractive group than in the high (30 vs. 15 percent).

There are other characteristics of the husbands of women in the sample—besides education and occupational status—which may affect the degree of homogamy, including physical attributes, handsomeness, and personality traits. These data were unfortunately not available for this study. If one or more of the above qualities are roughly equal in value to feminine beauty, a man who marries a low-status, attractive woman may possess fewer positive qualities of this kind than one who marries a woman of equal status and attractiveness. Exploration of these complex interactions presents many technical problems, but this research is needed to expand our knowledge regarding marital exchange in social mobility.

Summary

A woman's prospect for social ascent through marriage is dependent on her access to men of higher status and on the exchange value of her personal resources for marriage. Such access, or contact between persons of differing class origin, is provided by settings with entry requirements that emphasize individual merit more than ascribed characteristics, such as institutions of higher education. One of the oldest forms of exchange in hypergamous marriage involves the woman's attractiveness and the man's higher social status or potential status.

These two sources of marriage mobility—attractiveness and educational attainment—were explored in a longitudinal sample of women from middle- and working-class families. The subjects, born in the early 1920s, were intensively studied during the 1930s, and participated in at least one adult follow-up. The physical attractiveness and grooming of the women were measured in adolescence by observational ratings. Mobility through marriage was assessed by comparing family status in 1929 with husband's occupational status in 1958. In view of sample limitations in size and representativeness, the following results should be considered tentative.

1. Adolescent girls from the middle class were rated higher in attractiveness of physique and groomed appearance than girls from the working class. Although middle-class girls were higher than the working-class girls on IQ, the two groups were similar in status aspiration.

2. Physical attractiveness and status aspiration were significantly related to mobility through marriage, with the former most predictive of marriage to a high-status man among women from the working class. Socal ascent from the working class was also associated with a well-groomed appearance and with an avoidance of steady dating and sexual involvement.

3. Educational attainment was more strongly related to the marriage mobility of women from the middle class: they were more likely than women of lower-status origin to attend college, and a larger percentage in the college group (relative to lower-status women) were upwardly mobile. Marriages in which the wife had more education than the husband were most prevalent among women who were relatively low in attractiveness.

4. Mental ability and academic aptitude were related to husband's status primarily through the women's own educational attainment; and since attractive women in the sample were not brighter or significantly more likely to attend college, education and appearance are relatively independent sources of mobility through marriage.

5. Class origin was more strongly related to educational attainment than to husband's occupational status, and its effects on mobility were less than those of attractiveness, status aspiration, and level of education. As noted, however, the relative effects of attractiveness and education on mobility through marriage varied markedly by class origin.

Points of correspondence on class differences in the mobility of women and men emerge when these results are compared with those obtained in a study of occupational mobility among men in the same longitudinal sample. Intelligence was more strongly related to occupational mobility among men from the middle class, while the effects of achievement motivation were relatively greater among men from the working class. Educational attainment was more predictive of occupational mobility than any other variable (as it was for husband's status in the present study), and its effects were generally greater among men from the middle class, in part because they were brighter and achieved a higher level of education. For both men and women in the sample, intelligence and academic aptitude in adolescence primarily influenced the adult status they achieved through the educational system.

Bradley R. Schiller

THE LIMITED OPPORTUNITIES OF WELFARE CHILDREN

The conclusions of Bradley R. Schiller's research are clear. "Inequality of opportunity along class lines is responsible for much of the achievement lag of poor children." His methodology and analyses are likely to be less clear, particularly to readers with little background in mathematics and statistics. Since some of the best mobility research presently being done relies on techniques common to these disciplines, the serious student of social mobility has no recourse but to try to master these techniques.

In spite of extensive and continuing discussions of poverty in the United States, no concerted effort has been made to determine socioeconomic achievement of sons born into poverty. As a corollary to this neglect, there has been no convincing evidence to portray

Bradley R. Schiller, "Stratified Opportunities: The Essence of the 'Vicious Circle,' " *American Journal of Sociology* 76 (November 1970): 426–441. Copyright © 1970 by the University of Chicago Press. Reprinted by permission of the publisher. Footnotes deleted.

differential achievement patterns by economic class of origin. This [essay] moves to fill these voids by considering how much success is achieved by sons who grow up in welfare families. The analysis contrasts the achievement of welfare sons with that of the general population. Consideration is given both to the absolute levels of achievement and to the routes by which they were secured. The initial socioeconomic position of the respondents' families is also assessed, indicating how much the observed achievements of the two populations represent disparate integenerational status mobility. In this manner, some tentative insights are obtained into (1) the nature and strength of exits out of poverty, (2) differential achievement patterns of the poor and nonpoor, and (3) the achievement barriers confronting low-income families.

The basic data have been secured from a national sample of 1,653 males who grew up in families receiving Aid to Families with Dependent Children (AFDC). These individuals represent all sons sixteen years of age or older in every third AFDC case which the welfare agency terminated during the months of January, February, or March 1961. Comparative data on the general population are taken from Peter Blau and Otis Dudley Duncan's *The American Occupational Structure* (1967). For both sets of data, information is available on parental socioeconomic status and sons' educational and early occupational achievement.

The Stratification Hypothesis

Socioeconomic achievement of an individual may be conveniently regarded as a function of three separate phenomena. First is the opportunity structure to which the individual has access. This structure defines both the ultimate achievement possibilities for the individual and the channels by which those achievements can be realized. Moreover, the potential efficacy of each of the available channels is carefully designed. It is not necessary, of course, that the same matrix of opportunities apply to every individual. Instead, we are more apt to speak of a stratified opportunity structure, indicating thereby that distinctive matrices may confront identifiable individuals or subpopulations residing within the same society. In such a case, it becomes necessary to define that stratification, especially in relation to the accessibility conditions applying to the different strata.

The second component of the achievement function is the individual himself. In this regard, we refer to the personality characteristics which determine the individual's capacity for exploiting his available opportunity structure, for example, intelligence, motivation, motor skills, and value systems. Given the set of individual characteristics and the opportunity matrix to which he has access, we can approximate the levels of socioeconomic status he will attain.

The third component of the achievement function is the frictional factor. The purpose of this factor is to recognize that two identically equipped individuals confronting the same opportunity structure may nevertheless attain disparate achievement levels. These variables—commonly called chance or fortune—inhere neither in the individual nor the opportunity structure. Thus, each individual's success is at least partly dependent on the frictions and windfalls of the relevant societal complex.

Theoretically, we could continue to specify the component variables in the idealized achievement function and thereby construct a thoroughly deterministic model of socioeconomic mobility. More pragmatically, we can approach a quantitative understanding of mobility patterns by specifying the most prominent component variables and observing their predictive ability.

We can postulate, for example, that the family's economic circumstances are the key accessibility conditions for the various opportunity strata available to the sons. Under this interpretation, each economic class confronts a separate and distinctive set of achievement opportunities, and knowledge of the economic status of the family of origin is critical to the specification of the achievements obtainable from any given set of individual abilities. In this [essay], household income is regarded as the most meaningful measure of origin economic status.

When we turn to the component variables which define the individual's capacity to achieve within his relevant opportunity structure, we encounter more serious specification difficulties. Thus, while eschewing responsibility for a more complete specification of the relevant variables, we will view the education of the homemaker as the only immediately available guide to such presumably important factors as personality structure, intelligence, motivation, and social outlook. Within a model of occupational determination the education of the individual himself can also be regarded as a partial proxy for these same variables, so that education becomes an indicator of both capacity to achieve (within the occupational hierarchy) and available opportunity (within the educational hierarchy).

Although these approximations remain exceedingly crude from a theoretical viewpoint, they do avail themselves to ready tests of the underlying achievement function. Because all of the AFDC sons grew up in a common economic class we might anticipate that they collectively confront identical opportunity structures. As a corollary, we can anticipate that variation in the economic achievements of the AFDC sons is attributable to disparities in individual capacities or talents. Hence, on an intraclass basis and within the available data dimensions, we anticipate that mother's education will emerge as a relatively important determinant of an AFDC son's socioeconomic success.

Within the confines of the AFDC sample it is relatively simple to explain the variations in socioeconomic achievement. A more adequate and interesting test of the stratification model must incorporate data from other identifiable classes. Without anticipating later results, we can formulate here two possible tests of the validity of the stratified opportunity hypothesis: (1) on an intersample basis father's occupation should increase in relative significance as a determinant of socioeconomic achievement, reflecting the postulate that economic status determines access to opportunity.

Because the Blau and Duncan sample covers nearly the entire U.S. population, it necessarily encompasses a large cross-section of the family-income distribution. Within its confines we have individuals of widely different economic-status origins, thus subject to varying opportunity structures. It is not possible, however, to immediately distinguish among these individuals, since no direct measure of income origins is available. Consequently, we must look to other, less direct measures of economic status, such as the occupation of the head of household, a variable which is positively correlated with family income. Accordingly, father's occupational status should serve to approximate access to offspring opportunity, and we may look for a relatively important relationship between father's occupation and son's achievement where the income and occupational hierarchies are broadly sampled (as they are in the Blau and Duncan survey). Where the income distribution is not broadly sampled (as in the AFDC survey), we would anticipate that origin occupational status would lose its potency in explaining son's achievement.

Our second test can be formulated: (2) the confrontation of the opportunity structure of a higher economic class with the characteristics of the AFDC sons should result in an overestimate of the AFDC sons' achievements, reflecting the postulates that the opportunity strata are in fact distinct and predicted upon economic class. Thus, as we move from the AFDC survey to the Blau and Duncan study, we expect the significance of origin occupational status to increase markedly.

Sample Comparability

The problem of comparing the data of the AFDC sample and the Blau-Duncan study results from the disparate scope of the two samples. The latter survey, an adjunct of the March 1962 Current Population Survey, represents all men twenty to sixty-four years old for whom requisite intergenerational occupational data were available. The AFDC sample, on the other hand, includes only younger men sixteen to thirty-nine years old with 75 percent of the sample concentrated in the sixteen- to twenty-one-year age range. Accordingly, the younger AFDC sample entered the labor force at a later point in time, and thus confronted an improved educational and occupational structure. Hence, the comparative achievements of the AFDC sons are biased upwards vis-à-vis the data from the Blau and Duncan sample. How serious this bias is cannot be determined exactly, but other interage cohort comparisons suggest the bias is important (Duncan, Featherman, and Duncan 1968, Appendix tables B.5–B.8).

Compounding the upward bias of the AFDC achievement levels is the length of time which the AFDC sons have already spent in the labor force. The data from the Blau and Duncan sample refer to the respondent's first job after the completion of his education. Although we are approximating the same observation for the bulk of the AFDC sons, it is also true that a high proportion of these sons has accumulated some years of experience and seniority. The bias here operates on two different levels. To the extent that the AFDC sons have experienced upward occupational mobility during these extra years of labor toward their "first job," their first-job occupational achievements are clearly overstated. One may suspect, however, that these men have not advanced greatly. If this is true, then the pertinent question for comparative integenerational occupational mobility patterns is: how far would the non-AFDC population have advanced with an equivalent amount of lead time to first job? The latter comparison extends the horizon of comparison and perhaps renders a clearer assessment of intergenerational socioeconomic change.

Another important source of disparity in the intersample comparisons may be found in the uneven coverage of the two samples. While the Blau and Duncan sample encompasses nearly all prospective labor-force entrants, the data on AFDC labor force entrants constitute only 62 percent (1,017 sons) of the underlying sample population. If those AFDC sons who reported unknown occupation or out-of-the-labor-force status have the potential to achieve higher socioeconomic status than their brethren, then we are underestimating AFDC achievements. While more detailed consideration is given to this question elsewhere (Schiller 1969, chap. 5), the caveat offered here is that the excluded AFDC sons show little promise of upgrading general AFDC socioeconomic achievement levels.

A final discrepancy worth special notice is the diverse racial composition of the two samples. Disparate occupational achievements by race do exist within the AFDC sample. Similarly, Blau and Duncan (1967, chap. 6) found racial discrimination in status achievement to be a major manifestation of their data. Accordingly, different racial proportions in the samples will distort intersample comparisons. This distortion lends itself to correction, however, on the basis of available data (appropriate adjustments are made in a forthcoming paper contrasting the relative impacts of racial and income discrimination). For the time being, the essential imperviousness of the immediate results to diverse sample racial compositions is offered as an article of faith.

Tallying the major difference in the two samples, then, we can conclude that the biases in the ensuing comparisons are distinctly in the direction of overstating the socioeconomic achievements of the AFDC sons vis-à-vis the achievements recorded by Blau and Duncan (1967).

Differential Achievements

Because the Blau and Duncan study refers to the entire socioeconomic hierarchy it can well be regarded as pertaining to the non-AFDC population. While some recipients of AFDC may be included in their sample, the number involved is certainly too small to significantly influence the sample characteristics. Accordingly, the confrontation of the samples approximates a straightforward interclass comparison, the primary distinction between the classes being income.

TABLE 1
Means and Standard Deviation of Selected Variables, for AFDC and Non-AFDC Populations

	Mean Values and Standard Deviations	
Variable	AFDC	Non-AFDC
Father's occupation	14.06 (10.02)	27.33 (21.6)
Mother's education	3.173 (1.115)	—
Father's education[a]	—	3.421 (1.274)
Father's education[b]	—	3.105 (1.838)
Son's education	3.610 (1.168)	4.433 (1.77)
Son's occupation	14.87 (12.74)	25.50 (21.4)

Source: Non-AFDC values calculated from Blau and Duncan (1967, pp. 484–85).
[a] Computed on AFDC mothers' index (see Appendix).
[b] Computed on AFDC sons' index (see Appendix).

In Table 1 the mean values and standard deviations for the primary variables of the basic achievement functions are presented for both samples. It can be confirmed readily that the disparate income position of the two samples manifests itself in all of the basic socioeconomic variables. For the variable "father's education" it should be noted that the relevant values were calculated on two different indexes, the first to correspond to the index of the AFDC mothers, the second to facilitate comparison with the education of the sons. For the sons, the difference between the AFDC and non-AFDC populations is equivalent to approximately two and one-half years of high school, with the non-AFDC mean falling just short of graduation. On the occupational index, it is of some interest to note that two standard deviations above the mean for the AFDC population fail to reach the mean score of the lowest white-collar occupations, while only one standard deviation achieves this objective for the non-AFDC population.

While the actual occupational distributions of both samples are presented in the Appendix, it is important to note here the exceedingly low-status position of the AFDC fathers. These depressed origins approximate an occupational status floor, below which there is little room to fall. Consequently, the AFDC sons should enjoy the greatest likelihood of experiencing upward occupational mobility. What is disquieting is that these sons achieve, in fact, negligible upward mobility, considerably less than that dictated by a changing occupational structure alone. While the non-AFDC sons experience net downward mobility to first job, other research has indicated that this status loss is but a brief interval in their lifetime career patterns. The available evidence is not so promising for sons of low-status origins (Form and Miller 1949; Blau and Duncan 1967).

The grossly inferior occupational mobility of the AFDC sons is seen most clearly when the AFDC and non-AFDC sons are compared according to father's specific occupational category. As Table 2 reveals, holding origin occupational-status constant only accentuates the achievement differences between the two groups. In the context of this latter comparison the severely limited intergenerational occupational mobility of the AFDC sons is apparent.

Hypothesis 1. In order to better understand the process of socioeconomic achievement for both groups of sons, a causal link between family background factors and later achievement was developed within a path-analysis framework (Schiller 1969, chap. 3). The most salient results of that analysis are summarized in the regression equations of Table 3. The equations can be interpreted both as achievement functions and as representations of the relevant opportunity structures, for they clearly define both the potential for and limits to socioeconomic achievement.

The first postulate of the stratified-opportunity hypothesis was that

TABLE 2
Sons' Mean Occupational Index Score by Fathers' Occupational Category, for AFDC and Non-AFDC Sons

	Sons' Mean Occupational Score	
Fathers' Occupations	AFDC sons	Non-AFDC sons[a]
Professional and semiprofessional	36.600	45.900
Proprietors, managers, and officials	25.667	39.718
Clerical, sales, kindred workers	17.727	38.648
Craftsmen, foremen, and kindred	17.488	28.262
Operatives and kindred workers	11.397	25.522
Service workers	17.744	26.393
Unskilled laborers	13.623	21.339
Farm owners, renters, farm managers	15.857	17.907
Farm laborers	13.283	14.003

[a] The occupational distribution of the non-AFDC sons is taken from Blau and Duncan (1967, table J2.2).

TABLE 3
Regression Equations for Specified Variables, for AFDC and Non-AFDC Populations

Non-AFDC Population[a]	
(1) $W = -4.45 + .3027 V + .2120 X + 5.2350 U$	$R^2 = .33$
(2) $U = +2.8975 + .2931 V + .0229 X$	$R^2 = .26$

AFDC Population	
(3) $W = -.9220 + .4193 V' + .2419 X + 3.4524 U$	$R^2 = .13$
(.3570) (.0380) (.3398)	
(4) $U = +2.4916 + .3135 V' + .0088 X$	$R^2 = .10$
(.0317) (.0035)	

Source: Non-AFDC coefficients calculated from Blau and Duncan (1967, pp. 174, 484–85).
Note: V = father's education, X = father's occupation, W = son's occupation, V' = mother's education, U = son's education.
[a] Standard deviations not available for non-AFDC regression coefficients.

within the context of the basic achievement functions, father's occupation would increase in stature relative to mother's education as a determinant of the son's socioeconomic achievement if the functions were applied on an interclass basis. To recapitulate, our argument is that increased economic status for the father leads to higher opportunity strata for the son. While we contend that income is the basic determinant of economic status, we accept father's occupation as a tentative proxy for income where the income distribution is broadly sampled. Accordingly, the regression coefficients of the Blau and Duncan sample should move in the direction indicated vis-à-vis the coefficients taken from the homogeneous income class of AFDC recipients.

The validity of these conjectures can be confirmed in Table 3. Thus, in the functions explaining son's educational achievement (equations 2 and 4), the importance of father's occupation increases threefold relative to parental education as we move from the AFDC to the non-AFDC population. Similarly, the relative importance of father's occupation doubles in the same comparison for son's occupational attainment (equations 1 and 3). These same relationships are confirmed in a comparison of the relevant standardized regression (or beta) coefficients, but those calculations have been omitted here. Accordingly, the available evidence is wholly consistent with the postulate that family income is a prime determinant of achievement opportunities.

Reinforcing this inference are the markedly higher coefficients of determination obtained in the Blau and Duncan sample. As Table 3 indicates, the coefficients of determination in the equations explaining either son's education or occupation are two and one-half times larger in their sample than in the AFDC population. This is precisely what we would anticipate on the basis of the stratification hypothesis. Because income (economic) class is a prime determinant of opportunity and achievement, a sample population which encompasses considerable income variation will better explain observed variation in son's socioeconomic achievement. Naturally, a sample which explicitly included family income as an independent variable would still better account for the observed achievement variations.

Hypothesis 2. The second postulate takes a multilayered opportunity stratification as given, then collapses that stratification into a simple dichotomized structure. At this point the data for the Blau and Duncan sample are taken to represent the opportunity structure confronting the entire non-AFDC population. Thus, the structure itself is a synthesis of the opportunity levels available to the different income groups here lumped together under the rubric "non-AFDC." It must be emphasized that the aggregation does not assert the existence of a dichotomized opportunity stratification, but rather serves as a convenient test of the existence of at least two levels within the broader structure.

The unstandardized regression equations for the Blau and Duncan sample are accepted here as quantitative representations of the opportunity structure prevailing in the non-AFDC population. The second hypothesis asserts that the application of these equations to the characteristics of the AFDC population will result in an overestimate of the AFDC sons' actual socioeconomic achievements. This statistical procedure is tantamount to a demonstration of "cumulative disadvantage," in the sense employed by Blau and Duncan in their discussion of racial discrimination, and is discussed further below.

When, in fact, the mean characteristics of the AFDC population (Table 1) are applied to equation 1 of Table 3, the predicted occupational status for the AFDC sons is 18.39, which contrasts with their actual status of 14.87. How serious this discrepancy is can be deduced from the following considerations:

1. If within the blue-collar occupations all of the AFDC sons were to rise one step on the occupational hierarchy (as depicted in the Appendix), the net gain in status would be insufficient for the purpose of eliminating the overestimate.
2. It would be necessary for all of the 108 AFDC craftsmen-foremen and half of the 107 AFDC operatives to move into the white-collar class for the status deficit to be overcome.

How difficult this ascension might be is suggested by the high school diploma requirements associated with the bulk of lower white-collar positions.

Thus the overestimate of the AFDC sons' occupational status is a formidable one and cannot be dismissed on the grounds that it falls within one standard deviation of the actual mean. In addition, the biases in the data already discussed tend to diminish the size of the calculated overestimate.

The same situation applies to the educational achievements of the AFDC sons. When equation 2 is applied to the background characteristics of the AFDC sons, their predicted mean educational attainment is 4.149, which contrasts with their actual attainment of 3.610. This overestimate is equivalent to better than one year of additional schooling for each of the AFDC sons. Thus, it is observed that the AFDC sons suffer far more occupational and educational under-achievement than can be attributed directly to their deprived home environments, an observation that is perfectly consistent with the stratified opportunity hypothesis.

Another view of the opportunity mechanisms separating the two populations can be obtained by decomposing the gross achievement disparities observed above. In Table 1 the gross status index dif-ferentials between the AFDC and non-AFDC sons were observed to be .8231 in education and 10.63 in occupations. By again applying the regression values of Table 3, we can identify the component sources of these differentials as shown in Table 4.

TABLE 4
Socioeconomic Status Differences between AFDC and Non-AFDC Sons, Identified by Source

	In Education	In Occupations
Gross-status difference	.8231	10.63
Due to mother's education	.0601	.06
Due to father's occupation	.3039	2.81
Due to son's education	—	4.31
Residual difference	.4591	3.45

It will be noted again that the unaccounted for or residual status differential in education amounts to .4591, or over one year of schooling at the high school level. What the calculations of Table 4 reveal is that this residual difference accounts for approximately 60 percent of the observed gross disparity in educational attainments between the AFDC and non-AFDC youth, with the other 40 percent accounted for by home environment. Our earlier arguments, together with supportive evidence presented below, are intended to demon-strate that this residual is primarily the result of differential educa-tional opportunities, as conditioned by family-income status.

The observed differential in occupational status between the AFDC and non-AFDC populations can be apportioned similarly. While the residual differential in this case is only one-third of the gross status difference, the influence of income is mediated by both father's occupational status and son's education. Accordingly, we can estimate the total or compounded impact of family income on son's early occupational status as $D_{wi} = r(3.45) + e(4.31) + o(2.81)$, where the coefficients r, e, and o represent the proportions of the associated status shares (residual, education, and occupation, respectively) attributable to the influence of family income. If we tentatively and perhaps conservatively assign the values $r = .50$, $e = .65$, and $o = .75$, then we can say that the total impact of family income is 6.63 status points, or over 60 percent of the gross occupational difference between the AFDC and non-AFDC sons. Unless and until we can find other explanations for this difference, this estimate must be regarded as a measure of the impact of constricted opportunities on the socioeconomic achievement of impoverished youth.

Supportive Evidence and Conclusions

While the evidence reviewed above provides considerable substantiation of the stratified opportunity hypothesis, the case is not really complete. While the residual differences observed above are impressive, it must be shown that achievement determinants other than parental education, father's occupation, and own education would not serve, if included in the achievement functions, to severely reduce the status differentials here attributed to income disparities.

The most glaring omission from the list of potential achievement determinants is a direct measure of the respondent's native abilities. Unfortunately, neither the Blau and Duncan study nor the AFDC sample data includes a direct measure of this potentially important variable. While I have stated that both mother's education and son's education (in the occupation regression) served as partial stand-ins for son's native abilities and motivations, I am under no illusion that these proxies are fully adequate to the task. To approximate the impact of this incomplete specification, we must go to independent collections of data.

Considerable evidence on the relationship between ability, socioeconomic status, and college attendance and graduation rates was reviewed by Duncan for the Department of Health, Education, and Welfare Social Indicators Panel. What those data demonstrate is a clear and profound association between socioeconomic status and higher education, both across and within ability groupings. Thus, for example, only 48 percent of highest-ability males from low-status origins attend four-year colleges, while 87 percent of those with the same ability but high-status origins do (Project TALENT 1966). The achievement disparity is even greater when college graduation rates are contemplated. High-ability, high-status-origin males outpace their low-status counterparts by a better than three-to-one ratio (64 percent vs. 20 percent) (Sewell and Shah 1957). This evidence provides considerable substantiation for the hypothesis that income discrimination remains forceful even after differential abilities are accounted for. The same conclusion was formulated by Sewell, Haller, and Straus (1957) in a study of educational and occupational aspirations of high school juniors and seniors. If, as Duncan says, ability influences achievement primarily insofar as it is certified by the formal education system (1968a), then the extension of the hypothesis to occupational achievement seems reasonable. The high coefficients for education obtained in the occupational regressions above have already suggested the validity of this extension.

While a completely satisfactory understanding of the relationship between socioeconomic status and mental abilities has not yet been attained, Arthur Jensen has offered an interesting hypothesis to account for some of the conflicting data collected on this subject. He argues that "for a particular mental ability, realization of genetic potential depends on the presence of certain environmental influences. Beyond some threshold level of environmental influences, however, further increases do not make for appreciable increases in ability" (1968, p. 10). This threshold approach to the relationship between origin status, ability, and achievement offers an expedient resolution of the immediate specification problem, although it does circumvent the broader issue. We can argue, for example, that the typical AFDC socioeconomic environment does not meet the necessary conditions for the nurture of genotypic ability. Accordingly, the independent role of differential abilities, either on an inter- or intra-class basis, will be severely attenuated for the AFDC population.

While this argument relieves us of the necessity of including innate mental ability as an independent achievement determinant, it fails to confront the core issue of differential genotypic abilities across socioeconomic origin classes. While evidence on this central issue continues to collect, it appears relatively secure to argue that all socioeconomic classes demonstrate regression toward the interclass mean of genotypic mental abilities on an intergenerational basis (Jensen 1968; Anderson, Brown, and Bowman 1952). The two arguments combined thus indicate that (1) the interclass distribution of second-generation mental abilities is not as skewed as parental status, and (2) that what association does persist between parental status and son's mental abilities is exaggerated by environmental factors, especially at the extremes of socioeconomic status.

A second factor, here omitted from the achievement functions but alleged to be of some importance, is a measure of the son's motivations or aspirations. It has sometimes been argued that the poor remain poor because they lack the motivation to rise above their origins. Without an extensive discussion of this issue it is worth noting that Alvin Schorr (1966), responding to the argument that "the attitudes themselves produce their poverty," has said: "It would be hard to imagine a more comfortable mystique for those who are not poor. It is less flattering and more taxing to the mind to grasp the back-and-forth play between facts of life and attitudes toward life, between what seems practical and what one aspires to." In the same vein, Underhill (1967) and Wilson (1966) have assembled data which indicate similar motivations among poor and nonpoor once environmental influences are controlled, and Irelan (1968, p. 5) suggests that aspirations for improving one's socioeconomic position may be even stronger among those individuals of poor origins.

On the basis of these arguments and the impressive evidence collected on interclass college-attendance rates, it seems reasonable to conclude that the absence of a direct measure of ability does not seriously distort the achievement comparisons. On the contrary, substantial support can be mustered for the inference that the estimates of the impact of discriminatory opportunities are not significantly sensitive to alleged misspecifications of the underlying achievement functions. Thus, Beverly Duncan (1967) has additionally demonstrated that ethnic status, type of school attended, and place of residence add little to an understanding of educational attainment after basic family factors have been taken into account. Also, Scanzoni (1967) suggests that the relationship between n-achievement and occupational attainment is considerably less forceful than previously supposed.

The weight of accumulated evidence thus firmly supports the

stratified opportunity hypothesis. What we have observed is that there are tremendous achievement disparities between AFDC and non-AFDC youth, and that these disparities cannot be explained on the basis of parental educational or occupational statuses. Furthermore, we have assembled other available data demonstrating that additional measures of individual capacity are not capable of resolving the resultant residuals.

Together these data provide considerable, if preliminary, substantiation of the basic stratification hypothesis. Thus it is concluded that a substantial portion of the AFDC sons' underachievement can only be explained in terms of a relative constriction in opportunities, with that constriction itself based on the economic status of the origin family.

Appendix

The socioeconomic indices employed in the foregoing analysis are presented below, together with some of the underlying distributions.

The occupational index utilized here is a summary of that prepared by Duncan (see Reiss 1961) and is the same for both fathers and sons. A nonscalar transformation of this index yielded insignificant variation in the results obtained above.

TABLE 5
Occupational Index

Occupation	Index Score
Professional and semiprofessional	75
Proprietors, managers, and officials	57
Clerical, sales, and kindred	47
Craftsmen, foremen, and kindred	31
Operatives and kindred workers	18
Service workers	17
Unskilled laborers	7
Farm owners, renters, and farm managers	14
Farm laborers, including sharecroppers	9

TABLE 6
Occupational Distributions

	Fathers[a]		Sons[b]	
Occupation	AFDC	Non-AFDC	AFDC	Non-AFDC
Professional and semiprofessional	0.5%	5%	0.7%	8%
Proprietors, managers, and officials	0.9	12	0.6	2
Clerical, sales, and kindred	1.2	7	6.1	17
Craftsmen, foremen, and kindred	9.4	18	10.6	9
Operatives and kindred workers	19.5	16	10.5	27
Service workers	5.3	5	7.7	4
Unskilled laborers	38.3	6	55.8	14
Farm owners, renters, farm managers	4.0	29	0.7	3
Farm laborers, including sharecroppers	12.3	3	7.4	15

[a] Father's occupation was ascertained for the time when respondent (son) was about sixteen years of age.
[b] For the non-AFDC sons, occupation refers to first job after the completion of schooling. For the AFDC sons, occupation refers to job at time of interview (see text).

For the fathers and the sons, the educational index employed . . . [is shown in Table 7].

For the AFDC mothers, the index [shown in Table 8] was employed.

TABLE 7
Educational Index

Years of School	Value
0	0
1–4	1
5–7	2
8	3
9–11	4
12	5
13–15	6
16	7
17+	8

TABLE 8
Educational Index

Years of School	Value
0	1
1–4	2
5–8	3
9–11	4
12	5
13+	6

References

Anderson, C. Arnold, James C. Brown, and Mary Jean Bowman. 1952. "Intelligence and Occupational Mobility." *Journal of Political Economy* 60 (June):218–39.

Bernard, Sydney E. 1964. *The Economic and Social Adjustment of Low-Income Female-headed Families.* Monograph. Brandeis University.

Blackwell, Gordon W., and Raymond F. Gould. 1952. *Future Citizens All.* Chicago: American Public Welfare Association.

Blau, Peter M., and Otis Dudley Duncan. 1967. *The American Occupational Structure.* New York: Wiley.

Burgess, M. Elaine, and Daniel O. Price. 1963. *An American Dependency Challenge.* Chicago: American Public Welfare Association.

Duncan, Beverly. 1967. "Education and Social Background." *American Journal of Sociology* 72 (January):363–72.

Duncan, Otis Dudley. 1968a. "Ability and Achievement." *Eugenics Quarterly* 15 (March):1–11.

———. 1968b. "Inheritance of Poverty or Inheritance of Race?" In *On Understanding Poverty,* edited by Daniel P. Moynihan. New York: Basic.

Duncan, Otis Dudley, David L. Featherman, and Beverly Duncan. 1968. *Socioeconomic Background and Occupational Achievement.* Monograph. University of Michigan.

Form, William H., and Delbert C. Miller. 1949. "Occupational Career Pattern as a Sociological Instrument." *American Journal of Sociology* 54 (January):319–29.

Irelan, Lola M., ed. 1968. *Low-Income Life Styles.* U.S. Welfare Administration, publication no. 14.

Jensen, Arthur R. 1968. "Social Class, Race, and Genetics: Implications for Education." *American Educational Research Journal* 5 (January): 1–42.

Kriesberg, Louis, and Seymour S. Bellin. 1965. *Fatherless Families and Housing: A Study of Dependency.* Monograph. Syracuse University.

Lundberg, Ferdinand. 1968. *The Rich and the Super-Rich.* New York: Stuart.

McClelland, David C. 1961. *The Achieving Society*. Toronto: Van Nostrand.

Morgan, James N., et al. 1962. *Income and Welfare in the United States*. New York: McGraw-Hill.

Project TALENT. 1966. *One-Year Follow-Up Studies*. Washington, D.C.

Reiss, Albert J. 1961. *Occupations and Social Status*. New York: Free Press.

Scanzoni, John. 1967. "Socialization, n-Achievement, and Achievement Values." *American Sociological Review* 32 (June):449–56.

Schiller, Bradley R. "Class Discrimination vs. Racial Discrimination," forthcoming.

———. 1969. "The Permanent Poor: An Inquiry into Opportunity Stratification." Ph.D. dissertation, Harvard University.

Schorr, Alvin. 1966. *Poor Kids*. New York: Basic.

Sewell, William H., Archie O. Haller, and Murray A. Straus. 1957. "Social Status and Educational and Occupational Aspiration." *American Sociological Review* 22 (February):67–73.

Sewell, William H., and V. P. Shah. 1967. "Socioeconomic Status, Intelligence and the Attainment of Higher Education." *Sociology of Education* 40 (Winter):1–73.

Seymour M. Lipset and Reinhard Bendix

INTRAGENERATIONAL OCCUPATIONAL MOBILITY IN OAKLAND

Seymour M. Lipset and Reinhard Bendix are two well-known sociologists who have done a number of outstanding studies of social mobility. The following selection should indicate why their high reputation is merited. Drawing from their comprehensive study of Oakland, California, they not only offer a clear appraisal of the patterns of occupational mobility they found, but with equal clarity they draw attention to many flaws in sociologists' handling of occupational data. Lipset and Bendix "show by doing" how complex occupational analysis can be accomplished simply and sensibly. They report a mixed picture, in which an amazing quantity of job turnover coexists with a very modest rate of movement from jobs of one status to those of another.

From Seymour Martin Lipset and Reinhard Bendix, *Social Mobility in Industrial Society*, pp. 156–181. Copyright © 1959. Originally published by the University of California Press; reprinted by permission of the Regents of the University of California. Footnotes deleted.

Much sociological analysis based on survey data attempts to relate occupational status to opinions, values, and behavior patterns. Thus, studies of voting behavior speak of the differences between the "blue-collar" and "white-collar" workers. Analyses of class identi- fication and class consciousness relate subjective feelings about class position to occupational position. The major effort to construct a scale of social-status positions in America employs occupational position as one of the principal items in the scale. All of these studies are based on the frequently validated assumption that how a person thinks and acts, as well as how he is regarded by other people, is in large measure determined by his occupational ex- periences. Marxian sociology makes such experiences the key ele- ment in its effort to predict social behavior. Thorstein Veblen dis- tinguished the conventional and pecuniary frame of mind of the typical businessman from the radical matter-of-factness of the en- gineer. The Lynds in their studies of Middletown attempted to show the great differences in ways of life and thought between those who worked with their hands and those who used their tongues.

The pervasive influence of a common occupation on the mentality of all who are in it is unquestioned. And presumably, the more uni- form the career of individuals, the easier it should be to predict their thoughts and actions. It is curious, however, that with all the interest in social mobility in America, and the recognition that a large proportion of the population do actually move up and down the social hierarchy and that an even larger proportion move hori- zontally by shifting jobs and occupations at the same social level, there has been little effort to refine the character of occupation as an interpretive variable by securing data on past occupational ex- periences of individuals. *As most current research is done, the man who has been a skilled worker or an independent businessman for the past twenty-five years is classified in the same category as the man who has been in the occupation for six months!*

The life-career data collected in the Oakland study enable us to indicate some of the variations in occupational background which characterize men currently in the same jobs and hence the degree to which different occupational classes vary in the heterogeneity of their collective work experience. These materials bearing on intra- generational mobility and its significance for analysis of social structure constitute the major contribution of the study. [Here] we shall lay out some of the characteristics of "occupational career patterns."

Stability and Instability of Occupational Careers

A person's characteristic pattern of mobility was determined by ascertaining the frequency with which he changed from one job to another, shifted from one occupation to another, or moved from one community to another. The rate of individual mobility of each of the 935 respondents was computed by dividing the number of changes the person has made by the number of years he has been in the labor force. The calculated ratios were expressed in the form of rates per decade, and the results for the three different types of mobility are presented in Figure 1.

It is clear from the tabulated data that men are more likely to change from one job to another than to shift occupations, and that they are more likely to change occupations than to move to another community. One obvious question about these three types of mobility concerns their interrelationship. Are the same individuals mobile on all three dimensions, or are persons who move readily from occupation to occupation resistant to moving from one community to another, while men who change communities tend to remain in the same occupation? The members of the sample were divided into three categories—high, medium, and low—for each type of mobility, and the patterns were compared. (See footnote to Table 1 for classification system employed.) The results (see Table 1) indicate that there is a high degree of association among mobility rates of different kinds. Men who are mobile in one respect (e.g., shifting jobs) are also likely to be mobile in other respects. This finding is perhaps to be expected, but a further inference from these data suggests that resistance to geographical movement may be greater than the resistance to changing occupations, a datum which casts some interesting light on the problem of rigidities within the labor force.

In order to determine the homogeneity of occupational career patterns, we have calculated intragenerational mobility by determining the percentage of total job career which respondents spent in different occupational categories. When the proportion of time which the respondents spent in their present or in some other occupa-

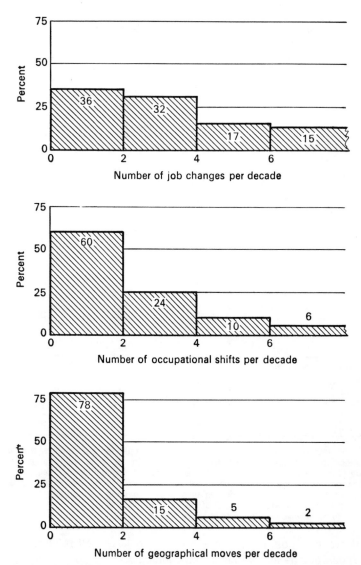

FIGURE 1. Percentage of the 935 respondents making job changes, occupational shifts, and geographical moves, by mobility rate.

TABLE 1
Relationship between Specified Types of Mobility Rates,
Expressed as Percentages

Range of Mobility Rates	Range of Mobility Rates		
	Low	Medium	High
Occupational Mobility Rates			
Job mobility rates			
Low	22	14	—
Medium	6	26	7
High	1	4	19
Total	30	45	25
Geographical Mobility Rates			
Job mobility rates			
Low	32	4	—
Medium	16	16	8
High	7	3	14
Total	54	23	22
Geographical Mobility Rates			
Occupational mobility rates			
Low	23	5	2
Medium	23	14	8
High	8	5	13
Total [a]	54	23	23

Note: Low mobility is here defined as 0 to 1.9 job changes per decade, 0 to 0.9 occupation or community changes; medium mobility as 2 to 4.9 changes per decade, 1 to 2.9 occupational changes, and 1 to 1.9 community changes; over 5 job changes per decade, 3 occupational changes, or 2 community changes are considered high mobility. The percentages shown in each cell of this table are expressed as a proportion of the total of the 935 respondents.
[a] Details do not always add to totals because of rounding.

tional group is computed, many turn out to have had relatively unstable careers, as the data in Table 2 indicate.

Although there are members of all occupational groups who have spent the largest portion of their careers in occupations other than their present ones, there are considerable differences among the various strata of the occupational hierarchy. Occupational careers

TABLE 2

Percentage of Respondents Who Spent Designated Proportions of Their Work Careers in Their Present Occupational Group

(Excludes female respondents and males 30 and younger)

Occupational Group of Present Job	Proportion of Work Career in Present Occupational Group			Number of Respondents
	80–100%	*50–79%*	*Under 50%*	
Professional	70	9	22	23
Semiprofessional	47	32	21	19
Own business	11	31	57	105
Upper white collar	14	21	65	72
Lower white collar	18	33	49	67
Sales	26	24	50	42
Skilled	22	35	43	169
Semiskilled	22	29	49	98
Unskilled	18	21	61	44
Manual	65 [a]	21	14	314 [b]
Nonmanual	58 [a]	23	19	343 [b]
All groups	22	29	50	657

[a] The proportion of all manual or all nonmanual workers who have spent 80–100 percent of their time in these categories is, of course, higher than the corresponding proportion for the separate occupational groups. Shifting between jobs may be frequent without entailing a cross-over from the manual to the nonmanual occupations, or vice versa.

[b] These figures include 15 business executives and 3 manual (odd-job) workers not shown separately.

appear to be more unstable among unskilled than among skilled workers, and among white-collar workers and the self-employed than among the professionals and semiprofessionals. Perhaps most interesting of all is the fact that there are more nonmanual workers who have spent a large proportion of their careers in manual employment than there are manual workers who have held nonmanual positions. It is clear that unskilled manual labor in America is not the cul-de-sac that it is reputed to be. The unskilled are the second most mobile group in the sample—if we measure mobility by the proportion of people who have spent more than half their careers in occupations other than their present one.

Thus far, we have discussed the proportion of career time which the respondents have spent in or out of their present occupation. Since we have data on every job which the sample's members can remember holding for more than three months, it is also possible to specify the variety of jobs characteristic of men currently in the various occupations. The data reported in Table 3 reveal a variety of job experiences which is staggering. Among the unskilled, one-third or more have held white-collar and skilled positions. A fifth of those now in professional or semiprofessional employment have at some time in the past been employed in semiskilled manual work, and the majority of those in lower white-collar and sales occupations have also held such low-level jobs.

In order to obtain an overall picture of the actual shifts between occupations, which are subsumed in the percentages given in Table 3, we have examined the 5,171 actual job changes reported by respondents (Table 4). This reveals that as a group, persons who own or manage a business have the most heterogeneous past experience. Thirty-six percent of the shifts into self-employment were from manual jobs of various kinds; slightly under 30 percent were from various nonmanual occupations other than business ownership; only one-fifth shifted from the ownership of one business to another. Conversely, changes from job to job at the "same" occupational level occurred most frequently in the high-status occupations—among professionals, semiprofessionals, and upper white-collar workers. In each of these groups over 60 percent of the changes took place within the category. Among manual workers, stable intragroup shifting has been most characteristic of the skilled workers.

Manual and Nonmanual Occupations

Though there are many shifts from one occupational group to another, especially in the lower strata, these are, on the whole, shifts between groups of similar status. There is, however, relatively little shifting between manual and nonmanual groups, as Figure 2 indicates: all those who work with their hands have spent 80 percent of their working lives in manual occupations; all in nonmanual employment have spent 75 percent of their careers in such positions.

The division between persons in the manual and in the nonmanual occupations has important ideological implications. Manual

TABLE 3

Percentage of Respondents Who Have Ever Worked in Designated Occupational Groups Other Than Their Present Ones

(Excludes female respondents and males 30 and younger)

Occupational Group of Present Job	Occupation Groups Other Than Present												Number of Respondents
	Professional	Semi-professional	Own business	Upper white collar	Lower white collar	Sales	Skilled	Semi-skilled	Un-skilled	Farm owner	Farm labor	Odd jobs, unemployed	
Professional	—	9	9	13	26	9	9	22	17	—	—	13	23
Semiprofessional	—	—	16	5	32	10	21	21	32	5	—	10	19
Own business	3	5	—	9	41	33	48	46	20	1	10	14	105
Upper white collar	3	7	17	—	78	29	15	26	18	3	10	17	72
Lower white collar	—	3	12	9	—	27	45	54	36	6	13	36	67
Sales	—	7	38	17	64	—	26	50	29	2	14	14	42
Skilled	—	1	24	—	22	11	—	73	40	4	18	30	169
Semiskilled	—	3	24	2	28	22	42	—	56	4	24	33	98
Unskilled	—	2	14	2	31	9	39	64	—	4	30	36	44
All groups	1	4	17	4	34	19	26	45	32	3	16	25	639

Note: Percentages based on numbers as small as some of these are quite unreliable, but are included for their suggestive value.

TABLE 4

Percentage Distribution of Job Shifts to Occupations Respondents Assumed, by Occupational Group of Previous Job

(Excludes all jobs of female respondents and of males 30 and younger)

Occupational Group of Previous Jobs	Occupational Group of Jobs Assumed										
	All groups	Professional and semi-professional	Farm	Own business and business executive	Upper white collar	Lower white collar	Sales	Skilled	Semi-skilled	Un-skilled	Casual Labor
Professional and semiprofessional	6	68	7	2	3	4	2	2	2	3	1
Farm	3	—	21	3	1	1	2	2	4	6	5
Own business and business executive	5	2	4	22	7	2	8	5	3	3	3
White collar	16	9	8	12	62	50	16	4	6	6	9
Sales	7	2	5	12	4	7	37	2	3	3	8
Skilled	18	4	7	18	2	4	5	54	9	6	14
Semiskilled	20	2	20	12	3	10	13	14	43	20	24
Unskilled	9	2	10	5	2	4	5	4	11	32	16
Casual labor	4	1	7	1	2	2	3	3	5	6	8
Unemployed [a]	10	9	8	9	8	13	8	7	11	14	10
War service	3	2	2	3	8	3	3	4	4	2	2
All groups [b]	100	100	100	100	100	100	100	100	100	100	100
Number of job shifts	5,171	240	137	426	120	855	390	1,118	1,168	498	219

[a] Unemployed includes also persons who have left the labor force.
[b] Details do not always add to totals because of rounding.

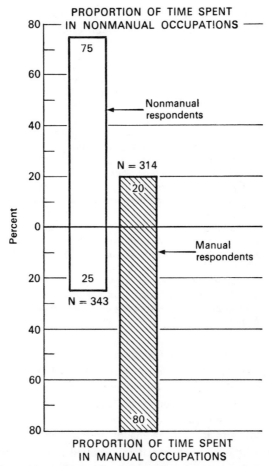

FIGURE 2. Proportion of career time spent in manual and nonmanual positions.
(Excludes female respondents and males 30 or younger.)

labor in the United States is not regarded as degrading, and the
dignity of manual work is frequently stressed. Nothing has contributed more, for instance, to the popular legend of Henry Ford
than the fact that this man who built an industrial empire worked
on a farm as a boy. But slogans cannot obliterate the great differences between the outlook and way of life of people on either side
of the barrier, some of which have been documented statistically

in chapter 2 [of *Social Mobility in Industrial Society*]. Some characteristics of working-class life have been tellingly stated by Gran-
ville Hicks:

> *Hunting and machinery—those are the two great topics of conversation
> when men get together. Sam Josephs loves to talk about both, and he is
> usually the central figure in any discussion. Being currently employed in
> a garage, he is regarded as an authority, and the session is likely to open
> with a question directed to him, but once the topic is launched, everyone—
> everyone but me—joins in. The talk grows more and more technical, but
> human interest is never excluded, for Sam is always being reminded of
> what some stupid customer said or what some incompetent mechanic did,
> and his anecdotes evoke others. Some of the men in our group are closely
> confined to things they have actually worked with, but others are inter-
> ested in general principles and capable of dealing with them. Stan Cutter,
> for instance, though he was unable or at any rate unwilling to finish the
> sixth grade, has a genuinely speculative mind, and has worked out cer-
> tain theories of mechanics for himself, just from handling machinery, even
> as he acquired some knowledge of physiology from the butchering of
> domestic and game animals. For all these men machinery is, among other
> things, a field of competence, and it is obvious that they enjoy talking
> about the subject simply because it is one on which they have something
> significant to say.*

Many people in the manual occupations have in common a way
of life in which men are judged in terms of what they do with their
hands and how they do it. The way of life of persons in the nonmanual occupations, however, is too varied, even in a small town,
to permit of such generalization. In the absence of a simple interest
in manual skill and the intricacies of animals and machines, their
concern, as Veblen has shown, is with social prestige and material
comfort, and this often overshadows the matter-of-fact aspects of
daily living.

> *The need of subsistence and of an increase of physical comfort may for a
> time be the dominant motive of acquisition for those classes who are
> habitually employed at manual labor. . . . On the other hand, so far as re-
> gards those members and classes of the community who are chiefly con-
> cerned in the accumulation of wealth, the incentive of subsistence or of
> physical comfort never plays a considerable part. . . . The dominant incen-
> tive was from the outset the invidious distinction attaching to wealth, and,
> save temporarily and by exception, no other motive has usurped the
> primacy at any later stage of development.*

But, although the barrier is high, the same sort of occupational shifts are found on either side of it. The manual workers in our sample have spent 80 percent of their work careers in manual occupations, but from 45 to 55 percent of their time has been spent in occupational groups other than their present ones. Nonmanual workers have spent 75 percent of their work careers in nonmanual occupations, but have spent from 20 to 61 percent of their time in occupational groups other than their present ones.

Moreover, shifts between manual and nonmanual occupations occur. Table 5 shows the proportion of male respondents, grouped by overlapping sociological categories, who have spent some time in occupations that are socioeconomically distant from their present position. The data indicate that 47 percent of the manual workers have held nonmanual jobs, and that 62 percent of the nonmanual workers have worked with their hands—clear evidence of the flexibility of the American occupational structure.

Another measure of the shift between manual and nonmanual occupations is obtained when all job shifts are cross-classified, as in Table 6. When all jobs held by the respondents are taken into account, one-sixth of the manual jobs are shown to have been filled by people from nonmanual occupations, while one-fourth of the nonmanual jobs have been filled by people who previously worked with their hands.

Upward and Downward Mobility

The amount of social mobility involved in the interchange between manual and nonmanual occupations can most easily be shown by considering the proportion of their total careers members of different occupational groups have spent on either side of the manual-nonmanual line. Although, as we have noted, there is considerable intragenerational mobility across this line in terms of specific job experiences, the data of Table 7 indicate that in terms of actual percentage of a work career such mobility is rather small. Nonmanual workers have spent 20 percent of their occupational careers working with their hands; manual workers have spent 11 percent of their job histories in nonmanual occupations.

These data indicate again that there is considerable variation in the stability of career patterns for different occupational groups.

TABLE 5

Percentage of Respondents Who Have Worked in Designated Occupational Groups Other Than the Present One
(Excludes female respondents and males 30 and younger)

| Occupational Group of Present Job | Occupational Group Other Than Present | | | | | | | Number of Respondents |
	All manual	Semiskilled and apprentice	Unskilled	All nonmanual	High status[a]	Lower white collar and sales	Own business	
All manual	—	—	—	47	26	33	23	314
Semiskilled and unskilled	—	—	—	47	26	37	21	145
All nonmanual	62	40	24	—	—	—	—	343
High status[a]	46	25	19	—	—	65	16	129
Lower white collar and sales	75	52	33	—	33	—	22	109

[a] "High status" includes professionals, semiprofessionals, business executives, and upper white-collar workers.

TABLE 6

Percentage Distribution of Respondents in Occupational Division of Jobs Assumed, by Occupational Division of Previous Job

(Excludes all jobs of female respondents, of male respondents 30 and younger and job shifts for which the previous job was not classifiable in an occupational division)

Occupational Division of Previous Job	Occupational Division of Job Assumed		
	Manual	Nonmanual	Farm
Manual	80	26	50
Nonmanual	16	72	27
Farm	4	2	23
Number of jobs	2,607	1,792	124

Among nonmanual workers, professionals who spend only 6 percent of their career in manual occupations are clearly the most stable in terms of this particular indicator, while independent businessmen and lower white-collar workers are notable for their greater career instability. Among manual groups, the skilled workers have spent the least percentage of time working in nonmanual occupations.

An important aspect of social mobility in American society may be obscured by speaking, as we have, of *all* moves from manual to nonmanual as upward, and of the reverse shift as downward. The test of a rise or fall in the socioeconomic hierarchy is clearly the permanence of the change, and our data indicate (Table 7) that there is relatively little *permanent* crossing between manual and non-manual occupations among the respondents.

Table 8 indicates, however, that a *temporary* change from one category to the other occurs with considerable frequency. Significantly, the temporary crossings are more frequently downward than upward. Workers in the lower job echelons of American society may well feel that their chances to rise in socioeconomic status are slight. Yet those in the middle and upper strata of the occupational hierarchy may continue to insist that ready opportunities for social and economic advancement exist, because from 40 to 80 percent of their numbers have at one time or another worked in manual occupations. Although this is not the place to explore the subjective aspects of social mobility, we want to emphasize the importance of considering the impact of casual job experiences on the subjective

TABLE 7
Percentage of Time Spent in Occupational Divisions Other Than Present
(Excludes female respondents and males 30 and younger)

| Present Occupational Group | Percentage of Time Spent | | Number of Respondents |
	In manual occupations	*In nonmanual occupations*	
Professional	6	—	23
Semiprofessional	13	—	19
Own business	26	—	105
Upper white collar	10	—	72
Lower white collar	30	—	67
Sales	21	—	42
Skilled	—	9	169
Semiskilled	—	14	98
Unskilled	—	13	44
Nonmanual	20	—	343 [a]
Manual	—	11	314 [a]

[a] These figures include 15 business executives and 3 manual (odd-job) workers not shown separately.

appraisals of opportunities and on the presence or absence of subjective class identifications.

Specific Avenues of Mobility

Though 935 job histories provide a mass of information, this mass is quickly reduced to insignificance when more than two or three breakdowns are attempted. It is nevertheless possible to analyze the upward and downward mobility of respondents in greater detail than we have done so far. "Areas" of high and of low mobility may first be distinguished, using the previous tabulations of job changes. Here again (Table 9) the pattern is similar to that found in the total job-history data. The self-employed have the greatest mobility from manual to nonmanual positions. Shifts from farm jobs are largely to manual labor, especially the unskilled and semiskilled positions. The lower white-collar and sales positions are those in which manual workers have the greatest opportunity to secure nonmanual work (if we exclude self-employment) and such positions do not usually bring

TABLE 8
Percentage of Respondents Who Ever Spent Time in Occupational Divisions Other Than the Present One
(Excludes female respondents and males 30 and younger)

Present Occupational Group	Respondents Ever Spending Time		Number of Respondents
	In manual occupations	*In nonmanual occupations*	
Professional	39	—	23
Semiprofessional	53	—	19
Own business	68	—	105
Upper white collar	46	—	72
Lower white collar	82	—	67
Sales	64	—	42
Skilled	—	47	167
Semiskilled	—	49	98
Unskilled	—	41	44
Nonmanual	62	—	343 [a]
Manual	—	47	314 [a]

[a] These figures include 15 business executives and 3 manual (odd-job) workers not shown separately.

TABLE 9
Percentage Distribution of Job Shifts to Occupations Assumed, by Occupational Division of Previous Job
(Excludes all jobs of female respondents and of males 30 and younger)

Occupation Assumed in Job Shift	Occupational Division of Previous Job				Number of Job Changes
	Nonmanual	*Manual*	*Farm*	*Total* [a]	
Professional and semi-professional	90	10	—	100	215
Own business	56	41	3	100	373
Upper white collar	89	10	1	100	102
Lower white collar	74	24	1	100	717
Sales	70	28	2	100	346
Skilled	14	84	2	100	995
Semiskilled	17	79	5	100	1,000
Unskilled	17	75	8	100	421

[a] Details do not always add to totals because of rounding.

about immediate upward economic mobility. The professional, semi-professional, business-executive, and upper white-collar positions are filled largely by persons from other nonmanual positions. As one would expect, skilled manual positions are seldom obtained by nonmanual workers.

It is difficult to estimate from the data how much genuine social mobility is reflected in these tables, since persons changing from manual work to lower white-collar and sales jobs or to ownership of small businesses may not actually be changing their status and income level. The fact remains, however, that a considerable amount of such shifting does occur. Table 9 suggests that the greatest social mobility occurs in the form of shifts into "own business," and that shifts into the white-collar occupations and sales rank next: these are the occupations of most of those who manage to pass from manual to nonmanual work. There is, however, a significant difference in the mobility patterns if "own business" is compared with the white-collar occupations. The majority of persons in white-collar jobs have always been employed in such jobs, though 24 percent of those employed in lower white-collar occupations have previously worked at manual labor. On the other hand, more than 40 percent of the persons who own their business have come from the manual occupations.

The type of social mobility represented by persons who establish their own businesses and that represented by those in the white-collar occupations—which may be called "old" and "new" types of mobility—present rather striking contrasts in our data. To run a business of one's own is still a much-cherished ideal, and those who achieve it are felt to have moved up in the social scale. But with the growth of large-scale organizations in all parts of American society small-business ownership has lost some of its meaning, though its ideological appeal has not necessarily been weakened thereby. Many persons still cherish the idea of success achieved through individual effort, though their own careers show little evidence that "private enterprise" has had much significance for them personally. Mobile persons in the white-collar occupations are mobile in a bureaucracy; the qualities which lead to the promotion of the salaried employee are radically different from those which would make him a successful independent businessman. The data reveal some significant differences between the idolized "free-enterprise" career of the businessman and the bureaucratic career of the white-collar worker.

The degree of mobility—determined by the "occupational distance" between the first and the present job—which characterizes these career patterns can be quite accurately assessed. Other data in this study reveal that the first job is a good predictor of the subsequent career. The "occupational distance" between first and present job is clearly greatest for business owners and sales people, almost as great for the lower white-collar workers, and least for persons in the upper white-collar positions. A number of other variables are associated with these differences. Business owners and executives are an older group than the white-collar workers: 7 percent of the first group, and 22 percent of the second, are thirty or under; 54 percent of the business owners and 43 percent of the white-collar workers are forty-six or older. The age of the business owners, together with the fact that many of them have had manual occupations, suggests that opportunities for manual workers to turn businessmen do not come to them until their middle and later years. In all other respects there is little difference between the mobility patterns of business owners or white-collar workers and those of the sample as a whole: mobility among jobs, occupations, and areas is greatest in the younger age groups and decreases with age.

The mobility of the middle-class occupational groups, considered as a whole, is, however, quite striking (see Table 10): between 40 and 50 percent of business owners and white-collar workers have had four or more different jobs. The similarity of the past patterns of mobility of these groups is upset when we consider the possibilities of future mobility that proprietorship and bureaucratic careers afford, as reflected in whether persons have known of other available positions since they began their present jobs. Answers to this question presumably reveal something of a person's potential mobility, since his mobility depends in good part on his awareness of alternatives (see Figure 3).

More than half of the semiskilled and unskilled workers and of the business owners state that they have not known of other jobs since starting on their present one: respondents in the other nonmanual and the skilled occupations have known of other jobs much more often. Business owners in particular are not at all concerned with other jobs but rather with how to make profitable their present,

TABLE 10
Percentages of Respondents in Selected Present Occupations,
by Number of Occupations in Career, and
Number of Jobs in Career

Number of Occupations and Number of Jobs	Present Occupation		
	Own business	*Business executive and upper white collar*	*Lower white collar and sales*
Number of occupations			
1	13	14	19
2 or 3	44	39	36
4 or more	43	47	45
Total	100	100	100
Number of jobs			
1 to 5	47	58	60
6 to 10	37	36	31
11 to 15	11	3	6
16 or more	5	3	3
Total	100	100	100
Number of respondents	119	108	162

mostly small-scale, investment. Thus, although business ownership is a goal of the socially mobile, especially for persons in manual occupations, it cannot be considered a step to other jobs. A significant difference between business ownership and bureaucratic position as a goal for the socially mobile lies in the fact that in modern society the first is the final step in a person's work career, and the second is at least potentially a means to a better-paying job in the same or another large-scale organization.

Changing Implications of Proprietorship. That there is a certain finality in proprietorship does not mean that persons in this group never move into other occupations. But, since a good proportion of these men come from the manual occupations, it is probable that their only choice is between manual labor and proprietorship. The self-employed businessman, so far as the data of this study represent him adequately, is today a very different person, both socially and economically, from his counterpart of two generations ago. Then

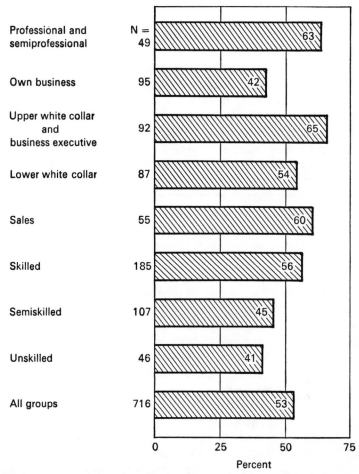

FIGURE 3. Knowledge of other jobs by respondents' present occupational group. Based on replies to question: "Since you began this job, have you known about any other jobs which you might have been able to get?"

he could hope and work for the real economic success which could result from the building-up of a large enterprise out of a small beginning. Then hope and work were meaningful, regardless of the individual's particular fate, because the social and economic distance between the small business and the large enterprise was nowhere near so great as it is today. Success in proprietorship today usually consists in the stabilization of an enterprise at a given social and economic level, because the opportunities for building large enterprises out of very small ones are relatively meager, though they have certainly not disappeared. It is in part a by-product of the predominance of large-scale organizations that those who head them have usually had a bureaucratic career. The "industrial bureaucrat," not the small independent businessman, is the one most likely to advance to the peak of the economic structure, both socially and economically. For these reasons the data on self-employed businessmen are of special interest.

The 105 individuals who were self-employed at the time of the interview had been so employed for less than half of their average working careers. Sixty-eight percent of the group had at some time been employed in manual work, while 74 percent of them had had jobs as lower white-collar workers or as salesmen. If one considers the lower-status occupations in American society to comprise lower white-collar workers and salesmen, as well as semiskilled, unskilled, and farm workers, then 89 percent of the self-employed business owners have spent some part of their work careers in lower-status occupations. If their work careers are considered collectively (rather than the proportion of the group that has been in the lower-status occupations at some time), then the group is shown to have spent, on the average, 36 percent of its work careers in these low-status jobs, which is only slightly less than the average time spent in self-employment (41.5 percent).

Although only about 10 percent of the American population are presently self-employed businessmen, it is obvious that a much larger part of the labor force has owned a business in the past, given the large turnover in this category. It is especially noteworthy that over one-fifth of the members of the Oakland sample who are currently engaged in manual work were at some time in business for themselves. The data on business turnover in the United States presented in chapter 3 [of *Social Mobility in Industrial Society*] corroborate the implication of the Oakland materials that somewhere between 20 and 30 percent of the urban work force have been self-employed for some time, although predominantly in very small, insecure enterprises.

The conclusion suggested by the objective data on the previous jobs of those who become businessmen—that this career is preponderantly a mobility path of manual workers and low-status, relatively unskilled, sales people—is reiterated by subjective materials obtained by questions concerning aspirations. The majority of every employed occupational group answers yes to the general question whether they had *ever* thought of going into business. This aspiration, however, is more widespread among all groups of manual workers and sales people than it is among the white-collar workers, the lower echelons of the managerial hierarchy, who presumably look forward to moving up within the company (see Table 11). Responses to the question "Have you ever tried to own your own business?" are similar, as Table 12 reveals. The proportion of persons who report that they attempted to own a business show that the aspiration documented in this table has its effect on business ownership. The contrast between the proportion who try and the proportion who succeed, according to the job-history data, show that the men least likely to carry through their attempts are those at the bottom of the entire occupational structure—the unskilled workers.

A recent report on mobility patterns in Sweden suggests that in that country also, small business tends to be an avenue of upward mobility for manual workers, while white-collar employees, if they move up, tend to do so through the ranks of large-scale industry. C. Arnold Anderson reports that, "The bulk of the 1930 big businessmen had in 1925 been functionaries [white-collar workers]. . . . Small

TABLE 11
Percentage of Respondents with Business Aspirations, by Present Occupation
(Excludes female respondents and males 30 and younger)

Present occupation	% with Business Aspiration	Number of Respondents
White collar	56	138
Sales	74	42
Manual	67	310
Skilled	63	168
Semiskilled	71	98
Unskilled	68	44

Note: Based on affirmative replies to question: "Have you ever thought of going into business for yourself?"

TABLE 12

Percentage of Respondents Who Attempted to Own Business, by Present Occupation

(Excludes female respondents and males 30 and younger)

Present occupation	Have Been in Business[a]	Attempted to Own Business	Did Not Try	No Answer	Total [b]	Number of Respondents
White collar	14	29	53	18	100	139
Sales	38	64	31	5	100	42
Manual	23	35	49	17	100	313
Skilled	24	36	46	18	100	169
Semiskilled	24	31	53	16	100	97
Unskilled	14	36	50	14	100	44

Note: Based on replies to the question: "Have you ever tried to own your own business?"

[a] Based on job history data; although 107 respondents have owned a business, 282 indicate that they have made attempts in this direction. The percentages in the first column are not added in the figures on the right.

[b] Details do not always add to totals because of rounding.

business recruited largely from urban labor groups. . . ." These Swedish materials yield some further evidence on the way in which educational attainment affects one's choice for bureaucracy or small business as a source of mobility. Those white-collar workers who became small businessmen instead of remaining in a bureaucracy were among the least educated of the white-collar workers, while those manual workers or small businessmen who shifted to white-collar employment were among the best educated in their previous occupational class.

Conclusions

Certain characteristics of an urban labor market emerge from this consideration of the occupational career patterns of our respondents. The first is that our respondents have had an extraordinary variety of occupational experience. A very large proportion of them have worked in different communities, in different occupations, and in many different jobs. By implication, this challenges the picture of the class structure derived from studies of small communities, which present it and the individual's position in it as pretty much "given."

It is important to note, however, that there are major areas of stability; there are certain limits to the variety of occupational experience of the respondents. In the first place, their mobility is largely confined to mobility on either side of the dividing line between manual work and the nonmanual occupations. There is little permanent occupational movement across this basic line. This means that although many persons have experience in a wide variety of occupations, most of it will be homogeneous to the extent that it will be either manual or nonmanual. The departures from this conclusion are generally of two major types.

1. Individuals whose occupational career is predominantly manual may have brief experience in nonmanual occupations, especially in small business, sales, and lower white-collar positions.
2. Individuals whose career is predominantly nonmanual quite often have spent some of their occupational career in manual positions, generally briefly and generally early in their career. This is particularly true of small businessmen. This type of mobility is somewhat more prevalent than the first.

The desire of American wage earners to become self-employed is still very strong, and the opportunity to become self-employed for at least brief periods of time is still open. Statistics on the small proportion of self-employed at any one time conceal the fact that many more than the present number have owned their own business at some time in the past, and many more will do so in the future. Self-employment is one of the few positions of higher status attainable by manual workers. That most of those who try it apparently fail does not change the fact that they do try.

We have indicated that studies of social mobility which only compare the father's occupation and the occupation of the respondent at the time of the study miss some of the most significant aspects of social mobility. What, for instance, are the characteristics of those individuals who have a highly mobile occupational career, as opposed to those who are stable? What are the consequences of the variety of occupational experience which a large proportion of American wage earners have? . . .

Otis D. Duncan and Peter M. Blau

WHAT DETERMINES OCCUPATIONAL SUCCESS?

Like Lipset and Bendix, Otis D. Duncan and Peter M. Blau are outstanding sociologists and students of social mobility. The essay that follows is a distillation from Duncan's and Blau's massive study of occupational mobility in contemporary America. The student should read it with particular care, precisely because it does not seem difficult. Its points are made simply but they are often subtle points that may be passed over if the essay is not read carefully. In effect, it contains some of the best fruits resulting from the most extensive digging yet done in the area of occupational mobility.

In this concluding chapter we summarize the main findings of our research and discuss some of their broader implications for social stratification. First, conditions that affect a man's chances of occupational success in the United States are reviewed, starting with an analysis of the factors that govern the process of occupational mobility directly, and proceeding to an examination of other factors that modify this process. Next, attention is centered on the relationship between family life and occupational life—how a man's ascribed status in his family of orientation influences his achieved status in the occupational structure, and what significance his career has for his family of procreation. After this overview of some antecedents and consequences of individual achievement, the focus turns to the analysis of the occupational structure itself, the patterns of movements characterizing it, and the historical trends that can be inferred. Reflecting on the research results in a more speculative mood, we attempt to distinguish between structural and historical causes of social mobility in contemporary industrialized society. Finally, our findings on mobility rates in the United States are compared with those from other countries in order to draw some implications about the significance of mobility and economic progress for social stratification and political stability in a democracy.

From Otis Dudley Duncan and Peter M. Blau, *The American Occupational Structure*, pp. 401–418. Copyright © 1967 by John Wiley & Sons, Inc. Reprinted by permission of John Wiley & Sons, Inc. Footnotes deleted.

Conditions of Occupational Success

A question often asked is, "What determines an individual's chances of achieving upward mobility?" This question can easily be answered, but the answer is not very meaningful. The main factor that determines a man's chances of upward mobility is the level on which he starts. The lower the level from which a person starts, the greater is the probability that he will be upwardly mobile, simply because many more occupational destinations entail upward mobility for men with low origins than for those with high ones. The trivial nature of the answer indicates that the question poses the issue poorly. To study what affects occupational mobility we must first decompose this concept into its constituent elements by examining how origins influence later achievements, and then proceed to investigate how several antecedent conditions interact in their effect on achievements. Regression and path analysis have been used to clarify the process of occupational mobility in this manner. All occupational categories for origins as well as destinations were transformed for this purpose into a status score based on the average income and education in each detailed occupation.

Whereas intergenerational mobility and intragenerational mobility are conventionally treated as two separate problems, we have investigated the two simultaneously because the influence of social origin (father's position) and that of career origin (first job) on occupational achievements are, of course, not independent. Given the crucial significance of education for careers in modern society, moreover, the variable of years of schooling has been included in the basic model of the process of stratification. This model dissects the process of occupational mobility by tracing the interdependence among four determinants of occupational achievement, two of which refer to a man's social background (father's education and father's occupation), and two of which refer to his own training and early experience that prepare him for his subsequent career (education and first job).

A man's social origins exert a considerable influence on his chances of occupational success, but his own training and early experience exert a more pronounced influence on his success chances. The zero-order correlations with occupational status are

.32 for father's education, .40 for father's occupation, .60 for education, and .54 for first job. Inasmuch as social origins, education, and career origins are not independent, however, their influences on ultimate occupational achievements are not cumulative. Thus the entire influence of father's education on son's occupational status is mediated by father's occupation and son's education. Father's occupational status, on the other hand, not only influences son's career achievements by affecting his education and first job, but it also has a delayed effect on achievements that persists when differences in schooling and early career experience are statistically controlled. Although most of the influence of social origins on occupational achievements is mediated by education and early experience, social origins have a continuing impact on careers that is independent of the two variables pertaining to career preparation. Education exerts the strongest direct effect on occupational achievements (the path coefficient is .39), with the level on which a man starts his career being second ($p = .28$).

Social origin, education, and career beginning account for somewhat less than half the variance in occupational achievement. One may interpret this result, depending on one's expectations and values, either by emphasizing that these three attributes of young men have nearly as much impact on their subsequent careers as all other factors combined, or by stressing that occupational success in our society depends not even so much on the socioeconomic and educational differences measured as on other factors. In any case, as a man gets older, the significance of his past career for his subsequent career becomes increasingly pronounced, and the influences of his social origin and his education as well as those of other factors not directly measured become less and less important. Making inferences about career stages from comparisons of age cohorts, we have estimated that the influence of his past career on a man's occupational status increases from a .30 path coefficient around age 30 to .89 when he is about 60, and the net influence of social origins decreases from .18 to nil, that of education decreases from .48 to .06, and that of all other factors decreases from .82 to .40.

The significance of other conditions, such as ethnic background, for occupational success is not independent of that of social and career origins and of education. It is well known that low social origins are associated with a variety of factors that have adverse effects on occupational chances. Disproportionate numbers of poor people are members of minorities who are discriminated against, have many children among whom their limited resources must be divided, and live in areas where educational and occupational opportunities are severely restricted, as illustrated by the Negro sharecropper in the South. Children who grow up in the lower strata tend to have not only poorer but also less educated parents, receive less education themselves, and must start work early in undesirable jobs. The assumption often made is that these multiple handicaps of men raised in lower strata have cumulative effects on their careers, creating a vicious circle through which poverty is perpetuated from generation to generation. Indeed the analysis has shown that low social origins are an impediment to occupational success (though most of the differences in occupational achievements are not a result of differences in origins but of other factors independent of origins). Yet these results by themselves do not reveal a vicious circle.

The concept of the vicious cycle of poverty implies not merely that growing up in lower strata affects occupational chances adversely but, more specifically, that the various conditions associated with low social origins reinforce each other and have cumulative adverse effects on occupational chances. The fact that several related factors have disadvantageous consequences for occupational achievements, however, does not necessarily indicate that each one adds a further impediment to those produced by the others. On the contrary, it frequently means that their combined effects are in large part redundant and not cumulative. Thus a man's career is adversely affected if his father had little education, if his father's occupational status was low, and if he himself has little education. But these three influences are not cumulative, as the preceding analysis showed. Father's low education only depresses occupational chances because it is associated with father's low occupational status and with son's low education. Once these two intervening factors that mediate the influence of father's education have been taken into account, father's education exerts no further influence on occupational achievements. The influence of father's occupational status on son's career, in turn, is in large part mediated by education, though not entirely. Given such minimum cumulation, it hardly seems justified to speak of a vicious cycle for the population at large, particularly in view of the fact that most of the differences in occupational achievements are not the result of differences in social origins. There are underprivileged groups in our society, however, who suffer serious occupational disadvantages as the result of cumulative handicaps, and whose situation may properly be described as resulting from a vicious cycle. The cases of three minorities—Negroes, Southerners, and sons of immigrants—illustrate the difference between background handicaps that are cumulative and those that are not.

A Negro's chances of occupational success in the United States are far inferior to those of a Caucasian. Whereas this hardly comes as a surprise to anyone familiar with the American scene, it is noteworthy that Negroes are handicapped at every step in their attempts to achieve economic success, and these cumulative disadvantages are what produces the great inequalities of opportunities under which the Negro American suffers. Disproportionate numbers of Negroes live in the South, where occupational opportunities are not so good as in the North. Within each region, moreover, Negroes are seriously disadvantaged. They have lower social origins than whites, and they receive less education. Even when Negroes and whites with the same amount of education are compared, Negroes enter the job market on lower levels. Furthermore, if all these differences are statistically controlled and we ask how Negroes would fare if they had the same origins, education, and career beginnings as whites, the chances of occupational achievement of Negroes are still considerably inferior to those of whites. Within the same occupation, finally, the income of Negroes is lower than that of whites. The multiple handicaps associated with being an American Negro are cumulative in their deleterious consequences for a man's career.

Whereas the uneducated Negro is the subject of the prejudiced stereotype that serves to justify discrimination, the better educated Negro, who is often explicitly exempt from the stereotype, seems to be the one who suffers most from discrimination. Education does not produce the same career advantages for Negroes as for whites. The difference in occupational status between Negroes and whites is twice as great for men who have graduated from high school or gone to college as for those who have completed no more than eight years of schooling. In short the careers of well-educated Negroes lag even further behind those of comparable whites than do the careers of poorly educated Negroes. This difference probably reflects in part discrimination in employment and in part discrimination in education, as the inferior educational facilities communities provide for Negroes make it likely that Negroes acquire less knowledge and fewer skills in the same number of years of schooling than whites. In any case, the same investment of time and resources in education does not yield Negroes as much return in their careers as it does whites. Negroes, as an underprivileged group, must make greater sacrifices to remain in school, but they have less incentive than whites to make these sacrifices, which may well be a major reason why Negroes often exhibit little motivation to continue in school and advance their education. Here we see how cumulative disadvantages create a vicious circle. Since acquiring an education is not very profitable for Negroes they are inclined to drop out of school relatively early. The consequent low level of education of most Negroes reinforces the stereotype of the uneducated Negro that helps to justify occupational discrimination against the entire group, thus further depressing the returns Negroes get for the educational investments they do make, which again lessens their incentives to make such investments.

The situation of Southern whites provides an interesting contrast with that of Negroes. The chances of occupational success of Southerners are inferior to those of Northerners, for both whites and Negroes, whether the Southerners remain in the South or migrate north to pursue careers there. Southerners have lower social origins than Northerners, they are less educated, and they start their careers on lower levels. Although the differences between Southerners and Northerners are not so great as those between whites and Negroes, there are parallel differences in respect to every variable under consideration. However, the handicaps of Southerners do not have cumulative effects on their occupational chances, whereas those of Negroes do. When social origins, education, and career beginnings are controlled the occupational level of Southern whites is, on the average, no longer any different from that of Northern whites. In other words, the inferior background and education of Southern whites fully account for their limited occupational chances, and there is no evidence of discrimination against Southerners once these initial differences have been taken into consideration; whereas the chances of Negroes remain inferior to those of whites under controls, which probably is the result of discrimination. Moreover the occupational chances of Southern Negroes remain inferior to those of Northern Negroes under controls, in contrast to the case of Southern whites, which undoubtedly reflects the more severe discrimination against Negroes in the South. Southerners have many competitive disadvantages in the struggle for occupational success, just as Negroes do, but the handicaps of Southern whites do not produce cumulative impediments for their careers, while those of Negroes do. It may well be that ethnic discrimination is at the root of such cumulative adverse effects on careers and that without discrimination there is no vicious cycle of poverty.

The case of a third minority—sons of immigrants—differs from that of Southerners as well as that of Negroes. The background of all three minorities creates hardships in their occupational lives. The initial handicaps do not fully account for the inferior occupational chances of Negroes but do account for the inferior chances of Southern whites. However in both cases the initial handicaps are accompanied by inferior subsequent achievements, whereas the occupational achievements of the second generation, despite its initial handicaps, are not inferior to those of Northern whites of native parentage. That is, sons of immigrants have lower social origins and less education than the majority group of Northern whites with native parents, yet their occupational achievements are on the average as high as those of the majority group, not only if initial differences are controlled but also without such controls. Although these results seem to indicate that white ethnic minorities do not suffer discrimination in the American labor market, a possible alternative interpretation is that some white ethnic groups are disadvantaged in their careers but the effects of these disadvantages are neutralized, and hence obscured in the data, by the overachievement of selected members of the white minority groups. There is some evidence in support of this interpretation. Thus second-generation men of northern or western European descent have slightly more successful careers than those with less prestigeful origins (primarily southern and eastern Europe). Besides the data on education show that the second generation has initial disadvantages, but those men among them who overcome these disadvantages are exceptionally successful.

Minority group handicaps are challenges for as well as impediments to achievement. They create obstacles to success and simultaneously provide a screening test of the capacity to meet difficulties, with the result that those members of the minority who have conquered their initial handicaps and passed the screening test are a select group with high potential for continuing achievement. The background handicaps of the second generation are evident in the finding that fewer of them than of the majority group complete eight years of schooling, go on to high school, and remain in high school until graduation. In order to graduate from high school sons of immigrants had to meet more serious challenges than sons of native parents. High school graduation, consequently, is a particularly effective screening test for the second generation, which is manifest in exceptional rates of proceeding to higher educational levels once the initial handicaps are overcome. The proportion of high school graduates who go on to college is larger among the second generation than among the majority group, and so is the proportion of college entrants who graduate and the proportion of college graduates who proceed to professional or graduate school. Men who had to overcome competitive disadvantages progress to higher levels subsequently than those never confronted by such difficulties, partly because having to pass through this screen selects men with high initiative or ability, and partly because success in meeting challenges steels men in further competitive struggles. For hardships to be such a spur to achievement, however, requires that those members of minorities who have conquered their initial handicaps are then permitted to enjoy the fruits of their success and that persisting disadvantages and discrimination do not rob them of these hard-won benefits. At least, this conclusion is suggested by the findings that Negroes, whose occupational chances remain inferior when education and background are controlled, do not have exceptionally high probabilities of continuing their education on advanced levels, whereas white minorities, whose occupational reward for given educational investment are not inferior, do have such high rates.

The significance of processes of selection for contemporary occupational life is most evident in migration. Migrants achieve generally higher occupational status than nonmigrants, whether reference is to a man's leaving the region of his birth or to his moving after age sixteen from the community where he was raised. To be sure, there are a few exceptions to the prevailing superiority of migrants, notably in the farm sector. For example, Southerners and, particularly, Negroes, though least qualified for urban careers, are most likely to leave farms. Nevertheless even migrants off farms are on the average superior in occupational achievements to the men who stay on farms, though not to the men in the communities to which they have come; and the achievements of urban migrants are superior to those of the nonmigrants in their place of destination as well as in their place of origin. Since the predominant stream of migration is from less to more urban places, where occupational opportunities are better, the greater achievements of migrants may be a result of the improvement in opportunity structure migration usually produces. Indeed migrants from all types of places achieve higher occupational status if they move to an urban community than if they migrate to a rural area. Contrary to expectations, however, the place in which a migrant grew up exerts a more pronounced and more consistent influence on his occupational chances than the place in which he now works. Regardless of the size of the place in which a migrant works, the more urbanized the community was where he grew up, the higher is the occupational status he attains. The superior education and early experiences more urbanized communities with their diversified facilities offer give men raised there a competitive advantage.

The question arises whether migration itself is associated with superior occupational achievements, quite independent of the type of community to which or from which a migrant moved. To answer this question, migrants from one to another large city are compared with nonmigrants in large cities, and parallel comparisons between migrants within the same community type and nonmigrants are made for small cities, rural communities, and farms. In both large and small cities such migrants are considerably superior in occupational status to nonmigrants. The status difference is smaller in rural communities, and it is reversed in farm areas, with migrants being inferior to nonmigrants on farms. Since the major variations in environmental opportunities resulting from degree of urbanization have been controlled in these comparisons, the findings suggest that urban migration is a process of selection of men predisposed toward occupational success, though this is less true for rural migration and not at all for farm migration. If this conclusion is correct, it would follow that urban migrants, but not rural ones, should be superior to nonmigrants already before the former actually leave their homes. The data confirm this inference. The social origins, education, and first jobs of urban migrants are superior to those of nonmigrants, whereas rural migrants reveal no such early superiorities. When the differences in these potentials for occupational success are statistically controlled, urban migrants continue to exhibit superior occupational achievements. The implication is that urban migration selects men with high potential for occupational success, and their actual migration raises their chances in fact to realize this potential.

Migration plays an important role for occupational mobility in urbanized society. The dominant stream of migration from rural to urban areas, which improves the opportunities of migrants, and the process of selective migration, which makes migrants particularly qualified for occupational success, combine to produce the superior occupational achievements of migrants. The communication facilities in modern society that make it easy to migrate enable men with initiative and ability but living in areas with restricted opportunities to translate their potential into actual achievements by migrating. To be sure, the poor preparation for urban careers men reared in rural areas tend to receive limits their occupational chances when they migrate to cities. As a result of this very fact, however, rural migration to metropolitan areas promotes not only the occupational mobility of the migrants themselves but also that of the urban natives.

Rural migrants to large cities achieve higher occupational status than the men who remain in rural areas but not so high status as the city natives. They are attracted to the metropolis because of the higher achievements the better opportunities make possible there, and their achievements fall short of those of city-raised men because of their poorer occupational preparation. The influx of poorly qualified rural migrants into the lower ranges of the metropolitan occupational hierarchy permits more of the better qualified city natives than would otherwise be possible to move into relatively higher occupational positions. Thus the role in the metropolitan structure once occupied by immigrants from Europe has been assumed today by migrants from rural areas. The metropolitan natives are advantaged by the inflow of rural migrants, and so are these migrants; even the men who remain in rural areas probably benefit some from the outflow of others, which lessens the competitive struggle for jobs. The rural migration to big cities in the United States has a structural effect on occupational mobility, for it furthers the chances of upward mobility of the natives who never migrated as well as of the migrants themselves.

Family and Occupational Life

Family life has important bearing on occupational life. Broken families spell lower occupational achievements for both the children and the husband, though it is not clear whether the husband's less successful career is a consequence of the marriage break-up or helps to precipitate it. The future occupational chances of children are not only affected by their parents' stable marriage but also by the number of siblings they have, their position among their siblings, and the educational encouragement the family provides.

Many siblings are a considerable occupational handicap. Men from large families are less likely to achieve high status in their careers than those from small families of the same socioeconomic stratum. The most likely reason is that parents of many children must divide their time and resources and cannot expend as much as parents of few children on the training and education or on the guidance and support of any one child. When educational attainments as well as social origins are held constant, the differences in occupational achievements between men from large and those from small families virtually disappear. Although family size affects occupational achievements primarily by affecting education, which in turn affects achievements, and not otherwise, this makes the ultimate depressing effect of large families on career chances no less real.

It is often assumed that oldest sons achieve higher status than younger sons. This assumption must be revised in the light of our findings. To be sure, eldest sons who are also the first-born child in a family have more successful careers than sons in intermediate positions. First-born sons who have older sisters, however, are not superior in occupational achievement to other sons in intermediate sibling positions. Moreover the occupational achievements of sons who are the youngest child in a family are just as high as those of sons who are the oldest child. In brief men in the two extreme sibling positions have more successful careers than those in intermediate positions. This difference is due to the better education oldest and youngest children receive, and it largely disappears when social origins and education are controlled. Parents appear to devote disproportionate resources to the training of their oldest child, who may also be particularly close to the parents and identified with adult values, and that of their youngest child, who benefits from their no longer having to economize for the sake of younger children. The consequent superior education of these first-born and last-born children enables them to surpass middle children in career achievements.

The relations among siblings in various positions also appear to influence achievements. An increase in the size of the family reduces the advantages of the oldest child and enhances that of the youngest one. In technical terms, number of siblings and sibling position interact in their effects on achievements. The adverse influence of a large family on future success is most pronounced for oldest children, less pronounced for middle children, and least pronounced for youngest children. These differences are manifest in educational attainments as well as occupational achievements, whether or not social origins are controlled, though not in achievements when both education and origins are controlled. The interpretation suggested for this finding is that the role relations and normative expectations in the family encourage older siblings to assume some responsibility for younger ones and assist them in their progress. The assumption that the future interests of older children are to some extent set aside in favor of those of their younger siblings could account for the asymmetry observed. The lower a child's position in the birth order, the more does the balance of receiving help from older and giving help to younger siblings turn in his favor, and the less disadvantageous it is, therefore, to have many siblings. To view it from a slightly different perspective, it is more of a handicap to have many younger than to have many older siblings, because older children are expected to make some sacrifices for their younger brothers.

The data on family size support the previous conclusion that men who successfully have overcome obstacles to their advancement are more likely to progress to still higher levels of attainment than those who had never to confront such problems. The disadvantage of men from large families is evident in their conditional probabilities of continuing education from one level to the next. At every step of the educational ladder up to college, the proportion of men who continue is not so high for sons from large families as for those from small ones. Among college graduates, consequently, large-family men are a more highly selected group than small-family men, and this finds expression in the greater tendency of men from large families to proceed to postgraduate levels of university education. Middle children, similarly, are less likely than youngest ones to continue their education at every level up to college, and they are more likely to go beyond college provided that they come from small families though not if they come from large ones, possibly because the compounded disadvantages of middle position and large family are too severe to be overcome by considerable numbers, just as the serious multiple disadvantages of the Negro are. In any case, the process of overcoming special difficulties, whether produced by many siblings or immigrant parents or, presumably, other handicaps that are not crushing, is selective of men with high potential for success, with the result that those members of the disadvantaged groups who have conquered their initial handicaps have better prospects of future success than other men.

The educational attainments of sons, and hence their occupational chances, may be assumed to be influenced by variations in the educational climate of their parental families, specifically, the extent to which conditions in the family stimulate an interest in learning and achievement. The family's educational climate depends undoubtedly in large part on the education of the father, which does, indeed, exert a considerable influence on his son's education. Within each educational origin level, however, the educational stimulation and encouragement children receive from their parents are not the same. Differences in family's educational climate within each educational class can be inferred from the educational attainments of the oldest brother when the father's education is held constant. Intraclass variations in the educational climates of families, so defined, have a pronounced impact on the educational attainment of sons. Even with race and some other conditions as well as father's education held constant, men with the most educated oldest brothers have, on the average, nearly four years more of schooling than those with the least educated oldest brothers. The introduction of a hypothetical variable representing their factor into the formal model of stratification reveals how this interpretation compares with alternative ones in terms of the plausibility of the assumptions made and the precise predictions advanced. The differences within educational classes in the degree to which family conditions stimulate the educational striving of children seem to have a profound impact on their progress in school.

One mechanism through which a favorable family climate apparently elevates the educational level of sons is by motivating them, or possibly the parents, to take full advantage of available resources to further educational attainments. Intraclass variations in family climate affect the education of sons more in small families than in large ones. Controlling father's education and other relevant conditions, the educational advantage of men from small over those from large families is zero if the oldest brother only went to elementary school and increases with oldest brother's advancing education. More resources are available for each child's education in small than in large families, but unless the family climate makes education an important goal there is no inclination to utilize the more abundant resources of the small family to remain longer in school. In brief the more favorable the family climate is to education, the greater is the tendency of men to divert available resources from other uses to attaining a higher education.

Occupational life has important connections with a man's family of procreation as well as his family of orientation. The phenomenon of differential fertility by occupational class is widely known. Higher occupational classes have fewer children than lower ones, though the relationship is not entirely linear because the lower rather than the top white-collar strata have the smallest number of children. The influence of occupational position on fertility extends over two generations. Classification by the occupation of either husband's father or wife's father reveals parallel differences in fertility, as does classification by husband's first job, except that in these cases the dip in the curve for lower white-collar strata is not evident. By and large, then, the higher a family's present social standing or social origins, the smaller is the number of children in it, though a decrease in this differential has accompanied the long-term downward trend in fertility.

These class differences in fertility have been interpreted by some as the result of the association between low fertility and upward mobility. The assumption is that a low birth rate is a prerequisite for upward mobility, inasmuch as a large family is an impediment for career success. Given this upward movement of families with few children, lower strata are depleted of small families and higher strata have an overabundance of them, and this is responsible for the lower fertility that can be observed in higher strata. It should be noted that this interpretation, which may be called the mobility hypothesis in its strong form, has been advanced in the absence of systematic empirical information on the relationship between fertility and mobility. The mobility hypothesis in its weak form merely asserts that fertility and mobility are inversely related, without assuming that this inverse relationship accounts for the observable class differences in fertility.

The strong hypothesis, according to which the lower birth rate of higher strata is due to the presence of upwardly mobile families with few children there, implies that the fertility of nonmobile couples does not differ by social class. The OCG data clearly show that the fertility of nonmobile couples in different occupational strata is not the same but varies parallel to that for all couples, whether mobility —or its absence—from first father's, or father-in-law's occupation is considered. On the contrary, class differences in fertility are more pronounced for nonmobile families than for all families, undoubtedly because the influences of present and origin status reinforce rather than counteract one another in the case of the nonmobiles. In its strong form the mobility hypothesis must be unequivocally rejected. The association between mobility and fertility does not account for existing class differences in fertility. The question arises whether the underlying assumption that upward mobility is associated with a low birth rate is correct, which is all the hypothesis in its weak form claims.

Upwardly mobile couples tend to have fewer children than others with the same origins. Whereas this finding is in accord with the weak hypothesis, it does not suffice to confirm it, for it does not necessarily reflect the significance of mobility as such. Upwardly mobile couples tend to have more children than others in their class of destination, and the fertility of downwardly mobile couples is also intermediate between that typical for their origin and that typical for their destination. As a matter of fact, the fertility of each origin stratum varies similarly by destination, and the fertility of each destination stratum varies similarly by origin. This pattern suggests that the additive effects of occupational origin and present occupation may account for fertility, with the experience of mobility itself playing no role. To test this inference a model incorporating the two additive effects was constructed, departures from which disclose the uncontaminated influence of mobility in its own right. The model accounts for most differences in fertility in the tables, but there are statistically significant departures, though they are usually very small. Upward occupational mobility appears to depress fertility slightly, and so does downward mobility. In sum the experience of mobility in either direction has a minor depressing effect on fertility, which is greatly overshadowed by the cumulative effects of present occupational status and origin status on fertility.

A number of conditions that reduce fertility simultaneously reduce class differentials in fertility. Thus men in towns and cities whose fathers were farmers, as well as men themselves living on farms, have higher rates of fertility than those two generations removed from the farm. Differences in fertility by occupational status are also more pronounced for men with farm backgrounds than for the second generation of urban dwellers, as fertility declines more sharply with rising status for men with farm background than for urban natives. Similarly the long-term historical trend has been toward lower fertility and lesser differences in it among social strata, as noted. The expansion of urbanization in modern society may well be responsible for this historical trend. An extreme instance of such a double effect on both fertility and its class differential is provided by age at marriage. Couples who married young have more children than those married when the bride was older than twenty-one. If the couple married early, husband's occupational status, education, and income are inversely related to fertility. If the couple married late, however, the birth rate is not related to either occupational status or education, and its relationship to income is reversed. In contrast to the otherwise observable tendency of lower socioeconomic strata to have more children than higher ones, couples who married late have more children if they are well off than if they are poor.

A clue for a possible interpretation of the observed patterns of fertility is provided by the significance of urbanization for them, whether reference is to the growing urbanization of society at large or the increasing urbanization of individuals as they become further removed in time from farm life. A distinctive characteristic of urbanized social structures is that *Gesellschafts* relations prevail over *Gemeinschafts* relations, to use Toennies's famous terminology. *Gemeinschaft* implies that men are imbedded in a matrix of close social ties most of which have existed since birth. In such a context human relations are conceived as part of the natural order, and they are valued for their own sake. Men do not judge their relations with fellow men by some external universalistic standard, but the established social bonds themselves define their particularistic significance. With slight exaggeration we may say that men look upon others as either friend or foe; there is hardly any middle ground. *Gesellschafts* relations differ decidedly from either extreme, involving social contacts that are neither of intrinsic significance nor hostile but simply means for a variety of ends. Urbanized society with its advanced division of labor requires its members in the course of their work and everyday life to enter into relatively superficial relations in segmental roles with many others. Few objectives of individuals in contemporary society can be accomplished without engaging in social interaction with others for this purpose. In these social relations, exemplified by those between buyer and seller or supervisor and subordinate, the objective sought is the external standard for evaluating their significance. As most social contacts of modern man are entered into as means for further ends, an instrumental orientation to social intercourse becomes pervasive and intrudes even on intimate human relations. Family life is not exempt from this tendency. Whereas the traditional view has been that getting married and having children are natural processes outside the realm of rational deliberation, men today are not merely permitted but normatively expected to base their decisions to get married and have children on rational calculation, as the disapproval of teen-age marriages and the high birth rate of the very poor illustrate.

The interpretation suggested is that the deliberate approach to human relations guided by rational calculation, which is embodied in the concept of *Gesellschaft,* is a major factor depressing fertility. Since the tasks of most white-collar workers entail dealing with people and achieving goals by influencing others, whereas blue-collar as well as farm workers primarily work on things, white-collar workers would be expected to be especially imbued with a calculating viewpoint toward social relations. Urbanization, which tears people out of the network of permanent social bonds in the small community and leads to social contacts among erstwhile strangers thrown together in close proximity, is assumed to foster more deliberate attitudes in social intercourse. Accordingly the trend toward increasing urbanization in the society at large and the degree of urbanization of its individual members both should be reflected in a more pronounced *Gesellschafts* orientation. The willingness to postpone marriage is a particularly straightforward expression of the inclination to permit rational deliberation to influence decisions about the most intimate human relations. All these conditions lower fertility rates. Class differentials in fertility, too, can be accounted for by the explanatory hypothesis advanced.

The paradox of class differences in birth rates is that the couples who can least afford it have most children. Calling this a paradox, however, itself reveals our calculating orientation toward family life, since it implicitly assumes that having children is not simply a natural process but ought to result from deliberate decisions based on rational economic considerations. Only people with a profound *Gesellschafts* orientation plan the size of their families in such a deliberate manner. Postponement of marriage manifests a calculating orientation toward family life rather directly, and couples who marry late not only have fewer children than others but also are rationally influenced by their financial resources in deciding how many children to have, as indicated by the positive association between income and fertility for them, in contrast to the negative association for other couples. There is reason to think that the social life of white-collar workers is most extensively guided by *Gesellschafts* principles, and the more affluent higher strata among them have more children than the less affluent lower ones, as rational deliberation would dictate. Thus a major consequence of a *Gesellschafts* orientation, late marriage, as well as a major determinant of it, white-collar work, finds expression in rational planning of family size. Less extreme forms of the calculating orientation toward human relations, like those produced by urbanization, merely attenuate the usual class differences in fertility without reversing them. The usually observable class differential in birth rate results, according to the interpretation, from the less deliberate and more spontaneous orientation toward family life of the lower social strata. The slight depressing effect of mobility regardless of direction on fertility, finally, may be due to the disruptions in social relations often engendered by mobility, inasmuch as men removed from a matrix of established social ties are prone to become more calculating in social intercourse.

What are the implications of differential fertility for society? It has been argued that the lower birth rates of the higher strata, as well as the lower birth rates of the more advanced societies compared to the less industrialized ones, are a deplorable waste of human resources and may spell the doom of civilized societies. Sorokin, who is not an extreme spokesman for this viewpoint, concludes his discussion of the topic in these words: "If we desire the continuation of our civilization, differential fertility and a generally low birth rate are scarcely favorable conditions for this purpose." This argument assumes that the sons of families in higher strata are better qualified for leading positions than men who have moved up from lower strata. There is no need to enter into a discussion of the significance of heredity here, since it can readily be granted that men raised in better educated and more affluent families are more likely than others to have superior qualifications, if only by reason of the advantage their environment creates for their development.

To say that the sons of the elite are superior in ability to the entire group of sons of other strata, however, does not imply that they are superior to those sons of other strata who succeed in moving up into the elite. The population of nonelite sons constitutes a large pool of human resources that is sifted in the process of selection entailed in upward mobility, which makes it likely that the ones who do achieve elite status are more outstanding than the initially superior but unselected elite sons, just as the more selected large-family college graduates are more successful in pursuing higher degrees than the initially advantaged small-family college graduates. Moreover Sorokin himself notes that "a greater versatility and plasticity of human behavior is a natural result of social mobility," and he points out that this encourages intellectual endeavors and creativity. These qualities would give the upwardly mobile a further advantage over those who have inherited elite status. Given the existing family structure it is hardly conceivable that men in the elite would not attempt to assure that their sons remain in this top stratum, and their resources and power often enable them to do so. Differential fertility makes it possible, without any change in the institution of the family, for the elite to be invigorated by fresh blood and for sons from lower strata to have opportunities to move into the elite. Unless we assume that the nonelite sons with the highest potential are inferior to the elite sons with the lowest qualifications, the process of selection inherent in upward mobility can be expected to have the result that the most successful men from lower strata bring not only new perspectives but also superior qualifications to the elite.

Bibliographical Essay

A good place to start, particularly for anyone interested in the history of social mobility studies, is with Pitirim A. Sorokin, *Social Mobility* (New York, 1927), a pioneering classic. For valuable summaries of subsequent research, see Bernard Barber, *Social Stratification* (New York, 1957); Raymond W. Mack, Linton Freeman, and Seymour Yellin, *Social Mobility: Thirty Years of Research and Theory* (Syracuse, 1957); and Melvin Tumin, *Social Stratification* (Englewood Cliffs, 1967). Particularly useful collections containing theoretical and methodological discussions as well as the fruits of detailed mobility studies are Reinhard Bendix and Seymour Martin Lipset, eds., *Class, Status, and Power: Social Stratification in Comparative Perspective* (New York, 1966); Neil J. Smelser and Lipset, eds., *Social Structure and Mobility in Economic Development* (Chicago, 1966); and D. V. Glass, ed., *Social Mobility in Britain* (London, 1967). Lipset and Bendix, *Social Mobility in Industrial Society* (Berkeley, 1963), is a modern classic.

Interpretive overviews are provided in a number of articles. (It should be noted that in this field most original work appears in highly concentrated articles rather than in book-length studies.) Among these are Charles F. Westoff, Marvin Bressler, and Philip C. Sagi, "The Concept of Social Mobility: An Empirical Inquiry," *American Sociological Review* (hereafter *ASR*) 25 (June 1960):375–385; Ely Chinoy, "Social Mobility Trends in the United States," *ASR* 20 (April 1955):180–186; J. O. Hertzler, "Some Tendencies toward a Closed Class System in the United States," *Social Forces* 30 (March 1952):313–323; Nelson N. Foote and Paul K. Hatt, "Social Mobility and Economic Advancement," *American Economic Review* 43 (May 1953):364–378; and Gerhard E. Lenski, "Trends in Inter-Generational Occupational Mobility in the United States," *ASR* 23 (October 1958):514–523. Future prospects are ably considered in Gideon Sjoberg, "Are Social Classes in America Becoming More Rigid?" *ASR* 16 (December 1951):775–783; and John Porter, "The Future of Upward Mobility," *ASR* 33 (February 1968): 5–19.

Several substantial studies of twentieth-century mobility patterns in different cities have come close to attaining classic status. These include Percy E. Davidson and H. Dewey Anderson, *Occupational*

Mobility in an American Community (Palo Alto, 1937), of San Jose, California; Sidney Goldstein, *Patterns of Mobility, 1910–1950: The Norristown Study* (Philadelphia, 1958); W. Lloyd Warner and Paul S. Lunt, *The Social Life of a Modern Community* (New Haven, 1941), of Newburyport, Massachusetts; Natalie Rogoff, *Recent Trends in Occupational Mobility* (Glencoe, 1953), of Indianapolis; and Lipset and Bendix, whose chapter 5 of *Social Mobility in Industrial Society,* is a study of Oakland, California. A major study that examines national trends rather than those of a single community is A. J. Jaffe and R. O. Carleton, *Occupational Mobility in the United States, 1930–1960* (New York, 1954). (What appears to be a disparity in the dates in the title is actually a projection into the future.)

Probably the best known studies are those that examined the social origins of business leaders or the elite. Still respected for its pioneering role, if suspect for its methodological limitations, is Frank W. Taussig and C. S. Joslyn, *American Business Leaders: A Study in Social Origins and Social Stratification* (New York, 1932). Good scholarly studies include Suzanne Keller, "The Social Origins and Career Lines of Three Generations of American Business Leaders" (Ph.D. diss., Columbia University, 1953); and Mabel Newcomer, *The Big Business Executive: The Factors That Made Him, 1900–1950* (New York, 1955). In two separate studies W. Lloyd Warner and James C. Abegglen tried to carry the story past where Taussig and Joslyn had left it: *Occupational Mobility in American Business and Industry, 1928–1952* (Minneapolis, 1955): and a popular version, *Big Business Leaders in America* (New York, 1955). The interpretation offered in the latter volume is even more roseate than that appearing in the scholarly version. A short, journalistic article, "The Nine Hundred," *Fortune* 46 (November 1952):132–35, 232, 234–36, reports the results of interviews of 900 "top executives." For iconoclastic studies of select numbers of big business leaders of the early twentieth century, see William Miller's "American Historians and the Business Elite," and "The Recruitment of the American Business Elite," in Miller, ed., *Men in Business: Essays on the Historical Role of the Entrepreneur* (New York, 1962).

Flawed but interesting studies of elite backgrounds over the centuries are Bendix and Frank Howton, whose examination of the origins of the elite, 1771–1920, appears in Lipset and Bendix, *Social*

Mobility in Industrial Society; C. Wright Mills, "The American Business Elite: A Collective Portrait," *Journal of Economic History* 5 (Supplement 1945):20–44; and P. M. G. Harris, "The Social Origins of American Leaders: The Demographic Foundations," *Perspectives in American History* 3 (1969), the data base for all of which is remarkably thin. Some of Harris's judgments do not inspire confidence.

The relationship between social or vertical mobility and geographical mobility has been treated by a number of historians and sociologists. Helpful studies are Peter R. Knights, *The Plain People of Boston, 1830–1860* (New York, 1971); Stephan Thernstrom, "Urbanization, Migration, and Social Mobility in Late Nineteenth-Century America," in Barton Bernstein, ed., *Towards a New Past: Dissenting Essays in American History* (New York, 1968), pp. 158–175; Gordon W. Kirk, Jr. and Carolyn Tyirin Kirk, "Migration, Mobility, and the Transformation of the Occupational Structure in an Immigrant Community: Holland, Michigan, 1850–1880," *Journal of Social History* 7 (Winter 1973); Howard Chudacoff, *Mobile Americans: Residential and Social Mobility in Omaha 1880–1920* (New York, 1972); Richard J. Hopkins, "Occupational and Geographical Mobility in Atlanta, 1870–1896," *Journal of Southern History* 34 (May 1968): 200–213; and Sidney Goldstein, "Repeated Migration as a Factor in High Mobility Rates," *ASR* 19 (October 1954):536–541.

The authoritative study on occupations as a measure of social mobility is Otis Dudley Duncan and Peter M. Blau, *The American Occupational Structure* (New York, 1967). Also valuable are Albert Reiss, Jr., *Occupations and Social Status* (Glencoe, 1961); Melvin M. Tumin and Arnold S. Freeman, "Theory and Measurement of Occupational Mobility," *ASR* 22 (June 1957):281–288; Elton F. Jackson and Harry J. Crockett, Jr., "Occupational Mobility in the United States: A Point Estimate and Trend Comparison," *ASR* 29 (February 1964):5–15; Paul K. Hatt, "Occupation and Social Stratification," *American Journal of Sociology* (hereafter *AJS*) 55 (May 1950):533–547; Edward Gross, "The Occupational Variable as a Research Category, *ASR* 24 (October 1959):640–649; Robert W. Hodge, Paul M. Siegel, and Peter H. Rossi, "Occupational Prestige in the United States, 1925–1963," *AJS* 70 (November 1964):286–302; Michael B. Katz, "Occupational Classification in History," *Journal of Interdisciplinary History* 3 (Summer 1972):63–88; and Edward Pessen, "The

Occupations of the Antebellum Rich: A Misleading Clue to the Sources and Extent of Their Wealth," *Historical Methods Newsletter* 5 (March 1972):49–52.

The varied backgrounds of professionals are instructively examined by Albert J. Reiss, Jr., "Occupational Mobility of Professional Workers," *ASR* 20 (December 1955):693–700; Robert C. Stone, "Factory Organization and Vertical Mobility," *ASR* 18 (February 1953): 28–35; and to particularly good effect by Robert Perrucci, "The Significance of Intra-Occupational Mobility: Some Methodological and Theoretical Notes, Together with a Case Study of Engineers," *ASR* 26 (December 1961):874–883; and in two articles by Stuart Adams: "Origins of American Occupational Elites, 1900–1955," *AJS* 62 (January 1957):360–368; and "Trends in Occupational Origins of Physicians," *ASR* 18 (August 1953):404–409.

At the other extreme on the status scale, the backgrounds of the lowly and drifters are considered in Donald J. Bogue, *Skid Row in American Cities* (Chicago, 1963); and Howard M. Bahr, "Worklife Mobility among Bowery Men," *Social Science Quarterly* 49 (June 1968):128–141.

There is an ample literature on the relationship between educational attainment and social position. Interesting studies are C. Arnold Anderson, "A Skeptical Note on the Relation of Vertical Mobility to Education," *AJS* 66 (May 1961):560–570; Otis Dudley Duncan and Robert W. Hodge, "Education and Occupational Mobility: A Regression Analysis," *AJS* 68 (May 1963):629–644; Carolyn Cummings Perrucci and Robert Perrucci, "Social Origins, Educational Contexts, ana Career Mobility," *ASR* 35 (June 1970):451–463; Samuel Bowles, "Schooling and Inequality from Generation to Generation," *Journal of Political Economy* (hereafter *JPE*) 80 (May/June 1972):S 219–S 251; Bruce R. Eckland, "Academic Ability, Higher Education, and Occupational Mobility," *ASR* 30 (October 1965):735–746; and Zvi Griliches and William M. Mason, "Education, Income, and Ability," *JPE* 80 (May/June 1972), S 74–S 103.

The somewhat related theme of the relationship between IQ or innate ability—whatever that is—and social achievement is dealt with in a number of studies of varying sensitivity. Most comprehensive is Kenneth Eells et al., *Intelligence and Cultural Differences* (Chicago, 1951). If C. Arnold Anderson, James C. Brown, and Mary Jean Bowman, "Intelligence and Occupational Mobility," *JPE* 60

(June 1952):218–239, is interesting but inconclusive, the latter trait is typical of work in this area. John C. Hause, "Earnings Profile: Ability and Schooling," *JPE* 80 (May/June 1972):S 108–S 138, treats IQ as representative of ability. A valuable empirical survey of the subsequent careers of 5,000 high school students is C. T. Pihlblad and C. L. Gregory, "Occupational Selection and Intelligence in Rural Communities and Small Towns in Missouri," *ASR* 21 (February 1956): 63–71.

The relationship between personal goals and aspirations, on the one hand, and the later standing of individuals, on the other, has been analyzed from a variety of angles. Influential and valuable are Harry J. Crockett, Jr., "The Achievement Motive and Differential Occupational Mobility in the United States," *ASR* 27 (April 1961):191–204; Russell R. Dynes, Alfred C. Clarke, and Simon Dinitz, "Levels of Occupational Aspiration: Some Aspects of Family Experience As a Variable," *ASR* 21 (April 1956):212–215; La Mar T. Empey, "Social Class and Occupational Aspiration: A Comparison of Absolute and Relative Movement," *ASR* 21 (December 1956):703–709; Richard M. Stephenson, "Mobility Orientation and Stratification of 1,000 Ninth Graders," *ASR* 22 (April 1957):204–212; Leonard Reissman, "Levels of Aspiration and Social Class," *ASR* 18 (June 1953):233–242; and Raymond W. Mack, Raymond J. Murphy, and Seymour Yellin, "The Protestant Ethic, Level of Aspiration, and Social Mobility: An Empirical Test," *ASR* 21 (June 1956):295–300. Two studies of special interest, whose analysis of the role of aspiration is partly masked by their titles are Margaret R. McDonald and Bernard C. Rosen, "Evaluation of Occupations: A Reflection of Jewish and Italian Mobility Differences," *ASR* 22 (October 1957):546–553; and Norman G. Keig, "The Occupational Aspirations and Labor Force Experience of Negro Youth," *American Journal of Economics and Sociology* 28 (April 1969):113–130.

The part played by emotional factors and maladjustment in allegedly spurring upward mobility has interested scholars since Sorokin first discussed the issue. The leading studies of this matter have been written by August B. Hollingshead. A good short treatment is Hollingshead, R. Ellis, and E. Kirby, "Social Mobility and Mental Illness," *ASR* 19 (October 1954):577–591. Robert W. Hodge, "Social Integration, Psychological Well-Being, and Their Socioeconomic Correlates," in Edward O. Laumann, ed., *Social Stratification: Re-*

search and Theory for the 1970s (Indianapolis, 1970), pp. 182–206 is excellent. Also worthwhile are Harry J. Crockett, Jr., "Psychological Origins of Mobility," in Smelser and Lipset, *Social Structure and Mobility,* pp. 280–309; Evelyn Ellis, "Social Psychological Correlates of Upward Social Mobility among Unmarried Career Women," *ASR* 17 (October 1952):558–563; Robert A. Ellis and W. Clayton Lane, "Social Mobility and Social Isolation: A Test of Sorokin's Dissociation Hypothesis," *ASR* 32 (April 1967):237–253; Mary H. Lystad, "Social Mobility among Selected Groups of Schizophrenic Patients," *ASR* 22 (June 1957):288–292; William H. Sewell and A. O. Haller, "Factors in the Relationship between Social Status and the Personality Adjustment of the Child," *ASR* 24 (August 1959):511–520; and R. Jay Turner and Morton O. Wagenfeld, "Occupational Mobility and Schizophrenia: An Assessment of the Social Causation and Social Selection Hypothesis," *ASR* 32 (February 1967):104–113.

The factor of family size is effectively discussed by H. Yuan Tien, "The Social Mobility/Fertility Hypothesis Reconsidered: An Empirical Study," *ASR* 26 (April 1961):247–257, albeit on the basis of Australian evidence; William J. Goode, "Family and Mobility," in Bendix and Lipset, *Class, Status, and Power,* pp. 582–601; Eugene Litwak, "Occupational Mobility and Extended Family Cohesion," *ASR* 25 (February 1960):9–21; and Carolyn Cummings Perrucci, "Social Origins, Mobility Patterns, and Fertility," *ASR* 32 (August 1967):615–625.

Ethnic, racial, and religious factors are considered in David Gottlieb and Jay Campbell, Jr., "Winners and Losers in the Race for the Good Life: A Comparison of Blacks and Whites," *Social Science Quarterly* 49 (December 1968):593–602, which is essentially a comparison of the motivations of youngsters; the previously mentioned article by McDonald and Rosen, "Evaluation of Occupations: A Reflection of Jewish and Italian Mobility Differences"; Humbert S. Nelli, *The Italians in Chicago, 1890–1930: A Study in Ethnic Mobility* (New York, 1972); Richard Raymond, "Mobility and Economic Progress of Negro Americans during the 1940's," *American Journal of Economics and Sociology* 28 (October 1969):337–350; Mariam K. Slater, "My Son the Doctor: Aspects of Mobility among American Jews," *ASR* 34 (June 1969):359–373; and Bruce L. Warren, "Socioeconomic Achievement and Religion: The American Case," in Laumann, *Social Stratification,* pp. 130–155.

Given its great significance, the factor of structural change is dealt with in all of the major mobility texts. Good shorter treatments include Phillips Cutright, "Occupational Inheritance: A Cross-National Analysis," *JAS* 73 (January 1968):400–416; and Donald J. Treiman, "Industrialization and Social Stratification," in Laumann, *Social Stratification,* pp. 207–234.

Important discussions of the effects on individual behavior and thinking of upward or downward social movement are Gino Germani, "Social and Political Consequences of Mobility," in Smelser and Lipset, *Social Structure,* pp. 364–394, based primarily on Latin American evidence; Elton F. Jackson and Richard F. Curtis, "Effects of Vertical Mobility and Status Inconsistencies: A Body of Negative Evidence," *ASR* 37 (December 1972):701–713; Joseph Lopreato, "Upward Social Mobility and Political Orientation," *ASR* 32 (August 1967):586–592, which challenges the thesis that the upwardly mobile become politically conservative; and Lopreato and Janet Saltzman Chafetz, "The Political Orientation of Skidders: A Middle-Range Theory," *ASR* 35 (June 1970):440–451.

General histories on the popularity of the rags-to-riches theme are Irvin G. Wyllie, *The Self-Made Man in America: The Myth of Rags to Riches* (New York, 1966); John G. Cawalti, *Apostles of the Self-Made Man: Changing Concepts of Success in America* (Chicago, 1965); and Moses Rischin, ed., *The American Gospel of Success* (Chicago, 1965).

For useful discussions of the problems attendant on studying social mobility historically, see Stephan Thernstrom, "Notes on the Historical Study of Social Mobility," in Don Karl Rowney and James Q. Graham, Jr., *Quantitative History* (Homewood, 1969); Stuart Blumin, "The Historical Study of Vertical Mobility," *Historical Methods Newsletter* 1 (September 1968):1–10; and Edward Pessen, *Riches, Class, and Power before the Civil War* (Lexington, Mass., 1973), Part II, "Social Mobility."

Historical mobility studies for the seventeenth through the nineteenth centuries are still in short supply. In addition to the selections in this book, the following are valuable: Charles S. Grant, *Democracy in the Connecticut Frontier Town of Kent* (New York, 1961); Donald Warner Koch, "Income Distribution and Political Structure in Seventeenth-Century Salem, Massachusetts," *Essex Institute Historical Collections* 105 (January 1969):50–71; T. H. Breen and Stephen Foster, "Moving to the New World: The Character of Early Massachusetts Immigration," *William and Mary Quarterly* 30 (April 1973):189–221; Allan Kulikoff, "The Progress of Inequality in Revolutionary Boston," *William and Mary Quarterly* 28 (July 1971):396–410; Philip J. Greven, Jr., *Four Generations: Population, Land, and Family in Colonial Andover, Massachusetts* (Ithaca, 1970); James T. Lemon and Gary B. Nash, "The Distribution of Wealth in Eighteenth Century America: A Century of Changes in Chester County, Pennsylvania, 1693–1802," *Journal of Social History* 2 (Fall 1968):1–24; Kenneth A. Lockridge, *A New England Town The First Hundred Years: Dedham, Massachusetts, 1636–1736* (New York, 1970); Clyde Griffen, "Making It in America: Social Mobility in Mid-Nineteenth Century Poughkeepsie," *New York History* 51 (October 1970):479–500; Pessen, *Riches, Class, and Power before the Civil War*; Merle Curti et al., *The Making of An American Community: A Case Study of Democracy in a Frontier County* (Palo Alto, 1959); Herman R. Lantz and Ernest K. Alix, "Occupational Mobility in a Nineteenth Century Mississippi Valley River Community," *Social Science Quarterly* 51 (September 1970):404–408; Paul B. Worthman, "Working Class Mobility in Birmingham, Alabama, 1880–1914," in Tamara K. Hareven, ed., *Anonymous Americans: Explorations in Nineteenth-Century Social History* (Englewood Cliffs, 1971); as well as the previously cited studies by Kirk and Kirk, Knights, Hopkins, and Chudacoff.

The methodological discussion among sociologists has quickened over the past decade. Nonspecialists are likely to find the going tough in Robert McGinnis, "A Stochastic Model of Social Mobility," *ASR* 33 (October 1968):712–722; David D. McFarland, "Intragenerational Social Mobility as a Markov Process: Including a Time Stationary Markovian Model that Explains Observed Declines in Mobility Rates," *ASR* 35 (June 1970):463–475; or Richard Hawkes, "Some Methodological Problems in Explaining Social Mobility," *ASR* 37 (June 1972):277–294. Important—if difficult—are Thomas W. Pullum, "What Can Mathematical Models Tell Us about Occupational Mobility?" in Laumann, *Social Stratification,* pp. 258–280; and Saburo Yasuda, "A Methodological Inquiry into Social Mobility," *ASR* 29 (February 1964):16–23. A methodological tour de force is Leo A. Goodman, "On the Statistical Analysis of Mobility Tables," *AJS* 65 (March 1965):564–585. Other contributions by Goodman are "On the Measurement of Social Mobility: An Index of Status Persistence," *ASR* 34 (December 1969):831–850; and "How to Ransack Social

Mobility Tables and Other Kinds of Cross-Classification Tables,"
AJS 75 (July 1969):1–40, based largely on English and Danish data.
More accessible to the reader are Judah Matras, "Social Mobility
and Social Structure: Some Insights from the Linear Model," *ASR*
32 (August 1967):600–614; Leo F. Schnore, "Social Mobility in Demographic Perspective," *ASR* 26 (June 1961):407–423, which stresses
the appropriateness of a demographic approach to the study of
mobility; and James M. Beshers and Edward O. Laumann, "Social
Distance: A Network Approach," *ASR* 32 (April 1967):225–236, which
offers a technique for measuring "gaps among social status categories." An excellent overview of the methodological controversy is
Otis Dudley Duncan, "Methodological Issues in the Analysis of
Social Mobility," in Smelser and Lipset, *Social Structure and Mobility,* 51–97.